Groups at Work

WILEY SERIES ON
INDIVIDUALS, GROUPS AND ORGANIZATIONS

Series Editor
Cary Cooper,
Department of Management Sciences,
University of Manchester Institute of
Science and Technology,
Manchester

Associate Editor
Eric J. Miller,

Tavistock Institute of
Human Relations,
London

Groups at Work

Edited by

Roy Payne

Medical Research Council/Social Science Research Council,
Social and Applied Psychology Unit,
University of Sheffield

and

Cary L. Cooper

University of Manchester
Institute of Science and Technology

JOHN WILEY & SONS

Chichester · New York · Brisbane · Toronto

British Library Cataloguing in Publication Data:

Groups at work—(Wiley series on individuals,
  groups and organizations).
  1. Social groups
  2. Social interaction
  I. Title   II. Payne, Roy
  III. Cooper, Cary L.
  301.18′5   HM131   80-41586

  ISBN 0 471 27934 X

Photosetting by Thomson Press (India) Limited, New Delhi and printed in the United States of America

Contributors

DAVID L. BRADFORD	*Graduate School of Business, Stanford University, California, U.S.A.*
LELAND P. BRADFORD	*Consultant, Pinehurst, N. Carolina, U.S.A.*
JOHN CARLISLE	*Consultant, Huthwaite Research Group, Penistone, Sheffield, U.K.*
CARY L. COOPER	*Dept of Management Sciences, University of Manchester Institute of Science and Technology, Manchester, U.K.*
ALAN DALE	*Brunel Institute of Organization and Social Studies, Brunel University, Uxbridge, U.K.*
GEORGE FARRIS	*School of Management, Rutgers University, New Jersey, U.S.A.*
FRANK FRIEDLANDER	*School of Management, Case Western Reserve University, Cleveland, Ohio, U.S.A.*
RONALD FRY	*School of Management, Case Western Reserve University, Cleveland, Ohio, U.S.A.*
DAN GOWLER	*Oxford Management Centre, Oxford University, Oxford, U.K.*
ROYSTON GREENWOOD	*Institute of Local Government Studies, University of Birmingham, Birmingham, U.K.*
HUGH P. GUNZ	*Manchester Business School, Manchester, U.K.*
WILLIAM I. JENKINS	*Interdisciplinary Studies, Darwin College, University of Kent, Canterbury, U.K.*
MALCOLM LEARY	*Consultant, Social Ecology Associates, Sheffield, U.K.*

KAREN LEGGE   *Department of Organizational Sociology, Imperial
                       College, University of London, U.K.*

ROY PAYNE   *Medical Research Council/Social Science Research
                       Council, Social and Applied Psychology Unit,
                       Sheffield University, Sheffield, U.K.*

ALAN W. PEARSON   *Research and Development Unit, Manchester
                       Business School, Manchester, U.K.*

MARK PLOVNICK   *Department of Management, Clark University,
                       Worcester, Mass., U.S.A.*

IRWIN RUBIN   *Situation Management Systems Inc., Honolulu,
                       Hawaii, U.S.A.*

BARBARA SCHOTT   *School of Management, Case Western Reserve
                       University, Ohio, U.S.A.*

Contents

Editorial Foreword to the Series

Over the last decade, there has been an enormous growth of interest in the social and psychological aspects of institutional and organizational life. This has been reflected in a substantial upsurge in research and training in the field of organizational behaviour particularly in Institutes of Higher Education and Research throughout the Western World. Attention in this development has focused on the interrelationship between the individual, the variety of groups to which he belongs and the organizational environment within which he and his group operate.

The purpose of this series is to examine the social and psychological processes of these interrelationships, that is the nexus of individual/personal development, group processes and organizational behaviour and change. Within this context, a wide range of topics will be covered. These will include: the individual, his role and the organization; multiple roles and role conflict; the impact of group processes on personal and organizational development; strategies for 'humanizing' the organizational environment to meet individual and group needs; and the influence of technical and economic factors on organizational life.

The series will attempt to draw together the main schools of organizational behaviour including, for example, the American behavioural science tradition as reflected by Harvard, UCLA and National Training Laboratories, and the British socio-technical and open systems approaches of the Tavistock Institute of Human Relations. It is hoped that this will add significantly to understanding the distinctive characteristics of the various approaches and also provide a link between them through which individual, group and organizational behaviour can be seen in fuller perspective.

CARY COOPER
ERIC MILLER

Introduction

Roy Payne and Cary L. Cooper

The title of this book, *Groups at Work*, is intentionally ambiguous. It is meant to convey that the book focuses on groups in work organizations, but also that it is concerned with understanding the dynamics of such groups when they are 'at work'. Since one of the classic volumes in the social psychology of groups is called *Group Dynamics* (Cartwright and Zander, 1960), one might wonder if the present volume has anything distinctive to contribute. Its distinctiveness is its concentration on groups in work organizations. Many of the classic books on groups draw heavily on research carried out in the social psychological laboratory and/or on the kinds of processes occurring in laboratory groups of the experiential kind. This book deliberately ignores these two literatures (almost anyway) and draws on studies of real, live, working groups located in real, live, working organizations.

Whilst the literature from the scientific laboratory and the experiential laboratory has its own validity as knowledge its direct relevance to groups in ongoing work organizations has yet to be convincingly demonstrated. Would a natural organization ever produce a perfect wheel communication structure (Bavelas's classic experiments)? Can the norms of trust, openness, and authentic emotional expressions which are strived for in sensitivity groups work in situations where politics and the struggle for scarce resources are real environmental constraints? We are not encouraged to believe in the transferability of knowledge generated in such situations when it can be shown that there is no correlation between driving performance on an automobile simulator and driving in normal traffic (Barrett, 1972). The work by Argyris and Schon (1974, 1978) also makes clear the difficulties involved in getting managers and professionals in work organizations to change the standards and norms guiding their interpersonal relationships which is essentially what T-groups and experiential learning is asking them to do. For these reasons we feel it is timely that a book should explore the literature on what actual work groups do.

One of the advantages of laboratory work is that it simplifies both the situation and the task. Handy (1976) lists the purposes for which groups are assembled in organizations and reveals the complexity of tasks and situations that natural groups encounter:

Organizations use groups, or team and committees for the following major purposes:
1. For the distribution of work, to bring together a set of skills, talents, responsibilities, and allocate them their particular duties.

2. For the management and control of work. To allow work to be organized and controlled by appropriate individuals with responsibility for a certain range of work.
3. For problem-solving and decision-taking. To bring together a set of skills, talents and responsibilities so that the solution to any problem will have all available capacities applied to it.
4. For information processing. To pass on decisions or information to those who need to know.
5. For information and idea collection. To gather ideas, information or suggestions.
6. For testing and ratifying decisions. To test the validity of a decision taken outside the group, or to ratify such a decision.
7. For co-ordination and liaison. To co-ordinate problems and tasks between functions or divisions.
8. For increased commitment and involvement. To allow and encourage individuals to get involved in the plans and activities of the organization.
9. For negotiation or conflict resolution. To resolve a dispute or argument between levels, divisions or functions.
10. For inquest or inquiry into the past.

In designing the structure of the book we have endeavoured to encompass this diversity of purpose whilst providing a meaningful organization of the material. This has been achieved by distinguishing between *ongoing groups* and *temporary groups*.

The ongoing groups probably perform all of the purposes listed by Handy but their emphasis is on activities which maintain current operations. In Morris and Burgoyne's (1973) neat summary of organizational activities into Breakdown, Maintenance and Development, ongoing groups spend most of their time and energy on Maintenance and Breakdown. They gather information, communicate information, allocate work, supervise work, do work, as well as solving problems and taking decisions. Some ongoing groups, however, also spend time on Development activities and to recognize these differences in purposes the section on ongoing groups is organized hierarchically and horizontally.

The hierarchical organization is reflected in the first two chapters. The first chapter by Royston Greenwood and Bill Jenkins reviews the literature about groups which make and take policy decisions. In this seminal book on organization structure, Mintzberg (1979) calls this the 'strategic apex'. These groups generate the structural and cultural contexts in which other groups function. The influence of these structural and cultural factors is explored by Ron Fry, Rubin Irwin, and Mark Plovnick in their chapter on groups that execute and manage the policy specified by those in the strategic apex. Mintzberg refers to such groups as the 'middle line' and they will actually span several hierarchical levels in medium to large organizations.

Following the logic of Mintzberg's breakdown of organizations we now need a chapter on groups which constitute what he calls the 'operating core'. In a factory they would be the machine operators, in a university the professors/lecturers, in a hospital the physicians, surgeons, and nurses, in government they would be the bureaucrats. Clearly, the task of generalizing about the dynamics of such groups is a formidable one, if not an impossible one, within the bounds of a single chapter. Since a volume in this series on Individuals, Groups and Organizations has already attacked this problem we decided to guide our readers there rather than attempt an inadequate summary. The volume is *Task and Organization*, edited by Eric Miller.

Two chapters in this section about 'ongoing groups' recognize horizontal relationships in organizations. The first is by Dan Gowler and Karen Legge who analyse the nature of the tasks faced by groups which provide specialist services to the hierarchical groups in the strategic apex, the middle line, and the operating core. They distinguish between specialist groups whose roles are largely *integrative* dealing with conflict management and coordination, and roles which are *differentiative*. The latter tend to provide specialist services rooted in particular skills and expertise: buying or research are examples.

Gowler and Legge point out that such distinctions are ones of emphasis since actual groups often perform both roles. This blurring of —roles and boundaries is acknowledged in the presence of George Farris's chapter on the informal organization. As Farris shows many groups/networks of relationships ignore the pristine neatness of organizational charts. These cliques and cabals may work to the advantage or disadvantage of the organization *qua* organization, but their pervasiveness makes it acutely apparent that they must be accounted rather than discounted in attempts to understand social relationships in organizations.

Informal relationships are not only horizontal, of course, but horizontal-like relationships probably dominate numerically, as well as psychosocially. So the informal organization makes fuzzy our organizational attempts to explain the structure of the book. It similarly blurs the distinction we have made between ongoing and temporary groups since many informal networks depend on individuals who constitute the central reason for the network's existence: liaison roles, gatekeepers, and product champions are illustrations. And since the groups disband when these socio-centric forces depart they might be classified as temporary. But the informal organization itself continues—*it* is ongoing.

Projects, committees, and working parties typically have more limited boundaries and time-spans. Part II of the book concerns itself with these *temporary groups*.

Bennis and Slater's book, *The Temporary Society* (1968) emphasizes the increasing role of temporary relationships in Western society. The first issue of the *Journal of Occupational Behaviour* (1980) documents the legislative changes in Scandinavia which give the workers the right to participate in decisions relevant to their work. Europe as a whole is moving towards increased industrial democracy and this inevitably increases the number of committees in organizations. These changes only accentuate the necessity for understanding, and improving, behaviour in committees. David and Leland Bradford reveal our knowledge of this area in the first chapter of Part II. Apart from analysing the nature of temporary committees, they provide examples, frameworks, and advice which facilitate the understanding and management of these ubiquitous groups.

Alan Pearson and Hugh Gunz also deal with a set of groups which have been growing steadily both in numbers and importance. They have various names but 'project teams' characterizes their nature, since it combines the intimate interdependence of teamwork with the specificity of goals embodied in the concept of 'project'. Pearson and Gunz describe the very different forms these groups can take and suggest the environmental factors which may determine whether or not particular forms are effective. They emphasize the need to pay more attention to the management and development of teams which combine a range of knowledge, skills, and abilities.

The fastest growing specialist role in organizations is probably the employee/industrial relations role. As the power of trades unions has increased, and the popular demand for democracy in the workplace has grown, so has the formalized management of conflict. John Carlisle and Malcolm Leary examine the natural history of bargaining groups. They distinguish between the negotiating group itself and the separate nature of the groups making up the negotiating group. They stress the importance of seeing these holistically and understanding the stages through which negotiating groups pass. Based on their research and experience as consultants they offer a description of the behaviours that characterize effective negotiation, and emphasize the value of having negotiating teams rather than single 'supermen'.

This chapter concludes the book's focus on specific types of work groups. Part III is concerned with problems which are common to all organizational groups. The first chapter by Frank Friedlander and Barbara Schott addresses the question of how to develop a viable group in the first place. What has to happen if a collectivity of individuals is to begin to identify itself as a distinctive psychosocial entity called a group/team? These authors demonstrate the issues and ways of resolving them by describing examples of their own attempts to develop effective teams. From this they are able to induce a most informative conceptual framework for analysing the group development process.

In the final chapter Alan Dale also starts from the reality of an actual group. Whilst dealing with the richness of its life, he is particularly concerned with a fundamental problem of organizational life—the management of the interface between a group and the other groups in which it is embedded. The very survival of a group depends on the successful maintenance of this boundary, and the growth of a group depends on its development.

In summary, the book expounds the literature relating to the major types of groups in modern work organizations. Apart from providing reviews of this literature, which will appeal to an academic audience, the book provides a rich variety of frameworks and prescriptions which will enable the practitioner to understand and manage the dynamics of groups at work.

References

Argyris, C. and Schon, D. (1974) *Theory in Practice: Increasing Professional Effectiveness*, San Francisco: Jossey-Bass.

Argyris, C. and Schon, D. (1978) *Organizational Learning*, Reading, Mass.: Addison-Wesley.

Barrett, G. V. (1972) 'Research models of the future for industrial and organizational psychology, *Personnel Psychology*, **25**, 1, 1–18.

Bennis, W. G. and Slater, P. E. (1968) *The Temporary Society*, New York: Harper and Row.

Cartwright, D. and Zander, A. (1960) (eds) *Group Dynamics: Research and Theory*, 2nd edn, Evanston, I11.: Row, Peterson.

Handy, C. (1976) *Understanding Organizations*, Harmondsworth: Penguin.

Mintzberg, H. (1979) *The Structuring of Organizations*, Englewood Cliffs, N. J.: Prentice-Hall.

Morris, J. and Burgoyne, J. G. (1973) *Developing Resourceful Managers*, London: Institute of Personnel Management.

PART I

Ongoing Groups in Organizations

Groups at work
Edited by R. Payne and C. Cooper
© 1981 John Wiley & Sons Ltd.

Chapter 1

Policy-making Groups

Royston Greenwood and William I. Jenkins

Introduction

Policy and Policy Making

It may be a cliché to argue that 'life is tough at the top' but one of the paradoxes of contemporary political and organizational life is that actors who seek and achieve power find it increasingly difficult to operate in an individual capacity when in positions of authority. While the buck may once have stopped on executive desks after a rapid journey up the organizational hierarchy, its passage now is often more complex, especially if important policy matters are involved. 'What I want', said President J. F. Kennedy at the time of the Cuban missile crisis, 'is a policy that all will support', and here in a time of unparalleled tension and decision complexity consensus was clearly the order of the day (Allison, 1971). Which is not to say that all leaders seek consensus but many move as near to it as they can, in particular since only occasionally can they achieve their own way easily (Crossman, 1979). In the world of policy, leaders are still important but whether they be president or prime minister, city mayor or private sector chief executive, it is often difficult to separate them from the groups that surround them. In national politics the role of adviser is as old as government itself, while top level groups such as cabinets have a long history. However, the current era is one where terms such as 'team', 'task force', and 'policy group' have become increasingly part of the language and reality of executive life to the extent, as some have argued, that it has become the usual practice to relegate important decisions to groups (Janis, 1972). The reason for this can be seen, in part, as being linked with the general development of organizations in the public and private sector, many of which have become considerably larger and taken on a variety of new functions. Nowhere is this clearer than in the case of government at national and local level where tasks have grown and differentiated in an environment that has been constantly changing over the last few decades. In such a world, the ability of organizations to cope, adapt, and anticipate becomes more crucial and, increasingly in such organizations, policies appear to be made or strongly influenced by small groups. As we will see, the roles of top level groups are many and various: to coordinate or interpret intelligence generated and gathered at lower levels of the organization; to bring together in one forum differing values and interests that exist within the organization itself; to legitimate current and projected actions; and to account for the past and to plan

9

for the future. Such groups also make decisions and, as is noted above, through such decisions shape and reshape policy. A study of policy and policy making within organizations is therefore inevitably caught up with an examination of the structure and functioning of organizations and organizational groups, yet on what conceptual issues should a study of policy making concentrate?

In recent years the study of policy making has become a focus of attention for both academic analysts and practising political actors. Much of this attention has been devoted to public policy as reflected in the action of central and local government, but this is not to deny work on policy in other areas such as business policy or at the intergovernmental level such as in the field of international relations (Allison, 1971; Allison and Szanion, 1976; Edwards and Sharkansky, 1978; Jenkins, 1978). A study of policy, runs the argument, provides a key to understanding how organizations work. It may also have practical implications, namely that in times of economic crisis and diminishing resources, better or more effective policy making can point the way to organizational survival. Given such thoughts, it is of interest to note that while normative guides to policy making abound, in empirical terms we really know very little on how decisions are taken and policies are made *at the top of organizations*. These observations hold for both public and private sector studies and would at once appear to place limits on the development of a viable conceptual framework in this area (Mintzberg *et al.*, 1976). However, while such caveats cannot be ignored, it is also clear that any understanding of policy making in an organizational context must consider the process through which policy is made, the policy itself, the organization involved, and the environment in which the latter operates.

A great deal has been written on the policy process where the latter is defined as 'the given set of strategies, methods and techniques through which a policy is made' (Jenkins, 1978, p. 16). It is a matter of doubt and debate that such a process would be uniform for all organizations and all policies. However, studies ranging from those of single decisions to more complex policy problems indicate that, to a degree, the policy process can be disaggregated into a number of discrete phases (Janis and Mann, 1977; Jenkins, 1978; Mintzberg *et al.*, 1976). Such phases may include the initiation of a particular issue, decision making with regard to the issue, the implementation of such a decision, and its evaluation. The phases are interrelated and the links between them complex. Hence we would agree with Mintzberg and others who, in the context of an empirical study of strategic decisions, argue that while there is a logic in delineating between phases of the decision process, there is no simple sequential relationship between them (Mintzberg *et al.*, 1976). But with this in mind it is also clear that the role of groups and leaders may vary according to the phase of the policy process with which they are involved (Kantor, 1976).

But what of the policy itself? Are all issues decided by the same group in the same way? The answer to this is clearly 'No' and it is neither sufficient nor adequate to observe that important issues are decided by top policy makers while unimportant ones filter below. Indeed, in some instances, it may be of interest to enquire why some issues never appear on decision-making agendas in the first instance (Crenson, 1971; Lukes, 1974). However, the latter point takes one down a road of some complexity away from the issue at hand which, simply stated, is that the content of a policy cannot be ignored and, in fact, may sometimes determine the process through which policy is made. Policies are not featureless; they reflect values and possess characteristics that may influence the way in which they are dealt with. As Lowi has observed, decisions that take from one group and give to another generally proceed through a different process from those that give to all (Lowi, 1964, 1970, 1972). Similarly, decisions not to act require less consensus building and involve fewer implementation problems than decisions involving new organizational ventures or a change in direction for established policy (Art, 1973). Policy making is, therefore, issue-dependent and the role and effectiveness of top policy makers may vary with the issue involved.

Yet policy and decision making do not take place in a vacuum. In both the public and private sectors, policy is organization-based which leads to the conclusion that any understanding of how policy evolves over time must pay particular attention to the organizational structures from which it emerges and the environment in which such structures operate. The argument for an organizational-based study of policy has been set out at length elsewhere by the authors and aspects of this argument are developed below (Greenwood and Hinings, 1977; Jenkins, 1978). For the moment we will simply observe that the vast majority of policy- and decision-making studies have either ignored or given low importance to the fact that decision makers operate within organizational environments. For example, leaders are far from free agents and, as has been frequently demonstrated, even powerful presidents may be constrained by both proximate and distant organizational forces (Allison, 1971; Kissinger, 1979). Organizational analysis may not be a coherent field but findings from it expose factors that influence policy-making and organizational performance: the nature of the organization's environment and the organization's dependency on such an environment for an allocation of resources; the size and structure of the organization; and the tasks the organization has to carry out and the demands such tasks make on the organization's internal structure (Child, 1972, 1977; Handy, 1976). But all this may neglect that organizations, large or small, public or private, are composed of groups, relatively permanent groups fashioned by the structure of the organization, less permanent ones that cohere around issues and personalities. Indeed, as many writers have argued, a group focus on organizations may be essential for understanding the political dimension of organizational life and, further, that without such a perspective organizational performance can only be poorly understood (Crozier, 1964; Dalton, 1959; Pettigrew, 1973). We will develop this point in more detail below. Here we briefly note that if a study of policy making is involved with a study of organizations then it will also, *ipso facto*, be involved in a study of groups.

Group Theory and Policy Paradigms

Before Richard Nixon moved into the White House in 1968, he announced his intention of bringing with him two teams: a 'big team' and a 'young team'. As things turned out, the big team, which he intended should be made up of well-known and experienced political actors, was difficult to recruit and even more difficult to sustain over time. In contrast, the young team was cohesive, loyal, and enthusiastic. It made sharp decisions and frequently acted in a decisive and forceful manner. It also, in no small way, laid the foundations for Nixon's downfall and eventual resignation (Raven, 1974). The negative effects of groups have been clearly demonstrated elsewhere; for example, top groups led Kennedy into the Bay of Pigs disaster, marketed the Ford Edsel, and at Pearl Harbor seemingly remained unmoved by overwhelming evidence of impending attack (Janis, 1972; Wohlstetter, 1962; Wilensky, 1967). Indeed, groups can demonstrate many pathologies; they can be slow, risky, generate pressures towards conformity and uniformity, and pose problems of coordination. Yet groups have access to greater resources than isolated individuals, can facilitate rapid communication between different parts of a complex structure and may even be creative (Kelley and Thibaut, 1969; Zander, 1979). In private sector organizations as well as governments, small decision-making groups are frequently found at the top level of the organization and some grasp of the logic of their operation is essential for an understanding of past policy and present action. Groups, however, may vary between organizations and within organizations; they may have different objectives, play different roles, and operate different procedures. Moreover, the same group may alter its operating methods over time and achieve differing levels of performance. How can one analyse such issues especially with regard to organizational policy making? The area of small group study, in particular the examination of group structure and group process, is the bailiwick of social psychology and a vast literature on these topics has emerged. However, much of this literature is experimentally based and, unfortunately, very little of it is directly concerned with actual studies of policy and decision making at the top of organizational hierarchies. Against this there is evidence that some of the findings from experimental work on small groups are capable of extrapolation and, indeed, may assist in interpreting wider phenomena in this area. But examples of this are rare and problems of fit clear. In brief, while the work on small groups is of massive proportions, little of it relates directly to high level policy making and little of it has developed out of empirical studies of policy making in organizations (George, 1974; Golembiewski (ed.) 1978; Maier, 1970; Shaw, 1976; Zander, 1979). Yet at other levels, decision making in general and group decision making in particular have been topics of interest to social psychology since the 1940s. How does decision making take place and, in group terms, what are the factors 'that lead a group to mobilize its resources most effectively in solving problems and in arriving at optimal decisions'? As Rubin and Raven argue, a study of these problems requires an examination of such factors as (a) the task at hand, (b) the group itself, and (c) the individuals that make it up (Raven and Rubin, 1976). As we have already observed, groups are paradoxical; they may facilitate decision making, they may offer better ways for an organization to manage its task environment, but they may also impose constraints leading to the shaping of policy (McWhirter, 1978).

Thus, any study of how policy is formulated in organizations must inevitably lead back to the influence of groups on the policy process.

But how does policy emerge? What paradigms do we have for understanding the formation, implementation, and evaluation of organizational policy? Undoubtedly, the most pervasive if not the most powerful perspective in this area is that which regards policy as the output of rational decision mechanisms. In both a descriptive and a normative sense the rational or analytical paradigm has dominated decision-making studies to the extent that both governments and organizations are frequently exhorted to be 'more rational' while decision-making innovations and organizational design procedures have unceasingly pursued rationality almost as a goal in itself (Jenkins, 1978). Yet, both in cognitive and in political terms there is an increasing body of work which indicates that rational perspectives on decision making may be both partial and dangerous. In the first instance it has been argued that for cognitive reasons decision makers, particularly when faced by what they perceive as complex problems, may consistently follow non-rational approaches (Steinbruner, 1974). However, the concept of a 'cognitive paradigm' of policy making may, as yet, be in its early stages. In contrast, in recent years the development of a political paradigm of policy making has grown apace. So, to terms such as 'satisficing', 'incrementalism', and 'bargaining' have been added others such as 'bureaucratic politics'. From this viewpoint an exploration of the internal dynamics of organizational behaviour becomes essential and associated with this is a study of the operation of groups (Caldwell, 1977; George, 1974; Halperin, 1974; Nathan and Oliver, 1978). The remainder of this chapter will attempt to develop some of these themes in more detail through an examination of policy (a) in terms of the rational or goal oriented paradigm, and (b) as political behaviour. In particular, we are interested in the involvement of groups in all this, especially how such groups operate within an organizational context.

Policy and the Rational Paradigm

The Rational Paradigm Introduced

'There is', argues John Steinbruner, 'a heavy investment of the culture in the concepts of rationality' (Steinbruner, 1974). Certainly, any discussion of descriptive or prescriptive theories of policy making in organizations is inevitably caught up with the rational paradigm and its central questions: to what extent are organizations rational in the decisions that they make and the policies they pursue? To what extent could they or should they be rational as they develop strategies for future conduct? The answers to these questions, of course, depend on what is understood by the rational paradigm. At its simplest and crudest the rational paradigm assumes that people and organizations (and the move from the individual to the group is not trivial) seek to maximize their values under the constraints they face. Thus, as Steinbruner notes 'although there is wide dispute over what values man typically pursues and over the interpretation of constraints, the basic rational thesis is rarely doubted and widely used' (Steinbruner, 1974, p. 8). It has been used in the field of strategic analysis where, according to Schelling, the very foundation of strategic theory is 'the assumption of rational behaviour—not just of intelligent behaviour but by behaviour motivated by a conscious calculation of advantages' (Schelling, 1970, p. 67), and it has been widely followed in policy and planning theory (Banfield, 1959; Faludi, 1973). Its expression in terms of both analytical and normative formula for the making of policy is available from a variety of sources (Dror, 1968; Etzioni, 1968; Lindblom, 1959) and the logic of the argument can be briefly summarized as follows. In the rational paradigm, policy is seen as emerging from a goal oriented, value maximizing strategy of either a single actor or group of actors. As Lindblom notes, the rational model is essentially a means–ends analysis 'first the ends are isolated then the means to achieve them sought' (Lindblom, 1959). Policy makers following the rational paradigm initially establish clear values and objectives and then survey alternatives in the light of comprehensive analysis and information. Following such analysis optimal policies can be selected since such a policy can be seen to maximize predetermined ends. In rational terms the policy process will be sequential beginning with the identification of objectives, moving through to decision (which will not be problematic if rational guidelines are followed) and proceeding to implementation which should also raise few difficulties since problems in this area would have been identified in prior analysis. Furthermore, for organizations that adopt the rational paradigm, policy, in organizational terms, will be centralized and hierarchical since it is only in such a way that organizational goals can be identified and comprehensive strategies fashioned and formed. The fact that such a model must operate under a system of constraints is generally widely accepted, as Banfield noted some years ago: 'for practical purposes a rational decision is one in which alternatives and consequences are considered as fully as the decision maker, given the time and other resources available, can afford to consider them' (Banfield, 1959). More fundamental and deeper seated limitations have also been identified, the constraints of organizational dynamics (Allison, 1971) or more specifically whether in many situations policy making may be structured not by rational procedures but by non-rational cognitive approaches. For example, the argument by Steinbruner that in many situations decision makers appear to suppress trade-off between values by constructing their world in such a way that trade-offs do not appear to exist (Steinbruner, 1976). The logic of the rational model and its applicability under varying conditions is therefore a topic that has generated extensive discussion (Allison, 1971; Etzioni, 1968; Steinbruner, 1974). Here, however, given the overall concern with policy groups in organizations, we should simply note the wealth of evidence indicating the search by many bodies, both public and private, to organize or reorganize their policy-making structures on a rational basis. For example, the rise of corporate planning in industry (Ansoff, 1979) and government (Greenwood and Stewart, 1974) or the development of strategic analysis in international relations (Allison, 1971; Hitch and McKean, 1960; Snyder, 1978) indicate attempts to alter both the process and structure of organizational decision making and, with it, often the composition and procedures of top-policy groups.

As a model for policy making, the rational paradigm, in its purest sense, offers seductively clear prescriptions and the promise of pay-offs (in terms of smooth internal processes and of policy achievement) in both the long and short term. By way of the paradigm a particular process model of policy emerges: information, sought in a structured manner, will be clear and complete, decision mechanisms unambiguous, implementation strategies linked to decisions and evaluations developed on a continuous basis, and in such a way that policies can be adjusted and amended as circumstances change. Through such a system organizations cope, respond, and adapt to fluctuating environments. Indeed, the absence of, or departure from, such a system would indicate imperfect structure and result in imperfect policy. Such a philosophy holds clear implications for the operation of policy groups. For example, the setting of goals will be a prerequisite to action, activities will follow a logical order identical to the stages in the policy process (see above), and organizational values, once identified, will permit the establishment of clear decision rules. But, how valid is the rational paradigm as a description of how organizations operate? Furthermore, should organizations seek to attain such a rational decision process?

As already outlined, the adequacy of the rational paradigm in both descriptive and normative terms has been questioned by a variety of authors some of whom have offered alternative models to account for organizational policy making (see, for example, Allison, 1971; Dror, 1968; Etzioni, 1968; Faludi, 1973; Snyder, 1978; Steinbruner, 1974). These authors argue that the idea of policy-making strategies based upon clear goals and the selection of optimal alternatives is fallacious on both cognitive and situational grounds. In terms of cognitive limitations there exists a stream of thought running from March and Simon (1958) onwards that indicates that for most organizations the idea of unitary goals and an accompanying hierarchy of decision must be rejected (Cyert and March, 1963; March and Simon, 1958). Rather, as will be noted in the next section, organizations struggle with multiple and changing goals. It is rare to find a single actor with clear and consistent goals straddling a hierarchy. Decision-making coalitions are more usual. However, even where a single executive actor does operate alone, there may by cognitive problems; George, for example, has argued that executive actors face difficulties when choosing between various values and alternatives as well as coping with situations where information and knowledge are inherently limited (George, 1974). Indeed, many organizational decisions are characterized by uncertainty rather than certainty, a fact that draws one into the arena of organizational politics discussed below.

However, the limits to rationality are not only cognitive but situational. The rational paradigm would seem to indicate a uniform model valid for all issues and all situations. Yet, as Yates has pointed out, in an area such as urban government it is *the environment of urban policy making* and *the nature of urban problems* that determine the shape of urban policy. Hence, in American cities mayors and their policy-making groups preside over a reactive, fragmented, and unstable system where demands and problems are incoherent and often insoluble. In such situations, rationality may be not just difficult but impossible. Indeed, to evaluate a policy group's effectiveness in terms of the rational paradigm may be to neglect the situational variables under which policy groups operate (Yates, 1977). Consequently, what constitutes an 'ideal' policy process is a matter of some debate and as George has pointed out in the context of foreign policy decisions, decision-making styles highly suitable in one political context may be highly disfunctional in others (George, 1974).

The thrust of the above argument, stated briefly, is that the realities of organizational life may at least modify and indeed render untenable the rational paradigm as an ideal model of decision making. We elaborate these arguments in the next section. Despite these weaknesses, however, the ideas embedded in the rational model have had and continue to exert a pervasive influence on the practice of organizational policy making. As such, it has influenced the design and operation of policy-making groups. Like all models, the rational paradigm offers prescriptions for organizational structures and organizational operation, with implications for the goals, roles, and procedures of policy groups. Following from it the task of the group is to establish the organizational goal or goals and then to work towards achieving it or their attainment. In such a model the group is a collective striving towards a collective objective, and operates in an organizational structure closely resembling the classical bureaucratic model. Roles are uniquely and clearly specified under an established hierarchy. Procedures, also sharply clarified, correspond or contribute to the sequential model of policy. Such a picture at once seems too artificial and static to typify organizational life, yet evidence of its existence arises from the operation of strategy and planning groups in a variety of organizations. Moreover, the search to achieve it is consistently exemplified by the reports of management advisers and consultants (Greenwood and Stewart, 1974; Eddison, 1973). Come what may, the rational paradigm still stands as the Holy Grail for many practising policy makers (if not of policy theorists) and it is against this search for purity that one can begin to explore in more detail the operation of policy-making groups.

Groups and Policy Making

It is a matter of some debate in both policy theory and policy practice, especially if the rational paradigm is followed, whether policy groups are really necessary. Why should groups be involved in policy making in the first instance? The key may be ambiguity and the continual search by organizations to resolve it. As Steinbruner argues: 'under conditions of complexity, decision making organizations arise which attempt to match the complexity of their environment by means of an internal complexity which is not the property of a single decision maker but rather of the collective' (Steinbruner, 1974, p. 69). In other words, ambiguity and uncertainty place organizations (and, in particular, their leaders) under stress. In such circumstances, ways of optimizing goals and of solving problems are no longer clear: hence leaders come to rely on others for psychological support and for the information resources needed to achieve at least a move towards organizational objectives (Steinbruner, 1974; George, 1974). If such points are correct, then one implication would be that the greater the ambiguity or uncertainty experienced by an organization, the greater the probability that policy making would become a group-based process. Moreover, since ambiguity and problem complexity also tend to increase as one moves up the organizational hierarchy, it would appear that in complex organizations the ability of individual leaders to act alone is severely curtailed. Decision and policy making for most organizations involve processes that are conducted under uncertainty, although the extent to which groups resolve this uncertainty is something that we need to examine.

This, in fact, leads in two associated directions: we must look first at the ways in which leaders involve themselves with groups in order to enhance their decision-making capability; and secondly look at the way such groups may or may not be related to the wider organizational context. Some effort to explore the broader aspects of these two issues is made below. However, in the first instance it may be useful to distinguish between *policy groups* and *groups for policy*. *Policy groups* are teams surrounding leaders whose particular tasks are directed towards policy decisions. Members are generally selected by the leader or internally by group members, and recruited on the basis of factors such as expertise; typical of such groups are inner cabinets such as those used by U. S. Presidents (Graff, 1970). In contrast, *groups for policy* are bodies where members appear as representatives of organizational interests. Here the group serves as a coordinating device for the organization itself as well as operating as a decision-making mechanism. Cabinets in the British political system typify such a group as do many policy boards in private sector management. It is clearly an error to make too sharp a distinction between these two types. It would also be unsatisfactory to assume that one form was automatically superior to the other. Yet the differences between them capture some of the dilemmas of organizational life. The small *policy group* promises openness, cohesion, and the opportunity for integrated attacks on problems. However, it may have a low degree of legitimacy in the wider organization often leading to problems of policy implementation. In contrast, *groups for policy* exist, at least in part, to guard specific and identifiable interests that exist at lower levels of the organization (see below). In such a situation, individual or sub-group goals, which may or may not correspond to overall organizational goals, are incorporated into the decision process to the extent that, as Wilensky has noted in another context, the very mechanisms that have been designed to increase rationality and an organization's ability to cope may in fact encourage intelligence failures (Wilensky, 1967; Betts, 1978). The question of whether better policy emerges from the formation and involvement of top-level groups is not an easy one to answer since any answer may depend on the circumstances. Such arguments which lie at the heart of contingency theories of organizations would seem to point toward the need to develop a similar perspective on policy-making groups. This issue is examined in the conclusion to this paper, but first it is of interest to explore what the study of group dynamics may add to the detail of policy studies.

Some Pathologies of Policy Groups

The study of small groups has generated and continues to generate a large literature within which the issues of decision and decision process are, in themselves, a substantial field. Is group decision more effective than individual decision? As many have argued, this may pose the question too broadly and in many situations decisions emerge from a combination of both individual and group processes. Still, there is evidence to indicate that, for decisions that demand extensive or unusual information or deal with ambiguous or uncertain situations, groups appear superior to individuals (Collins and Guetzkow, 1964; Handy, 1976; Hellriegal and Slocum, 1976). The reasons for such conclusions are complex but may result from the superior resources the group offers in addition to the fact that group membership may be a source of influence and motivation (Collins and Guetzkow, 1964). In short, under certain circumstances, groups provide an organization with a greater problem-solving capacity and act as devices to increase an organization's power. That is to say, groups enable the organization to move closer to the rational model discussed earlier.

Yet groups have another 'face'. The presence of groups may result in unforeseen consequences, and actually retard the process of rational decision making. For example, power is rarely distributed evenly amongst group members; indeed, such distributions may vary over time and according to situation. From such a seed-bed, organizational politics may develop and spread (see below). However, this is only one consequence of groups. Another relates to the social structure within groups. Take, for instance the issue of group norms with particular regard to how such norms may affect group productivity. Could such norms influence the policy process of the organization to the extent of leading it towards an irrational policy? In his discussion of the Johnson administration's conduct of the Vietnam war, Janis argues that there exists considerable evidence that key policy makers were constrained by their membership of an inner policy group from advocating innovative policy stances especially any that ran against group norms which stressed loyalty to past decisions and placed a high value on conformity (Janis, 1972). As George has contended elsewhere, the problem-solving capacity of a group is 'a variable that takes many forms, some of which may not be conducive to rational decision making' (George, 1974). If this is the case, this Janus-faced nature of groups needs more thought. In particular, in the world of policy the extent to which the problem-solving and legitimation function of groups are supported or threatened by social mechanisms arising within the groups themselves requires attention. Even in the rational model, where the goals of the group may appear to coincide with the goals of the organization, group roles and procedures may direct or steer decision mechanisms down unexpected paths. A key aspect here is the way a group may generate pressures towards conformity which is not, as has frequently been pointed out, to say that small groups necessarily produce uniformity (Cartwright and Lippitt, 1957). However, there is a great deal of evidence from small-group studies to indicate that groups may pressurize individuals towards conformity and that conformity may arise as a product of group cohesion. This is particularly likely in conditions of extreme crisis. It is such a possibility, termed by Irving Janis 'groupthink', which raises interesting questions concerning the role of small groups in top-level policy making and certainly poses problems that have rarely been considered in the wider compass of policy studies (Janis, 1972). Hence, Janis deliberately challenges the conventional wisdom that a highly cohesive group is, inevitably, a high performance group. Indeed, in Janis's eyes, the goal of 'group agreement' may displace other goals of policy making to the point where 'efficiency', 'rationality', or even the 'morality' of a policy may run a poor second to the pressures for group agreement (George, 1974). Thus, Janis's concern has been with what can be termed 'policy failures', particularly in the field of international relations.

Is it possible that, in the highest echelons of government, the small policy groups gathered around leaders may 'close' rather than open the policy process? That there is likelihood of such an occurrence has already been indicated by our earlier discussion, and using a variety of empirical evidence derived from historical records, observers' accounts of events and participants' memoirs, Janis demonstrates that in many cases policy groups have (a) often operated *a selective bias* with regard to the gathering and interpretation of information, (b) considered few alternatives in the decision process, and (c) either neglected or rarely considered the issue of policy implementation. In rational terms such decision making is clearly defective, yet evidence of it can be found in a variety of organizations. The importance of Janis's work, however, is not to give a blanket explanation of departures from the rational paradigm but rather to point to the possibility of groups initiating or accelerating such trends:

> Yet the potential advantage of having decisions made by groups is often lost because of the psychological pressures that arise when the members work closely together, share the same values and above all face a crisis situation in which everyone realises at the outset that whatever action the group decides to take will be fraught with serious risks (Janis and Mann, 1977, p. 133).

The stipulation of crisis decision making clearly places limitations on Janis's analysis but this should not detract from his impressive arguments that processes and procedures in small groups may have a direct effect on the conduct and content of policy. In particular, he draws attention to possible pathologies in policy groups arising from (a) group insulation, (b) group cohesiveness, and (c) leadership style. Some of the arguments for this position have already been rehearsed above; however, they would benefit from being restated and briefly elaborated. Thus, the issues of insulation and cohesiveness are linked to the development and maintenance of group norms. In cohesive groups, members are more dependent upon each other in psychological and social terms. Such dependence is often accompanied by attempts to isolate the group from outside influences and, in particular, to reject external information that either challenges the group's position or threatens current policy. In support of such arguments one may note examples such as the Kennedy group involved in the Bay of Pigs invasion while, in another context, Raven has drawn attention to the insulation of the White House group that surrounded Nixon in his second term as U. S. President (Janis, 1972; George, 1974; Kissinger, 1979; Raven, 1974). Leadership is also clearly important since, as wider studies have shown, group performance may well be linked to situation and leadership style (Fiedler, 1967; Fiedler and Chermers, 1974) and these and other factors combine to form what Janis terms 'concurrence seeking tendencies'. These tendencies manifest themselves as groupthink: the illusion of the invulnerability of the group, stereotypes of out-groups, direct pressures on dissenters, illusion of unanimity, etc. So, does the appearance of a small policy group inevitably lead to defective decision making in a crisis situation? Not necessarily, argue Janis and Mann. Not all cohesive policy groups can be assumed to operate in this fashion. For example:

> A group not insulated from outside evaluations, and subject to traditions and norms facilitating critical enquiry and non-authoritarian leadership practices is probably capable of a better decision than any individual in the group working on the problem alone (Janis and Mann, 1977, p. 133).

Such a statement may be open to question since the intrusion of external influences (especially from other parts of the organization) may not, *ipso facto*, lead to critical enquiry and rational decision. However, issues such as this aside,

Janis's work is clearly important in its attempts to relate group processes and procedures to policy and decision making in organizations. But, what of organizational politics itself? As George has noted, 'few attempts have been made to study ways in which primary relationships within decision making groups affect political attitudes and, more generally, the political process' (George, 1974, p. 10). For George the group relationships may affect political behaviour within organizations, yet the reverse may also be true in that organizational politics may be an influential factor in both the process of top-level policy making and in determining organizational policy itself which leads us towards a political model of how policy groups operate.

Policy and the Political Model

The Political Model—Basic Features

The thrust of the above section has been (a) to describe the rational method of policy making, (b) to outline the conditions favouring the setting up of policy groups, and (c) to discuss some of the unanticipated ways by which group norms can prevent policy groups from attaining goal optimization even where members share goals and values. The purpose of this section is to describe a model of organizations which stresses the divergent interests and commitments of groups within the organization, and the problems of those interests. That is to say, we shall consider groups whose members do *not* share common goals or hold the same values. Policy making in this model is seen largely as the interplay of groups, and policies are largely a function of (a) tactical skill on the part of group representatives and (b) their relative influence within the organization.

As we have seen, one of the central concepts assumed within the rational paradigm is that of organizational 'goal'. Or, as Burns (1966) has eloquently put it, 'desired end states'. Organizations are supposedly structured to attain goals, and policies are framed according to the relationship between the content of the policy and the organizational goal. Unfortunately, the idea of an organizational goal is not as clear-cut as the rational model implies, for several reasons. First, goals (if they exist) are rarely drawn in less than ambiguous terms and are often too vague to provide clear yardsticks against which alternative policies might be evaluated.

Furthermore, attempts to turn ambiguous goals into more precise statements run into a second difficulty, namely that organizations usually have multiple goals which are frequently inconsistent. Even a private enterprise with the apparently straightforward aim of securing profit maximization will find itself subject to a set of pressures from a diverse array of interested parties, each of which holds particular definitions of what the organization should be doing (Stagner, 1969). One of the dilemmas facing all organizations is the need to reconcile multiple goals valued to differing extents by significant parties. Thirdly, there is never a sure appreciation of the relationship between organizational goals and alternative courses of action. The means-end continuum, fundamental to the rational model, is not certain and decisions on the relative merits of policy options have to be taken on the basis of reasoned estimation of how far they will reach stated goals, always assuming that goals could be formulated in relatively precise and operational form.

Recognition that organizational goals, far from providing an accepted framework within which decisions and policies can be taken, are themselves a matter of conjecture and dispute is the starting point for the political model. This model accepts that it is not possible to appeal to goals in justification of a single policy option because other options may be linked, with equal facility, to the same goal (differently interpreted) or to other equally legitimate goals. Furthermore, the model accepts that it is usually impossible to demonstrate conclusively what are the consequences of a proposed policy, a fact that tends to separate both cognitively and organizationally the stages of decision and implementation.

The problem with organizational goals is linked in the political model with another characteristic of organizations, the development of units or departments within the organization committed to functional interests which often appear contrary to the interests of other units or departments. The rational model of organizations recognizes the advantages of specialization created by a division of labour. Work is facilitated if the organizational task is broken into a series of discrete and interdependent activities each made the responsibility of separate individuals and suborganizational units. What the rational model does not recognize, however, is that these units become increasingly committed to the particular set of activities for which they are responsible. Individuals find themselves pursuing sub-organizational responsibilities, and interpreting issues of policy, in terms of its effects upon their work unit. As Dalton (1959, p. 3) noticed: 'Isolation of personnel in this way provokes a given group to magnify the importance of its function in the system and to ignore and minimise that of others. This leads to challenges and defences.' The tendency for both individuals and groups within such sub-units to identify with the unit task, rather than with the organization, is an inevitable consequence of the division of labour (Strauss, 1962; Lawrence and Lorsch, 1967). In one sense it is inevitable because individuals are familiar only with a part of the overall task (and, naturally, perceive directly the importance of that part). But the issue is more complicated than that. There is increasing evidence that the structures, management styles, and methods of working appropriate for organizational tasks vary according to the nature of the task, the scale of the operation, and the conditions within the environment. The literature on this topic is not always consistent but the thrust is that organizations vary in methods of operation because of the situational contingencies bearing upon their task. That is to say, this literature argues that organizational performance is impaired or enhanced by the choice of structural

Table 1

Departmental type	Formality of structure	Task orientation	Time orientation	Interpersonal orientation
Legal	3.7	5.2	4.7	1.2
Finance	4.0	4.5	4.3	1.7
Social Services	3.9	6.2	5.0	1.5
Engineering	4.2	4.7	5.3	2.0
Architecture	2.3	2.5	3.9	3.9
Planning	3.4	4.6	4.7	2.7

Note: A difference of 0.5 or greater was statistically significant.

arrangements, and that the choice of arrangements is a direct function of the organization's size, the technology used, and the stability or otherwise of the environment (Kast and Rosenzweig, 1973; Greenwood *et al.*, 1975). (Further on this, see the conclusion.)

The importance of this for operations *within* an organization was recognized by Lawrence and Lorsch (1967) who analysed the extent to which the division of labour within industrial companies produced groups whose situational contingencies were sufficiently different to warrant different styles of management. That is, they recognized that parts of the organization face their own contingencies and, in order to achieve optimum performance, adopt different styles and methods of operation.*

The same is frequently, but not always, true of public agencies. An unpublished study of local authority departments by Greenwood and Hinings (1978) examines differences between them along dimensions similar to those used by Lawrence and Lorsch. The results were as shown in Table 1.

There is a clear indication that along the four dimensions used local authority departments exhibited different patterns which could be explained by their differences in task and organizational size. As such these results from local government confirm the underlying thesis presented by Lawrence and Lorsch. That is, it would appear that organizations both in the public and private sectors are composed of groups which, for reasons of technical advantage, have each developed significantly different methods of working. Departments are differen-

---

* These differences were assessed in terms of four dimensions:

1. *formality of structures*, i.e. the extent of bureaucratization;

2. *goal orientation*, i.e. the extent to which managers in different departments are concerned with different objectives (e.g. sales volume versus low manufacturing costs);

3. *time orientation*, i.e. the time scale of analysis (e.g. are production departments more pressed by immediate problems than design engineers?);

4. *interpersonal orientation*, i.e. the extent to which managers emphasize task attainment or maintenance of relationships with peers. Lawrence and Lorsch demonstrate that departments within the same organization do vary in terms of these four dimensions. They refer to these differences as the extent of organizational *differentiation*.

tiated in terms of their structural formality, time orientation, task or goal orientation, and the emphasis upon interpersonal relationships. All of this compounds the natural tendency of organizational members to become committed to departmental goals at the expense of wider organizational goals. Personnel within the sales department perceive sales volume as more important than manufacturing costs: education officers are more likely to favour the development of teaching facilities than the construction of houses. And so on.

Given their identification with departmental goals members of a department work to attain those goals. That is, departments seek to protect or enhance their share of critical organizational resources because of a commitment to the perceived importance of the group's activities. Differences between groups, caused by virtue of their specialization and varying methods of working, are not eased by the ambiguity of multiple goals. Inevitably, organizations are composed of functional groups with differing views about the relative importance of particular sets of activities, and of how those activities can be advanced.

These 'internal combustics' (Dalton, 1959, p. 232) and the lack of a clear framework of superordinate goals by which to resolve them, means that *policies are the product not of measured rational calculation but of political negotiation between competing groups seeking to translate departmental interests into organizational policy.* An interesting example of this is provided by Pfeffer and Salancik's study of resource allocation within the University of Illinois. These authors begin by separating

two classes of decision variables which can be employed in determining resource allocation. First, there are variables that represent universalistic or bureaucratic criteria. Second, there are those variables which represent particularistic or political criteria that are used in decision making (1974, p. 138).

An example of bureaucratic criteria might be staff–student ratios as a determinant for the allocation of scarce teaching resources. Political criteria, on the other hand, would involve the application of sub-unit power. Pfeffer and Salancik use several indicators of subunit power, including (a) access to, and membership of, important committees, and (b) power as perceived by departmental heads. The results of the study indicate that departmental power is significantly related to the successful acquisition of resources. That is to say, powerful departments were able to obtain resources despite their comparatively low workload. Therefore, Pfeffer concludes: 'when consensually agreed upon, objective standards are missing from the situation, social power and influence affect the outcome of decisions' (1978, p. 12). What we are emphasizing is that the rational model, with its focus upon the use of rational, objective bureaucratic criteria for resource allocation and policy making, is frequently inappropriate because of (a) the existence of multiple, rather vague organizational goals, and (b) the process of organizational differentiation which creates sub-units motivated to defend and enhance departmental goals. The existence of several departments seeking to advance departmental rather than organizational interests implies that policy making is an essentially *political* activity. Not surprisingly, therefore, the role of 'groups' within the organization, as interpreted by the political model, is significantly different from that described for the rational model.

At least two crucial differences should be noted: first, the reasons for setting up groups differs between the rational and bureaucratic models and, secondly, they differ in how the groups operate. In the rational model groups are formed in order to pool the expertise distributed throughout the organization. We noted earlier that groups in the rational model are formed because of the ambiguity and uncertainty involved in policy making within complex organizations. Recognition that the hierarchy of authority within a complex organization is not synonymous with a hierarchy of expertise implies that some vehicle is required to pull together the disparate pools of expertise required for policy making. One such vehicle is the policy group composed of members drawn from the disparate pools. Thus, in the rational model the focus is legitimately placed upon how that kind of group functions. The important questions are: How are decisions affected by group size? What procedures are appropriate for different kinds of policy issues? What is the appropriate style of leadership? The focus within the political model, on the other hand, has to be different. Much more attention has to be placed upon decision making involving groups that takes place *outside* of a formal policy making group.

To illustrate this point it is convenient to discuss policy making in an English local authority. English local authorities are composed of several departments each responsible for a particular service. There may be ten or more departments, providing housing, education, social welfare, recreation, highways construction, refuse collection, and so on. To a large extent these services are administratively self-contained, but there are significant instances where policies are required that cover several if not all of the authority's departments. Certain planning decisions—the location of a housing estate, or city centre redevelopment, for example—may affect all services. Similarly, the annual process of resource allocation affects all departments in that resources for one department are no longer available for others. For these issues the majority of local authorities have set up inter-departmental teams of officers, culminating in the management team of chief officers. In other words, the local authority operates with an *explicit* framework of *policy groups*. (Why these groups are set up will be explored below.) The intention is that these groups should analyse issues affecting more than one department and prepare a programme of action that will ensure a coordinated approach. Thus, in determining the annual budget, departments would analyse their respective priorities, consider the financial and policy implications of the expenditure proposals of one service department for those of others, and hammer out coherent and consistent policy advice for elected representatives. That is, the management team is intended to behave as a *policy group* along the lines assumed in the rational model. But, the reality is somewhat different. There will be considerable negotiation between two or three departments as chief officers prepare and test out their case before formal meetings of the management team. Negotiations are begun, bargains struck. Moreover, proposals put forward at the management team are framed to anticipate likely objections and to meet the requirements of affected influential parties. The preparation of reports for the management team is not one of rational analysis but of anticipated reaction, compromise, and expediency. The discussion, moreover, takes place not *in* the formal policy group but *outside* it (Greenwood, 1980).

Similar experiences are documented in a variety of sources. Burns (1977), for example, has traced the interaction and negotiations between functional groups at the BBC. Beard (1976) and Sapolsky (1972) provide evidence concerning the military. Pettigrew (1973), Dalton (1959), Woodward (1965) and, to a lesser extent, Mintzberg (1973) illustrate the same theme from industrial organizations. Baldridge (1971) and Pfeffer and Salancik (1974) have studied universities. These accounts demonstrate that policy making within organizations is a function of the interplay between departmental groups with interdependent and competitive interests. In that sense groups play a considerable role in the formulation of policy within organizations. The same accounts also show, however, that *formal groups charged with ratifying policy options are much less important than assumed within the rational model. The study of groups in the processes of policy making is a matter of analysing the interactions that occur between functional groups outside the formal decision process.* Policy making, in other words, is the product of subgroup commitments and divergent interests, but the reconciliation of those commitments and divergent interests takes place *outside* of formal groups as well as inside.

This is not to suggest that formal *policy groups* are not found. We have already mentioned the management team within the English local authority. Similarly, the BBC has formal policy-making bodies (Burns, 1977) as does the military (Beard, 1976) and the university (Baldridge, 1971). Indeed, to consider organizations in terms of the political model is not to deny the structural existence of the apparatus found within the rational model. *Policy groups* exist at least formally. There is a difference, however, in why they are set up and in how they operate. *Policy groups* are set up under the rational model to bring together pools of expertise distributed throughout the organization. The complexity of decision making defies the limited ability of single decision makers: therefore, representatives of relevant skills are pulled together to formulate a coordinated policy stance. Under the political model this same rationale is often put forward to explain the existence of groups. For example, the management team of chief officers in a local authority is expected to have:

a corporate identify and a positive role to play in the corporate management of the authority . . . its members do not attend primarily as representatives of particular departments, though on occasion it will be necessary for them to speak in that capacity; they are there as members of a body created to aid the management of the authority as a whole . . . (Bains, pp. 48–49).

That is, the management team is pooling the skills of several departments in order to promote the corporate interests of the authority. But underlying this bureaucratic rationale is a more political one. It is recognized that any attempt to resolve the differences that exist between departments stands a greater chance of success if those departments are formally involved in the policy-making process. That is, there is the belief that commitment to the wider organizational goals, or to a particular course of action, is more attainable if affected and powerful interests are directly involved and, more fundamentally, that consensus on decision will smooth the path to policy implementation. Thus, when one looks at the composition of formal policy groups within the political model, the powerful departments will be represented. The management team of chief officers does not always involve all chief officers—but those excluded are excluded not because their skills of judgement are any less than other chief officers, but because they are seen as less important politically.

In summary, the supposedly *policy group* established within the political model are in fact *groups for policy*. The terms of references given these groups may well stress the need for rational analysis and objective evaluation of policy options in terms of organizational purposes, but in practice there are strong undertones of commitment to departmental interests.

Groups for Policy: Problems of Operation

The second principal difference between groups under the political and rational models concerns the ways in which they operate. Rational groups, we have suggested, operate in terms of 'computational' analysis (Thompson and Tuden, 1956) and seek to relate policies to goals without undue concern for departmental interests. The problems of these groups are in the area of 'groupthink'. Groups within the political model are rather different. Here the clash is not one of intellect and ideas, but of commitment and interests. The problem is not one of reaching a policy that incorporates the technical constraints and opportunities available, but of securing *acceptance* from affected interests. How do *groups for policy* reach policies acceptable to those represented?

The political model emphasizes the importance of departmental power as a determinant of policy making. But naked power is rarely used in organizations. Instead, organizations develop 'rules of the game' (or standard operating procedures) which constrain which policy issues will be discussed, what options will be raised, in what form, and how they will be treated (Cyert and March,

1963). That is to say, the open conflict of departmental interests is contained by a set of understood (but rarely codefied) rules that effectively structure how groups will behave. To illustrate this it is worth summarizing the ideas of Wildavsky (1964, 1974) which, although focusing exclusively upon the problem of resource allocation, are equally relevant to more substantive policy areas (Lindblom, 1968; Garlichs and Hull, 1978).

The starting point of Wildavsky's analysis is to question how decision makers arrive at resource allocation decisions given their inability to pursue comprehensive rational analysis. How, asks Wildavsky, do officials go about 'their staggering burden of calculation' (p. 10)? Part of the answer is the adoption of 'rules of the game', or 'standard operating procedures' which serve to limit both the *attention* of actors and the *actions* they are expected to adopt. Two rules in particular stand out. First, existing policies are rarely reviewed. Instead, attention is focused upon the proposed changes. Thus, in referring to budgetary appropriations Wildavsky (1964, p. 15) concludes that:

The beginning of wisdom about an agency budget is that it is almost never actively reviewed as a whole every year in the sense of reconsidering the value of all existing programs as compared to all special attention given to a narrow range of increases or decreases.

Secondly, decisions on the allocation of resources are taken, not to pursue optimal achievement of objectives, but to provide a 'fair share' for each claimant. In other words, resources are allocated in a way that provides each claimant with his previous expenditure (i.e. the 'base') plus a reasonable ('fair share') proportion of additional resources. Wildavsky describes it thus:

'Fair share' means not only the base an agency has established but also the expectation that it will receive some proportion of funds, if any, which are to be increased over or decreased below the base of the various governmental agencies. 'Fair share', then, reflects a convergence of expectations on roughly how much the agency is to receive in comparison to others (p. 17).

Here, then, are two norms, or rules of the game, that shape policy making over the budget. First, officials accept that existing expenditures (the base) should be left more or less untouched. Secondly, any additional resources will be allocated on a 'fair share' basis. These rules of the game are necessary, emphasizes Wildavsky because (a) comprehensive analysis is impossible, and (b) departmental interests are fundamentally in conflict. These rules of the game *work*, in that budgets are prepared on time, and they have the important advantage of *minimizing conflicts*: 'Conflict is reduced by an incremental approach because the area open to dispute is reduced' (p. 136). *Groups for policy*, then, if Wildavsky is correct in his analysis (and there is considerable evidence that this is the case, e.g. Danziger, 1978; Heclo and Wildavsky, 1974; Garlichs and Hull, 1978) produce policies which are unlikely to deviate from existing policies. Attempts to change existing policies run the risk of reopening old battles by threatening departmental interests. Therefore, changes tend to be incremental rather than fundamental. *Groups for policy* are constrained by the outcomes of previous struggles, and are essentially conservative in their stance.

Clearly, however, policy shifts do occur. There are instances of departments and government receiving significantly increased allocations. There are instances of new departures in policy, both by business corporations and governments. What is less clear is whether these shifts in policy are the product of groups or of more individual initiative. Much more research is necessary before this question can be satisfactorily explored. What seems likely from available evidence is that *groups for policy* are highly unlikely to produce radical departures from existing policies. Groups within a political environment tend not to produce new policy departures. In this they appear similar to the small policy group described earlier that becomes ensnared in the web of 'groupthink'. In the present case, however, pressure for consensus is more an organizational property than a group phenomenon but in both cases it would seem that other than in exceptional circumstances innovative policy is unlikely.

Clearly the Wildavsky thesis does not remove the possibility for some departments to achieve a larger share of resources than others. The actual amount of resources will in part reflect the skill of the agency advocate in exploiting opportunities and pressing the agency case. Wildavsky, in fact, documents at some length the tactics adopted by budget officials. In this respect his analysis is not dissimilar to the work of Christie and Geis (1970) on 'Machiavellian' workers. But, the important theme underlying Wildavsky and Lindblom is that decisions within groups concerned with policy making are constrained by a conservative acceptance of previous decisions (the 'base') as the appropriate starting point, and a conviction that new policies, and resources, should be acceptable to all participants: 'Agreement on policy thus becomes the only practicable test of the policy's correctness. And for one administrator to seek to win the other over to agreement on ends as well would accomplish nothing and create quite unnecessary controversy' (p. 71).

Let us be clear. Policy making in groups is constrained by the limited ability of groups to appreciate all the complexities involved in the issue at hand. Inevitably there will be sub-group loyalties and divergent interests. Reconciliation of divergent interests on matters of policy occurs through agreement on basic *rules of the game*. These include an unwillingness to reconsider previous policy decisions. Previous policies are accepted as the starting point for discussion. In this way latent conflicts are kept within bounds. There is no attempt to reopen old wounds.

Some evidence to this end is provided by Greenwood *et al.* (1976). In their study of local authority management teams they constantly note the apparently trivial nature of the items found on the agenda. Indeed, members of the management team were frequently critical of the items discussed:

we discuss trivia much of the time. It's all nuts and bolts—we have not yet achieved one of the basic aims of corporate management, that is, sorting out priorities.

And:

Oh God, we discuss everything from planning to the repair of the house with the thatched roof . . . here is a typical agenda: student expenses, control of dogs, fire precautions in the town hall, departmental lunch times and so on' (Greenwood *et al.*, 1976, p. 113)

The *reason* why management teams discuss these issues but ignore priorities is because of an unwritten acceptance that heads of department should not be forced to bring policy matters to the management team. To do so runs the risk of opening serious divisions of view between members of the team, and would act as a precedent whereby any department could be asked to report to the team. That is to say, chief officers tacitly agree to support each other by not bringing forward items, and by not raising issues involving other departments. The result is an agenda of largely uncontentious items. As a consequence policy making by the management team within the local authority is essentially *incremental* both in style and effect. The range of policy options considered is restricted to those close to existing arrangements and thus to those unlikely to disturb existing interests. This is typical of the political model. Groups involved in the policy-making process are *groups for policy*, despite their formal appearance as *policy groups*. In order to reconcile divergent interests they adopt group norms that produce highly conservative and incremental policies.

We have used the ideas of Wildavsky and Lindblom to illustrate the conventions that operate within policy-making groups. That these ideas operate within the public sector is beyond doubt. Numerous studies of policy making and resource allocation within government agencies have demonstrated the empirical utility of these ideas (Crossman, 1979, Danziger, 1978; Heclo and Wildavsky, 1974). There is also some evidence that similar principles are operative in business organizations. The ideas of Lindblom and Wildavsky are not dissimilar to the model proposed by Cyert and March. More directly, Mintzberg's (1973) study of managers at work reached the following conclusion:

current strategy-making practice cannot be characterised as 'grand planning'. Although the incrementalists play down the role of entrepreneurship, and underestimate the power of the manager and the ability of the organization to impose major change on itself there is little doubt that they present the better description of current strategy-making behaviour (p. 153).

The picture that emerges from the political model, therefore, runs as follows. Organizations are made up of interdependent but loosely coupled functional groups each with its set of interests. Policy making is the product of interplay between those groups or, at least, interplay between groups whose interests are affected. Much of the interplay occurs in the 'corridors of power' in the way described by C. P. Snow and not in formal policy groups. Formal groups become involved in policy making only after much initial negotiation has taken place. These groups, moreover, are characterized by an unwillingness to review existing policies, and a tendency to base policy decisions on previous decisions because they are less likely to disturb existing interests, and which therefore have more chance of securing agreement. The net effect is a highly incremental process of policy making.

We have referred so far to the peculiar role of groups within the political model. That is, we have stressed that policy making within the political model is a function of negotiation between functional units and departments each with a discrete set of interests and commitments. Negotiations take place outside the formal arena. Policy groups may be set up but are in practice *groups for policy*. These groups operate with rules of the game that serve to minimize the outbreak of considerable latent conflict and as a result produce essentially incremental changes in policy stance. We have intimated that this kind of behaviour is found in all organizations, whether they be public agencies, universities, or business corporations. However, the political model may be more appropriate under certain circumstances than others, and it is worth concluding this section with an interesting line of research that has occurred in recent years.

Pfeffer and Salancik (1974) in their study of budgeting within a university make the point that universities are 'loosely coupled' organizations (Weick, 1976). That is, various departments are not directly affected by what happens to other departments. The same is true of multi-purpose local authorities: it would be possible to disband a recreation department (for example) without damaging the activities of the education department. Indeed, the history of governmental organizations is replete with such changes. Under such conditions suggest Pfeffer and Salancik, the characteristic behaviours of the political model may be more evident—departments that are not reciprocally threatened by damage imposed upon other departments may feel less compunction about inflicting such damage! 'Internal interdependence among subunits . . . limit the utilization of subunit power in organizational decision making' (Pfeffer and Salancik, 1974, p. 150).

Perhaps a more important limitation on the political model, however, is the state of the environment. Child (1972) has demonstrated that organizations may choose to operate at less than optimum performance, a strategy which is feasible in a benign resource environment. Under conditions of resource abundance there is less pressure to remove organizational 'slack'. Therefore, the politics of interdepartmental bargaining may be less constrained, and norms of 'fair share' and 'base' less threatening to organizational survival. However, a more threatening environment may change the performance standards applied within the organization with one of two results. On the one hand, loosely coupled organizations may find that powerful departments use that power to shape policy and resource decisions to their advantage. The norms constraining open promotion of departmental interests will be less in force. Pfeffer and Salancik reached this conclusion in the study cited earlier. On the other hand, a more threatening environment confronting a highly interdependent organization may reduce the level of interdepartmental conflict and politicking. The absence of organizational 'slack' will make it more difficult for departments to develop and push policies that do not accommodate the technical interests of other departments.

In conclusion, then, the political model of organizations is based upon the absence of clear goals and the commitment of functional departments to subunit goals and interests. It is a model which emphasizes the politicking that occurs between subunits outside the formal apparatus for determining policy, and which recognizes that policy groups may well be groups for policy. There are, however, limits to this behaviour, set by the extent of interdependence within the organization, and the tightness of the resource environment.

Policy Groups: A Contingency Perspective

Towards a Contingency Framework

A central factor to be grappled with in any attempt at policy analysis is the explanation of policy outputs. What factors within and outside the organization account for the emergence of some policies rather than others, or explain the changes (or lack of change) in policy over time? In this chapter we have been particularly concerned with the place top-level groups may play in explaining these issues, although, as was seen in the previous section, it becomes extremely difficult to consider such groups separate from their organizational context. Are different types of policies the result of differing policy processes? If so, can the differences between these processes be linked to the presence and operation of particular types of top-level groups? Findings outlined above indicate in a tentative way that the causal sequence indicated could be accurate. Rational policy, in terms of optimal decisions that maximize single and uniquely identified goals, may be the product of small integrated policy groups surrounding a leader although Janis's work indicates that even this is not inevitable. Similarly, complex organizations with highly differentiated structures may be associated with incremental policies which are the expected product of more broadly based groups whose operating procedures are directed towards consensus. Again, though, as was indicated earlier, in certain circumstances different outcome patterns may be possible. In brief, policy outputs do appear to be influenced by top-level groups, but the way they are influenced varies with the type of group involved and with the roles and procedures adopted by a group at a particular point in time. To reverse the casual direction of the argument it would seem that there exist top-level groups with characteristic styles and operating procedures which have distinctive effects both on the *way* organizational policy is made and on the *character and form* of that policy. Policy performance may therefore be affected by the appearance and operation of top groups. But what factors determine the appearance of such groups and their mode of operation? It is in an effort to grapple with these issues that we turn to theoretical perspectives already identified, namely contingency approaches to both organizations and groups.

The contingency approach to organizations, introduced above, is well rehearsed and developed in the literature (Child, 1972, 1977; Warner (ed.), 1977). The main argument is that an organization's performance is related to the way the organization accommodates to a set of contextual constraints (in particular, the constraints of organizational size, environment, and task). If this perspective is correct then it clearly has policy implications in that policy performance will be related to the way organizations adjust to their contingencies (Jenkins, 1978). The examination of groups in similar terms has been advocated by a number of writers (Handy, 1976; Hellriegel and Slocum, 1977). Thus, Handy would see group performance as dependent upon the way that factors such as leadership styles and group processes are able to modify wider contingencies such as group size, task, and environment. The application of this perspective to the problem at hand can be briefly stated: first, policy outputs may be explained by the ways that organizations cope with their contingencies; and, secondly, top policy groups can be an important factor in such operations, i.e. top groups may emerge as the result of organizational attempts to accommodate to the pattern of constraints operating on them; therefore over time, the presence of such groups and their mode of operation become an important factor in influencing policy.

A simplistic contingency exploration of why top-level groups develop would see the appearance of policy structures (e.g. planning mechanisms) as an organizational response to the contingencies of environment, task, and size. Uncertainty and complexity are generally key terms here; for example, in uncertain environments with tasks of increasing complexity, organizations will restructure themselves and indeed may attempt to move to the rational model (see above). In all this, size is important since, as an organization grows, further problems of coping emerge, in particular the tensions between the decentralization of operations as against a centralization of decision making (see above). Increasing size, task differentiation and complexity, and uncertain environments (in the extreme instance, 'crisis') result in a variety of pressures on the policy framework of organizations to which the establishment of a group basis for policy is one possible response. That is to say, the increasing complexity of decision making is handled by removing the locus of decision making from an individual to a group. Such a response has advantages both in simple cognitive terms (increasing the intellectual capacity) and, in a more organizationally based way, may increase the scope of the organization for environmental management.

Evidence that such organizational strategies are to be expected can be illustrated by a variety of examples from both public and private sector organizations (Chandler, 1962; Galbraith, 1974; Hage, 1977). We would expect, therefore, that top policy groups may be created as a direct response to distinct patterns of internal and external contingencies. If such a thesis holds, then certain limits on the group's mode of operations become apparent because the contingencies influencing the organization are those with which the group *must* cope (e.g. rational planning may be demanded in the most irrational circumstances) (Caiden and Wildavsky, 1974). This, in itself, has implications for the roles and procedures of such a group. However, the idea that, given certain situational circumstances, planning groups *will* emerge is clearly too simplistic because it neglects organizational history. Organizational responses to structural contingencies cannot be taken as automatic and, as Burns (1977) pointed out, the ability of an organization to cope with one particular form of environment may, over time, make it difficult to cope with another. In part, this may be because 'managerial elites can try to be innovative in a mechanical structure but they cannot get very far' (Hage, 1977). However, the point is wider than this since, to quote Hage again, in both the public and private sector 'success may breed failure'. Generally, the evolution of organizational structures leads to biases in organizational processes that are difficult to alter. Hence, in the specific instance of top policy groups, an initial problem is that their appearance can neither be easily predicted nor their performance be taken for granted. In part, they do seem to be the product of environmental contingencies but their presence (or absence) is also influenced by the internal and external history of the organization itself.

However, if we were to pursue a theme, it would be that certain patterns of environmental and organizational contingencies favour the appearance of top policy groups. Top-level groups constitute a reasonable strategy for coping. Clearly, however, there are other strategies. Types of groups, indeed other policy mechanisms, exist, and those who control organizations face a choice of what strategies to adopt. Whatever form of groups are created will, in turn, have consequences for the processes of policy making, and the nature of the policies that emerge. This was the principal theme in earlier sections. It is not within the scope of this chapter to pursue these links further.

It is a major point of our argument, however, that much of the work on groups and group decision making neglects the organizational and contingency dimension. Group dynamics are undoubtedly important in explaining the behaviour of top-level groups and may have a measurable influence on policy but it is only rarely that such groups can be separated from the wider organizations in which they operate. Furthermore, if the operation of top-level groups does need to be viewed in an organizational context, it follows that contingency perspective is also important. In brief, the group–organizational interaction must be considered in terms of a wider set of variables, in particular the structure of the organization and the environment in which the latter operates. Evidence for this is apparent from our analysis of the political model of policy making (see above) although clearly the issue requires more detailed theoretical and empirical investigation.

Conclusion

This chapter has attempted to deal with the problem of how small top-level groups in organizations can affect both the process and nature of policy. In looking at this problem we have outlined two major approaches to the study of policy making, the rational paradigm and the political model, and attempted to show the functions and dysfunctions of top policy groups with respect to these. Finally, we have argued that a more complete understanding of such groups in organizations may come from viewing organizational policy making in a contingency framework and by attempting to relate group and organizational processes within this. Given this focus, we briefly offer here some final thoughts on what might be termed rationality and the paradox of groups. Rationality is still a key goal for many writers and practitioners in the organizational world and top-level groups are often seen as a way to achieve it. Thus, while writers such as Janis (1972) and George (1974) would recognize the existence of pathologies such as 'groupthink', the existence of bureaucratic politics, the cognitive limitations of groups as well as individuals, and of 'maladaptive' coping mechanisms, they still inherently believe that these constitute deficiencies which can either be overcome or eliminated. Janis would prescribe a variety of strategies for minimizing groupthink. George offers the idea of 'optimal mutual advocacy' to move executive structures away 'from the detrimental vagaries of bureaucratic politics' (George, 1974, p. 218). Our position is not to downgrade such ambition but rather to deny some of the foundations of its overall logic. There is, within such arguments, a flavour of there being one best way to organize for policy. The idea that a cost–benefit analysis of top policy groups is possible to the extent that more information, less conflict, and clearer decisions are all desired end-states, while organizational politics and suchlike are 'pathologies' to be minimized or dispensed with, seems to neglect the organizational context in which policy making takes place. 'The beginning of administrative wisdom', wrote Burns and Stalker some years ago, 'is the awareness that there is no one optimal level of management system' (Burns and Stalker, 1961). This remark underlines the basis of contingency perspectives on organizations and, we would contend, holds in the context of policy systems and policy groups. To talk of an effective and efficient policy in organizational terms demands a wider frame of analysis than might be currently available. The same holds for any evaluation of top policy groups in that the performance of such groups can only be understood and evaluated by identifying the constraints under which they operate and in particular how the group relates to the wider organizational context. To our knowledge, there has been little analysis to date that has examined the operation of top policy groups in such terms but it is clearly an objective that must be worked towards.

References

Allison, G. T. (1971)*The Essence of Decision*, Boston: Little Brown.
Allison, G. T. and Szanion, P. (1976) *Remaking Foreign Policy*, New York: Basic Books.
Ansoff, H. I. (1979) *Strategic Management*, New York: Macmillan.
Art, R. J. (1973) 'Bureaucratic politics and American foreign policy: a critique', *Policy Sciences*, **4**, 467–90.
Bains Study Group (1972) *The New Local Authorities*, London: H.M.S.O.
Baldridge, J. V. (1971) *Power and Conflict in the University*, New York: John Wiley and Sons.
Banfield, E. (1959) 'Ends and means in planning', *International Social Science Journal*, **11**, 361–68.
Beard, E. (1976) *Developing the ICBM: A Study in Bureaucratic Politics*, New York: Columbia University Press.
Betts, R. K. (1978) 'Analysis, war and decision: why intelligence failures are inevitable', *World Politics*, **31**, 61–89.
Burns, T. (1966) 'On the plurality of social systems', in J. R. Lawrence, ed., *Operational Research and the Social Sciences* London: Tavistock, pp. 165–77.
Burns, T. (1977) *The BBC: Public Institution and Private World*, London: Macmillan.
Burns, T. and Stalker, G. M. (1961) *The Management of Innovation*, London: Tavistock.
Caiden, N. and Wildavsky, A. (1974) *Planning and Budgeting in Poor Countries*, New York: John Wiley and Sons.
Caldwell, D. (1977) 'Bureaucratic foreign policy making', *American Behavioural Scientist*, **21**, 87–110.
Cartwright, D. C. and Lippitt, R. (1957) 'Group dynamics and the individual', *International Journal of Psychotherapy*, **7**, 86–102.
Chandler, A. (1962) *Strategy and Structure: Chapters in the History of Industrial Enterprise*, Cambridge, Mass.: M.I.T. Press.
Child, J. (1972) 'Organizational structure, environment and performance: the role of strategic choice', *Sociology*, **6**, 1–22.
Child, J. (1977) *Organization: A Guide to Problems and Practice*, London: Harper & Row.
Christie, R. and Geis, F. L. (1970) *Studies in Machiavellianism*, New York: Academic Press.
Collins, B. E. and Guetzkow, H. (1964) *A Social Psychology of Group Processes for Decision Making*, New York: John Wiley & Sons.
Crenson, M. (1971) *The Unpolitics of Air Pollution*, Baltimore: John Hopkins.
Crossman, R. (1979) in A. Howard, ed., *The Crossman Diaries*, London: Magnum Books.
Crozier, M. (1964) *The Bureaucratic Phenomenon*, Chicago: University of Chicago Press.
Cyert, R. M. and March, J. G. (1963) *A Behavioural Theory of the Firm*, Englewood Cliffs, N. J.: Prentice-Hall.
Dalton, M. (1959) *Men Who Manage*, New York: John Wiley & Sons.
Danziger, J. D. (1978) *Making Budgets*, London: Sage Library of Social Research.
Dror, Y. (1968) *Public Policy Making Re-examined*, San Francisco: Chandler.
Eddison, P. A. (1973) *Local Government: Management and Corporate Planning*, Aylesbury, England: L. Hill.
Edwards, G. C. and Sharkansky, I. (1978) *The Policy Predicament*, San Francisco: W. H. Freeman.

Etzioni, A. (1968) *The Active Society*, New York: Free Press.

Faludi, A. (1973) *Planning Theory*, Oxford: Pergamon Press.

Fiedler, F. (1967) *A Theory of Leadership Effectiveness*, New York: McGraw-Hill.

Fiedler, F. and Chermers, M. (1974) *Leadership and Effective Management*, Glenview: Scott, Foresman & Co.

Galbraith, J. K. (1974) *Economics and the Public Purpose*, Harmondsworth, England: Penguin Books.

Garlichs, D. and Hull, C. (1978) 'Central control and information dependence: Highway planning in the Federal Republic of Germany', in K. Hanf and F. W. Scharpf, eds., *Interorganisational Policy Making*, London: Sage Modern Politics Series, vol. 1.

George, A. (1974) 'Adaptation to stress in political decision making', in G. V. Coehlho, G. E. Hamberg, and J. E. Adams, eds., *Coping and Adaptation*, New York: Basic Books, ch. 9.

Golembiewski, R. (ed.) (1978) *The Small Group in Political Science*, Athens, Georgia: University of Georgia Press.

Graff, H. F. (1970) *The Tuesday Cabinet: Deliberation and Decision on Peace and War under Lyndon B. Johnson*, Englewood Cliffs, N. J.: Prentice-Hall.

Greenwood, R. (1980) 'The local authority budgetary process', in B. A. Booth, ed., *Planning for Welfare*, London: Basil Blackwell/Martin Robertson.

Greenwood, R. and Hinings, C. R. (1977) 'The study of local government: toward an organizational analysis', *Public Administration Bulletin*, **23**, 2–24.

Greenwood, R. and Hinings, C. R. (1978) *'Organization of local authority departments'*, Final Report to Social Science Research Council (U.K.).

Greenwood, R. and Stewart, J. D. (1974) *Corporate Planning in English Local Government*, London: Charles Knight.

Greenwood, R. and Hinings, C. R. and Ranson, S. (1975) 'Contingency theory and the organization of local authorities', *Public Administration*, **1975** (Spring), 1–23.

Greenwood, R., Hinings, C. R., Ranson, S., and Walsh, K. (1976) *In Pursuit of Corporate Rationality*, Institute of Local Government Studies, Birmingham, England: University of Birmingham Press.

Hage, J. (1977) 'Choosing Constraints and Constraining Choice', in M. Warner, ed., *Organisational Choice and Constraint*, Farnborough, England: Saxon House, pp. 1–56.

Halperin, M. H. (1974) *Bureaucratic Politics and Foreign Policy*, Washington, D. C.: Brookings.

Handy, C. B. (1976) *Understanding Organisations*, Harmondsworth, England: Penguin.

Heclo, H. and Wildavsky, A. (1974) *The Private Government of Public Money*, London: Macmillan.

Hellriegal, D. and Slocum, J. (1976) *Organisational Behaviour: Contingency Views*, New York: West Publishing Co.

Hitch, C. and McKean, R. (1960) *The Economics of Defence in the Nuclear Age*, Cambridge, Mass.: Harvard University Press.

Janis, I. L. (1972) *Victims of Groupthink*, Boston: Houghton Mifflin.

Janis, I. L. and Mann, L. (1977) *Decision-Making*, New York: Free Press.

Jenkins, W. I. (1978) *Policy Analysis*, London: Martin Robertson.

Kantor, P. (1976) 'Elites, pluralities and policy arenas in London', *British Journal of Political Science*, **6**, 311–34.

Kast, F. R. and Rosenzweig, J. E. (1973) *Contingency Views of Organisation and Management*, New York: Science Research Associates.

Kelley, H. H. and Thibaut, J. W. (1969) 'Group problem solving', in G. Lindzey and E. Aronson, eds., *The Handbook of Social Psychology*, Reading, Mass.: Addison Wesley, ch. 29.

Kissinger, H. (1979) *The White House Years*, London: Weidenfeld and Nicolson, and Michael Joseph.

Lawrence, P. R. and Lorsch, J. W. (1967) *Organisation and Environment*, Boston: Harvard University Press.

Lindblom, C. E. (1959) 'The science of muddling through', *Public Administration Review*, **19**, 70–88.

Lindblom, C. E. (1968) *The Policy Making Process*, Englewood Cliffs, N. J.: Prentice Hall.

Lowi, T. (1964) 'American Business, Public Policy, Case Studies and Political Theory', *World Politics*, **16**, 677–715.

Lowi, T. (1970) 'Decision making vs public policy: Toward an antidote for technocracy', *Public Administration Review*, **30**, 314–25.

Lowi, T. (1972) 'Four systems of politics, policy and choice', *Public Administration Review*, **32**, 298–310.

Lukes, S. (1974) *Power: A Radical View*, London: Macmillan.

McWhirter, D. A. (1978) 'Testing for groupthink', in R. Golembiewski, ed., *Small Groups in Political Science* Athens, Georgia: University of Georgia Press, pp. 210–20.

Maier, N. R. F. (1970) *Problem Solving and Creativity in Individuals and Groups*, Belmont, California: Brooks Cole.

March, J. G. and Simon, H. A. (1958) *Organisations*, New York: J. Wiley and Sons.

Mintzberg, H. (1973) *The Nature of Managerial Work*, New York: Harper & Row.

Mintzberg, H., Raisinghani, D., and Theoret, A. (1976) 'The structure of unstructured decision processes', *Administrative Science Quarterly*, **21**, 246–75.

Nathan, J. K. and Oliver, J. (1978) 'Bureaucratic politics: academic windfalls and intellectual pitfalls', *Journal of Political and Military Sociology*, **6**, 81–91.

Pettigrew, A. (1973) *The Politics of Organisational Decision Making*, London: Tavistock.

Pfeffer, J. (1978) *Organisational Design*, Arlington: AHM Publishing Corporation.

Pfeffer, J. and Salancik, G. R. (1974) 'Organisational decision making as a political process: the case of a university budget', *Administrative Science Quarterly*, **19**, 135–51.

Raven, B. H. (1974) 'The Nixon Group', *Journal of Social Issues*, **30**, 297–320.

Raven, B. H. and Rubin, J. (1976) *Social Psychology: People in Groups*, New York: John Wiley and Sons.

Sapolsky, H. M. (1972) *The Polaris System Development*, Cambridge, Mass.: Harvard University Press.

Schelling, T. (1970) *Strategy for Conflict*, Cambridge, Mass. Harvard University Press.

Shaw, M. E. (1976) *Group Dynamics* (2nd edn), New York: McGraw-Hill.

Snyder, J. L. (1978) 'Rationality at the brink: The role of cognitive processes in failures of deterrence', *World Politics*, **30**, 345–65.

Stagner, R. (1969) 'Corporate decision making', *Journal of Applied Psychology*, **53**, 1–13.

Steinbruner, J. D. (1974) *The Cybernetic Theory of Decision*, Princeton, N. J.: Princeton University Press.

Steinbruner, J. D. (1976) 'Beyond rational deterrence: the struggle for new conceptions', *World Politics*, **28**, 223–45.

Strauss, G. (1962) 'Tactics of lateral relationship: the purchasing agent', *Administrative Science Quarterly*, **7**, 161–86.

Thompson, J. D. and Tuden, A. (1956) 'Strategies, structures and processes in organisational decision making', in J. D. Thompson, ed., *Comparative Studies in Administration*, Pittsburgh: University of Pittsburgh Press, pp. 195–206.

Warner, M. (ed.) (1977) *Organisational Choice and Constraint*, Farnborough, England: Saxon House.

Weick, K. E. (1976) 'Educational organisations as loosely coupled systems', *Administrative Science Quarterly*, **21**, 1–10.

Wildavsky, A. (1964) *The Politics of the Budgetary Process*, Boston: Little Brown.
Wildavsky, A. (1974) *Budgeting: A Comparative Theory of the Budgetary Process*, Boston: Little Brown.
Wilensky, H. (1967) *Organisational Intelligence*, New York: Basic Books.
Wohlstetter, R. (1962) *Pearl Harbor: Warning and Decision*, California: Stanford.
Woodward, J. (1965) *Industrial Organisation*, London: Oxford University Press.
Yates, D. (1977) *The Ungovernable City*, Cambridge, Mass.: M.I.T. Press.
Zander, A. (1979) 'The psychology of group processes', *Annual Review of Social Psychology*, **30**, 417–51.

Groups at Work
Edited by R. Payne and C. Cooper
© 1981 John Wiley & Sons Ltd.

Chapter 2

Dynamics of Groups that Execute or Manage Policy

Ronald Fry, Irwin Rubin, and Mark Plovnick

Introduction

Dilemmas faced by the middle manager are well known. For example, Aram (1976) has observed that this person must motivate, but also alter, individual needs of others in order to achieve collective actions; must exercise authority with humaneness; must apply rules and policies with equity, yet allow for special needs and considerations of individuals in order for them to develop; and as a leader must both adhere to and change group norms in order to maintain effectiveness over time. Occupants of such roles are caught betwixt and between. The executive washroom lies some distance above: a constant source of aspiration and motivation. The keys are few, however, so the competition will be stiff. Some distance below lies the old gang: a group perhaps recently left. The middle manager is no longer one of the troops and is not yet one of the generals. S/he lives in a state of limbo . . . a kind of no-man's land. Zander (1979) has argued further that the better the occupants of these positions practise 'good management techniques' the more vulnerable they become to coercive derisive tactics of others. In the face of such hostility or unfair treatment, they must remain cool, calm, and dignified. The better the manager, the more s/he tends to be 'on stage' all the time.

Our intent in this chapter is to examine a class of groups in organizations whose life space and dynamics parallel, in many ways, those of the manager caught in the middle. These are groups that execute or manage policy. For the sake of convenience we will refer to these groups as *middle groups.*

Since no group—top, middle, or bottom—exists totally in isolation, we will begin by looking at the organization as a whole . . . as a series of interlocking groups. This will provide a picture of the unique environment in which middle groups function. In so doing, we shall focus heavily on a concept which we label the *mirror image.* This is a phenomenon whereby a middle group experiences the effects of a problem reflected upon it by a group above it in the organizational hierarchy, usually an executive level, policy *setting* group. After a focus on the ways in which the functioning of a middle group is influenced by its environment (primarily top groups), we will then look within the middle group itself. The focus will be upon factors that influence a middle group's ability to execute or manage policy. Key examples will be illustrated in actual case vignettes. The final section will deal with a description of the individual and group level skills needed to cope with the particular problems faced by middle groups.

A Framework for Analysis

Beckhard's (1972) general model of task-group functioning provides the basis for
our analysis of middle group functioning. Basically, this model says that task
groups meet in order to manage issues related to their goals, roles (allocation of
work), procedures (ways work gets done), and relationships. To this notion we
would add two key propositions. The first is that a task group also meets to
manage issues resulting from its surrounding *system* or environment. As we shall
see for middle groups in particular, it is impossible to conceive of a group existing
in a vacuum. Thus, in addition to goal, role, procedure, and interpersonal issues
these groups experience and manage internally, they will also experience, and
thus need to manage, issues resulting from organizational structure, reward and
promotion systems, training policies, interfaces with other groups at their own
and other organizational level, and sometimes interfaces with the environment
outside the organization. Rubin and Beckhard's (1972) field studies of interdisciplinary health care teams supports the resulting model of factors
influencing work-group functioning shown below.

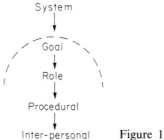

Figure 1

The vertical arrows speak to the second addition to Beckhard's basic model. In
essence, these five factors are thought to be causally linked in the sense that
interpersonal conflicts are more often than not *symptoms* of real conflicts in
system, goal, role, or procedural areas (Plovnick *et al.*, 1975). Similarly,
disagreement over how to make a decision, a procedural issue, is often the result
of unclear or conflicted expectations over who does what, i.e. a role issue. Even
goal conflicts are sometimes symptoms of conflicting mandates given the group
by others in the overall organization, i.e. a systems issue. For the sake of
convenience we shall refer to this hierarchical model as the SGRPI model (S for
system, G for goal, etc.). Using this model, let us move to the particular kinds of
dilemmas faced by middle groups: those groups that lie somewhere beneath the
chief executive and corporate planners, and who must execute and manage
policies set by the executives for the majority of the employees in the total system.

System Issues Faced by Middle Groups

The major 'systems' issue, or environmental factor, that influences a middle
group is the top group (or groups) from which it receives the policies it must

manage or execute. Many lower level groups have tasks which are highly constrained or, at least defined, by the technology they use (e.g. an assembly group or programming group). Furthermore, they can make their own decisions about roles (who operates what), procedures (scheduled maintenance, speed of operation), and interpersonal issues. On the other hand, a middle group derives its primary work from others above it and often does not have *any* impact on this task (i.e. policy to implement). Indeed, whether or not the middle group can or will influence its basic mandate is a crucial goal issue to be addressed, as we will discuss in the next section. Beyond setting the basic task for the middle group, the top group also greatly influences the role, procedural, and interpersonal factors a middle group experiences in its daily life. The structure of the organization and/or executive fiat often dictates *who* is on the middle group and thus can create desirable role complementarity or undesirable role confusion or conflict. Structurally, a middle group often is not alone, particularly in larger systems. There are several middle groups executing or managing various policies set down by upper groups. Hence, any one middle group may find itself competing with another in order to succeed in its policies,* often at the expense of another middle group's policies. This is often seen in situations where a marketing group, trying their best to execute given policies, runs into resistance from a production or research and development group who are also trying to operate in their own best interests. Procedurally, the top group often influences the middle group's ways of doing things via the middle group's leader or manager who is typically a member of that top group: what Likert (1961) has labelled the 'linking pin'. As such s/he is accustomed to 'a way of doing things' which may be best for determining policy, but may also be less desirable for managing policy. Thus, in middle groups, styles of decision making, ways of running meetings, how conflicts are dealt with, etc. can often *mirror* the way things are done in the top group(s) from which the middle group's leader comes. Similarly, interpersonal conflicts in middle groups are typically handled as they are in top groups because members at the middle level are attuned to the norms, or what it takes to get ahead, of the 'executive suite'. This is not as true for lower groups who exist in areas more distant from the executive suites and have norms and standards that reflect more their function or physical technological environment.

In essence, what is being suggested is that the main systems issue that middle groups face is the danger(s) inherent in *mirroring* the key environmental force acting on them, namely the top group. Using the SGRPI model, this is akin to saying that one group's management (or lack of it) of goals, role, procedural, and interpersonal issues creates a set of influences that become a systems force for groups below them. This systems force can have a facilitative or dysfunctional impact on the lower group's GRP or I issues as it goes about its work.

---

* One need only look at the way budgets get handled in most organizations. A middle group which underruns its budget may well get chastized for poor planning and take a cut in next year's budget. Neither of these responses can be construed as a reward for good performance.

For the middle group, this mirroring dynamic creates a sort of Catch 22: they are tying to do a completely different task (manage or execute policy) from the top group (who set the policy), but feel pressure to function in a manner akin to the top group with respect to problem definition, role allocations, decision-making procedures, conflict management, etc. They are also trying to do this in a collaborative environment while coping with the competitive pressures created by so many in the middle striving for so few positions at the top. For the middle group to manage its goals, roles, procedures, and relationships in fundamentally different ways from how things are done above it may get the job done better, but may also cause its members to look like deviants and become less desirable for promotion.

Mintzberg (1979) illustrates this Catch 22 well in his analysis of divisional structures. In the headquarters attempts to monitor divisional behaviour on a personal basis, the group executive visits the middle group (Division Management) often to 'keep in touch' or to 'avoid any surprises'. Tensions can often develop around doing things 'his way', thus tending to more centralization or doing things differently in ways better suited to the specific tasks at hand. If the executive 'wins', the middle group emulates the top and may not get its task (executing and managing) accomplished most effectively. If the middle group 'wins', headquarters distances themselves and evaluates only on output, and usually only the economic measure of it. So even if a good job is done, the personal relationship and understanding between middle and top group members that may be the key to any promotion for members of the middle group, is lost.

Given this mirroring tendency, or dilemma, of middle groups, we now turn to a more specific analysis of issues these groups will face in trying to manage their own work.

Internal Characteristics of Middle Groups

Middle groups experience a series of dynamics that are unique from other groups in the organization. In terms of the SGRPI model, the goals, roles, procedures, and interpersonal factors can be used to understand some of these peculiarities facing middle groups.

Goals

Goal issues are perhaps the most difficult problems faced by middle groups. Further more, because of the subsequent impact of goal ambiguity and conflict on role, procedural and interpersonal issues, goal problems are also the most critical for these groups to resolve. In the middle group the primary source of difficulty in determining goals stems from the group's hierarchical location—being in the middle.

Middle groups tend to experience great difficulty in establishing an identity or philosophy. Top-level groups, by comparison, are generally recognized as needing to deal with the highly ambiguous task of setting overall organizational mission, policy, and strategy (e.g. to increase sales and profits). Their rewards are predicated upon overall organization success. They recognize that theirs is an ambiguous task and the power and control they enjoy in being at the top takes some of the anxiety out of the fuzziness of their goals.

Lower level groups likewise experience relatively low goal ambiguity. Their task is generally clearly and operationally defined. The parameters of effective performance are also usually fairly explicit (e.g. increase widget production by 15 per cent).* The first-line supervisor does experience some problems in having to relate both to management and labor simultaneously, but these issues are generally felt in the role, procedural, and interpersonal areas rather than goal areas.

The middle group, however, is often fundamentally unclear as to whether their goals are, or should be, fuzzy and abstract, or concrete and operational. Partly this results from unclear or inconsistent expectations communicated by top management. Even with clear mandates, however, most middle groups are still faced with the challenge, ultimately, of interpreting higher level expectations and molding them into an acceptable statement of their group's core mission, goals, and priorities for others to use.

The very description of these groups—'groups that execute or manage policy'—suggest inherent goal conflicts. To *execute* policy is to carry out well-defined operational objectives—yourself. To *manage* policy is to infer objectives and to see to it that others own them clearly, and carry them out. Essentially a middle group must decide if it is more of a doer group or more of a support group. At one extreme, a middle group's primary mission might revolve around 'helping employees to understand/internalize/prioritize organizational policies'.† At another extreme, the mission might revolve around 'announcing and insuring strict compliance to policies set from above'. The role and procedural implications both within a middle group and between a middle group and lower groups are dramatically different depending on which of these two mission-orientations most represents the reality.

As implied in our model, if a middle group is experiencing what appears to be a mission or goal-related conflict, one natural place to look for the cause would be the environment or system which surrounds it—the group(s) above it. What expectation has the policy-setting group sent (through its linking-pin

---

* This is often true, even in the face of unclear policy from the middle group, because of the constraints or demands of the technology. That is, certain objectives related to output, rate, or quality are tied to the type of process, degree of automation, type of task interdependency, etc. all dictated by the particular kind of technology in use.

† Further to this, as one staff under a general manager put it, 'We're here to protect the people in the plant from his (the GM's) personal style'.

representative—the formal boss) to the middle group? Is it clear, unambiguous, and free of internal incompatibilities and inconsistencies? If not, then the middle group is bound to experience difficulty in working through its own GRPI issues and its functioning will suffer accordingly. Since the cause lies in its environment, in this case the policy-setting group above, so too does the ultimate solution. And hence, another mission dilemma for a middle group: to influence or consult the policy *setters* above (an often risky venture for people in no-man's land), or to dutifully serve as interpreters and administrators of what is given to them (also risky *vis-à-vis* the subordinate workforce).

Suppose that the policy-setting group has clear, unambiguous, unconflicted expectations of the middle group enabling the middle group to define its mission clearly. This represents the essential start but it is not, in and of itself, sufficient. There remains the issue of the consistency or congruence between the middle group's goals, and several related procedural issues under the control of the top group. Consider the effects of an incongruity between a mandated mission from the top and another system issue—the reward system in the organization. A mandated mission to a middle group such as 'develop new products' may require very high levels of interdependence both within any one middle group and between various middle groups. Yet, in most organizations the typical formal reward system—which reflects a *policy* decision of a procedural type from the top group to the entire organization—strangles collaboration and nurtures competition. To behave collaboratively in most organizations, over any length of time, is thus highly irrational. This 'rationality' of successful managers is reflected in Schein's (1978) study of MIT Alumni. In categorizing his sample by type of career anchor (a pattern of self-perceived talents, motives, and values that serve to guide, constrain, stabilize, and integrate a person's career) only 18 per cent were identified as having 'managerial' career anchors. In this category, 'interpersonal competence' to work with others to achieve organization goals was only one of three foci: the other two being analytical competence and emotional competence to address crises. The remaining 82 per cent of the sample were seen to have even less collaboratively oriented career anchors labelled as technical/functional, autonomy, creativity (i.e. entrepreneurial), and security. The real pay-offs, typically, come from individual success and achievement. Thus, corporate procedures may further complicate middle group goal setting and achievement.

Roles

As the SGRPI model indicates, problems with goals often lead to problems with roles. The middle group's dilemma regarding their mission, executor, or manager of policy, translates into ambiguity and conflict regarding functional responsibilities of middle group members. For example, a product manager must decide whether his/her role is personally to make and oversee the implementation of all decisions regarding the product, or to organize and coordinate those responsible for the product (i.e. marketing, manufacturing, engineering, research and development, etc.) into a team that can make and implement product-related decisions. In the latter case the product manager is a coordinator and many day-to-day decisions can be made without her or his personal presence. However, the product managers within an organization (a middle group) may be unclear as to how they are to function in this regard—doers or coordinators.

With increased supervisory responsibility and high personal aspirations to succeed in high status jobs added to the above demands for innovative problem solving and decision making, role conflict would seem inevitable. This is supported in Kahn *et al.*'s (1964) study of role stress where they found middle managers reporting the largest amount of role conflict (90 per cent of sample above median score on conflict index). This was much higher than either the group above (54 per cent of top management cases over median score) or the group below (60 per cent of second-level supervisors over median score). It appears that such large role conflict scores reflect a goals–roles paradox for middle groups: by attending to their aspirations to do well in the eyes of top managers, the middle group may tend toward the 'executor' role to fulfil the goal they perceive the top wants to achieve and in a way the top might do it. In so doing, however, they subject themselves to increased demands to change their supervisory, decision-making, etc. behaviour from peers and subordinates who may prefer the more 'managerial' or coordinative role.

Often the skills and experiences of middle group managers also limit their flexibility in these role areas. As 'graduates' of lower level management they may rely heavily on the skills that made them successful in previous positions. Frequently these earlier jobs were highly technical (versus managerial) in nature and lead the middle group to behave more like implementors than managers. More often than not what is learned from past experience in lower level groups is the message: 'if you want it done right, do it yourself!'. This is particularly true in professional groups like physicians, engineers, or teachers. Engineering managers may prefer to work at the bench rather than at the meeting table. An M. D. in an administrative position, director of emergency services for example, may find it difficult to delegate decision making to the staff since all of a physician's professional training emphasizes that the doctor is the only qualified authority for most decisions.

Because the managers comprising middle groups come from a variety of backgrounds and orientations their perceptions of appropriate roles often conflict. Middle groups may, for example, find it difficult to manage areas of overlapping responsibility between group members, each accustomed to clear operational responsibilities, or whose prior work required them to be individual contributors and, when successful, individual recipients of praise or reward.

Procedures

Many of the procedural problems a middle group faces regarding decision making, communicating, conflict resolution, etc. are symptomatic of unresolved goal or role issues. Suppose, however, the goal and role issues were well in hand. Procedural decisions—the how we should work together issues—are meant to flow from and be consistent with the nature of the task (goal) and role allocations.

The particular danger in a middle group is the pressure which can be felt to mirror the procedure of the group above it—when the tasks of the two groups are different. In subtle but powerful ways the linking-pin boss brings in norms of behaviour learned while s/he is a member of the top group. It is the dilemma of those in the middle.

The sense of limited opportunities which is more evident in middle managers than elsewhere adds to the competitive pressure to look good to the top. Lower level groups perceive a large number of middle level jobs available and see the quality of aspirants as 'mixed'. In the top management groups there is a sense of having 'made it' and the competition for the one job available, Chief Executive Officer, is fairly 'up-front' and manageable. Middle group managers may not feel as though they have made it yet and perceive limited promotional opportunities with much talented competition for those few opportunities.

Interpersonal Issues

Again, the existence of interpersonal issues, or personality conflicts, is often a consequence of unresolved system, goal, role, or procedural issues. In the summary of research on conflict in organizations, Katz and Kahn (1978) find that personality and other predisposing factors have been shown to have weak and irregular effects on organization conflict in comparison to the influence of situational/organizational factors related to the administration of rules and procedures.

The ambiguity and conflict in middle group goals and roles can lead to relatively high levels of stress and anxiety in these groups which can exacerbate any real or potential interpersonal conflicts. Yet middle groups can still have some very real interpersonal issues stemming from their position in the organization. The juxtaposition in middle groups of managers from differing backgrounds and with differing orientations creates potential stylistic incompatibilities. Finally, the struggle to the top of the organization can set the stage for some fierce clashes over conflicting personal goals and ambitions. While some of these same conditions can be found in other groups, middle groups seem to provide unusually fertile turf for interpersonal conflict.

The preceding discussion describes some of the types of problems middle groups experience internally in their goals, roles, procedures, and interpersonal relationships. It is usually the case that the conditions creating a problem in any one category tend to lead to difficulties in the other categories as well. The following two case studies illustrate this dynamic.

The CD Case

This case deals with the Construction Division (C.D.) of a large, high technology electronics company. The Construction Division was responsible for the building and maintenance of the organization's physical plant. There were six major facility sites within the company. The C.D. had a Site Manager at each of these locations who reported directly the C.D. Manager. Three functional specialists from staff groups and staff assistant to the C.D. Manager rounded out the C.D. team as shown in figure 2.

As part of a systematic team development effort, based on the SGRPI model (Rubin *et al.*, 1978), the team very early on had to address the question of the C.D. team Core Mission. In preparation for this, each individual member (eleven in total) wrote out their own response to the question:

'As *I* see it, our Core Mission as a team is. . . .'

During a team development session the team would share and discuss their individual perceptions. They would then work toward one synthesized statement which reflected an agreed upon view of the team's Core Mission. The output, in other words, would be an agreed upon response to the following:

'As *we* see it, our Core Mission as a team is. . . .'

Exhibit 1 contains each individual's actual response to the pre-meeting homework assignment: 'As *I* see it, our Core Mission as a team is. . . .'

While at first glance this may look like a surprising conglomeration of unrelated perspectives, it is not at all atypical. Several very predictable patterns can be seen in these individual 'answers' to the same question.

Diagnostic Confusion

One thing which becomes immediately clear is the tendency all groups have to mix and lump SGRP and I issues. The diagnostic questions was intended to focus on Core Mission—'What business are we in, as a team?'—a goal-level question. What comes out are goal-type responses *and* role-type responses *and* procedural-type responses *and* interpersonal-type responses. This type of confusion is

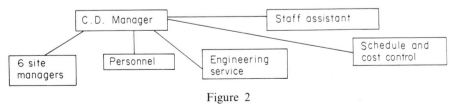

Figure 2

particularly prevalent in middle groups and speaks to the general difficulty they experience in setting goals.

One of the first things this group would need to learn is how to sort out different types of issues. Role, procedural, and interpersonal issues could then be addressed in sequence after the goal issues had been identified and resolved.

Conflicting Internal Orientations

The C.D. team became involved in a team development effort in the first place in part because there seemed to be a host of persistent interpersonal conflicts—particularly between the C.D. Manager and the Site Managers, and the staff representatives. As mentioned previously, there are a variety of issues that increase the likelihood of interpersonal conflict in middle groups. Many of the interpersonal issues identified in this case were symptomatic of more fundamental goal, role, and procedural conflicts that can be inferred from these Core Mission inputs.

The C.D. Manager, a civil engineer from the 'old school', saw the team's Core Mission being 'to *construct all* site. . .'. Several of the Site Managers with more formal management training (notably Site Managers 4 and 5) saw the team's Core Mission being 'Complete responsibility for the *management* of all new. . .'. These differences are not all unlike the difference between managing policy or executing policy discussed earlier. In the past, given this team's conflict avoidance tendency, this difference was passed off as one of semantics. It is anything but a semantic difference. Rather, it reflects a very basic boundary definition issue. The role and procedural implications of 'to construct. . .' versus 'to manage the construction. . .' are dramatically different. The inability to resolve this basic mission-related issue in the past resulted in the C.D. team having to continuously deal with problems that pop up in procedural areas (Should/should not staff people attend our meeting?), role areas (Who decides whether or not to have a subcontractor?), and in interpersonal areas (What is taking you guys so long to get started?). The ultimate decision, in this case to be responsible for the *management* of all construction, served to clarify and unblock a host of previously persistent energy drains.

Conflicting External Expectations

As discussed earlier, a middle group's functioning is influenced by its surrounding system or environment, particularly the goal, role, and procedural-type inputs it gets from the groups above it. We can see a small but nonetheless notable example of this in the case of C.D. team.

The Corporate mandate to the C.D. team included elements of quality and cost and, as Site Manager 4 pointed out, the employment of minority (primarily Black) contractors. The C.D. team, in other words, had a piece of the larger organization's social responsibility mission. Hiring minority contractors could easily conflict with highest quality, lowest cost expectations.

The source of this conflict lies outside the C.D. team itself. A policy-setting group above it has sent what is potentially an incompatible set of expectations. The C.D. Manager, through his linking-pin function, must try to clarify this conflict within the top-level group of which he is a member. Then, as the formal leader of the C.D. team, he can input a clearer mandate from the group above. Ultimately, however, the C.D. team must interpret its mandate in its own way, and integrate top management's expectations into the C.D. core mission.

Line/Staff Conflicts

Because the C.D. consisted of managers with diverse backgrounds (engineering, finance, personnel) there was considerable confusion regarding the contributions various team members could and should make. The site managers went so far as to question the relevance of the staff representatives at team meetings. The staff people in turn complained about under-utilization, being left out of important decisions and communications, etc. What was necessary was to examine the potential contribution of each team member, and negotiate a level of involvement. Untimately the team did this as part of their team-building program. In general the site managers were pleasantly surprised by the contributions the staff people were capable of making.

The C.D. case demonstrates some of the S–G–R issues middle groups experience and must manage, particularly in the areas of identity and goal-setting. The following case describes important problems in the areas of roles and procedures.

The B. P. Case

This case centres around the management team of a body parts (B.P.) division of an automobile manufacturer. In this particular case, this middle group has a clear and agreed to goal of *managing* policies set down by corporate executives and interpreted by the general manager of the B.P. Division (and leader of this group). These policies concern the number, type, and quality of body parts to be designed, engineered, manufactured, and shipped to the automotive assembly division of the corporation. During a formal, 'task-oriented' team development program (Rubin *et al.*, 1978), this group determined their mission to be one of 'managing' policy and in discussing role and procedural issues they faced, they essentially developed a communication and problem-solving structure as shown below.

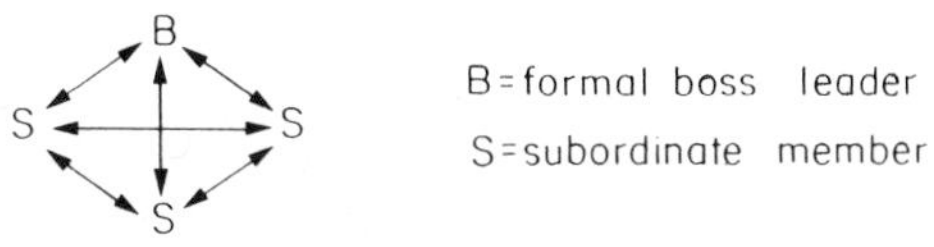

B = formal boss leader
S = subordinate member

Figure 3

With this team structure, divisional policies would be discussed collectively so that engineering, quality control, finance, personnel, and manufacturing heads could all engage with one another in an *interdependent* atmosphere to best *manage* the policies mandated to them. It was also mutually decided by this team that because their 'core mission' was to manage policy, their efforts should be focused on selling, guiding, and helping subordinates to do work, not doing the work themselves (something they were each good at, or they would not have been in this group in the first place).

This philosophy and agreements about goal, role, and procedural issues helped this middle group to lead its division to one of their most profitable years and increased status and recognition in the large corporation. It was also felt by the group's members to have contributed to reduced turnover in the group and better interpersonal feelings, as our SGRPI model would predict.

This rather bright picture began to change as the sale of automobiles diminished due to rising energy costs, cyclical decrease in demand, and a general economic slowdown occurred. Gradually, this group's environment (the top group) began to operate in a 'crisis mode'. If inventories were not being turned as frequently, if production schedules slowed, if quality standards fell, if deliveries to assembly plants were late, executives (who set the policies) would call down to various members of this team to get an answer to the problem. Consequently, as the mirroring phenomenon discussed earlier would predict, each member would act on his/her own to either solve the problem (thereby doing the work versus managing it) or by calling someone else below to gather information without consulting any other members of the team. Thus, their internal dynamics changed as a result of system forces on them. Now they behaved as in the figure below.

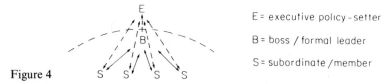

E = executive policy-setter

B = boss / formal leader

S = subordinate /member

Figure 4

As a consequence, role expectations that had been clear before now became conflicted as any member might call someone into another's area to get an answer for someone higher up, thereby going into another member's 'turf' without consent or consultation. Collaborative procedures gave way to one-on-one conferences or publicly reporting one's 'findings' about some problem in the group before the problem had ever been discussed by the group. Lastly, and probably most importantly, the mutual trust and cohesiveness of this group began to break down as the causal effects of system–goals–roles–procedural issues finally resulted in increased anger and frustration with each other. Members began to resent others for finding answers for the top group first, for calling their people without their knowledge, and for not doing things that had been agreed to or scheduled previously because they were reacting to the unilateral and crisis-oriented requests of the top group.

Thus, several aforementioned aspects of the SGRPI model came into play in the B. P. group. First, by working through their own GRPI issues (and not automatically mirroring their top group) they achieved a good, productive atmosphere with minimal symptomatic interpersonal issues. As the system around them changed, however, so did their ability to manage their GRPI issues. And as they mirrored an autocratic, crisis-oriented, do versus manage climate around them, their work as a group began to falter. Agreed to tasks were not done on time while members were busy reacting in a one-on-one fashion to top group requests.* Role ambiguity led to more private and competitive procedures which finally resulted in interpersonal mistrust and anger.

With both the C.D. and B.P. cases in mind, let us now turn finally to a discussion of what group and individual skills can help to anticipate and manage these dilemmas that can and do occur in middle groups.

Implications and Summary

The hierarchical SGRPI model and the mirror dynamic discussed above have important implications for middle groups and their formal leaders. The power of the hierarchical SGRPI model lies first in its usefulness as a diagnostic tool to help group leaders and groups, themselves, to understand factors that may be getting in the way of doing their work effectively. The typically chaotic and ambiguous world of the middle group described in this chapter can thus be made more predictable, if not more manageable.

In addition to providing diagnostic clarity, the model provides a built-in intervention sequence: goal issues to be dealt with before role issues, the latter prior to procedural issues, and so on. The author's experiences with their task-oriented team development programme (Rubin *et al.*, 1978), developed from the SGRPI model, has shown this sequence of interventions to be particularly useful to middle groups and their managers where, as we have argued, the definition of task (e.g. manage versus execute) and allocation of role responsibilities are typically ambiguous. The tendency of most persons in these groups to attribute their inability to address this ambiguity to interpersonal conflicts has, in our experience, immobilized any potential energy to overcome the negative effects of such confusion and ambiguity. In Argyris and Schön's (1974) terms, their 'espoused theories' are to do what is best to accomplish tasks, meet objectives, etc. but their 'theories in use' are rather to scapegoat someone as being the block to team effectiveness, or to wait for the system to transfer, recruit, or otherwise readjust the team's personnel to achieve a better mix of personalities. By

---

* Both the formal (salary increases, etc.) and informal (norms about pleasing one's boss) reward system in most organizations guarantees and reinforces this dysfunctional pattern.

providing these managers and groups with a conceptual model and skills that help them focus on goal, role, and procedural issues *before* trying to deal with true interpersonal conflicts (which are seldom resolved—only managed), this task-oriented approach to team development has helped these managers to develop more congruent espoused and in-use theories.* They can get to a position where, if they espouse goal, task, and other organizational criteria to be the most important, they can behave in conjunction with these beliefs by applying the SGRPI model.

The sequential nature of the SGRPI model also helps the formal leader to see his/her choice points about what to work on, and when. In the role of linking-pin or boundary spanner, she/he has the opportunity and responsibility to work on the system(s)-level forces impacting on his/her group's functioning. To do this the formal leaders of middle groups will find that they must interface with others who sit below, along side, and above them in the organizational hierarchy. The personal influence and negotiation skills required to operate effectively in the midst of such potentially conflicting cross-currents must be learned and practised. These influence skills are particularly critical when, as we have seen, a middle group may need to consciously resist the pressure to function like a top group. The manager of a middle group must first be able to diagnose the influence behaviour demanded by the situation and second have the behavioural flexibility to respond.†

The formal manager is also the key to avoiding dysfunctional mirroring of the top group. First, the dynamic of mirroring must be understood and its symptoms noticed or diagnosed. The task-oriented approach to team building helps in this regard for it forces an explicit focus on appropriate ways to organize the undertaking of a task and thereby minimizes inappropriate attention to issues of politics, style preferences of top managers, and the like.

Acting on the kinds of awareness noted above is easier said than done, however. To do any of what has been suggested as necessary to improve middle groups requires that the group leader often go against some fairly deeply entrenched attitudes or assumptions. One such assumption we have con-tinuously observed regarding groups is that 'over time things will work themselves out'. In our view, groups left to their own devices will not likely reach anywhere near their full potential. Some form of systematic, planned development intervention is essential. It is time to treat groups/teams as the complex pieces of human machinery they are and to train them to work well.

---

* It should be noted that this task-oriented approach to team development differs in focus from other interpersonal and group-process oriented technologies currently in use. Comparisons of these basic approaches to team building, focusing on goal, role, procedural, or interpersonal issues are offered by Beer (1976). For a comprehensive view of alternative team building techniques focusing more on P and I issues, see Dyer (1977).

† For a further description of training efforts designed to develop these personal influence and negotiation skills see Berlew and Harrison (1977).

If the wishful thinking mode is to become passé, so too must the tendency to focus on persons versus situations. The typical strategy for a poorly functioning middle group is a transfusion of new blood—the 'Red Cross' approach—or individual training—'a Statue of Liberty' approach—where in the 'poor, weak, tired' individual members are sent to a training program of some sort. While individual training is important and mismatches do occur necessitating these 'transfusions', the SGRPI model points to the critical importance of addressing specific situational or environmental issues—S, G, R, P—before assuming inter- or intrapersonal issues are causal to the problems at hand.

This environmental focus again puts great pressures on the formal leader of a middle group. Because managers of middle groups are almost to the top, they are often rather resistant to raise S, G, R type issues within the group of which they are a member. To do so in most organizations is to run the risk of being seen as disloyal and/or questioning the wisdom of one's superiors. Yet it is exactly the raising of these issues which is essential to the management of the interface between top and middle groups and the effective functioning of the middle groups themselves.

We are reminded, in closing, of a brief Sufi parable which captures the essence of what life must be like for middle groups and their managers. A snake says to a frog: 'If you carry this message to my friend at the top of the mountain, you can eat all the flies which are buzzing around me'. The frog reflected for a moment and responded very thoughtfully: 'The job seems fine but I'm not sure I can handle the compensation'.

Exhibit 1.
C.D. team
Individual Core Mission Input

C.D. Manager
To construct all site and building facilities and chemical installation from information supplied by the engineering departments and/or customers.

This construction to be performed within quality, cost, and time schedules as specified and agreed upon. The actual physical work to be performed in the field by either our own shops or outside contracting firms.

Personel Representative
To construct facilities in the most efficient manner possible, utilizing the talents of the organization.

Engineering Service Representative
Manage all space and facilities construction as defined by engineering services to insure least cost, highest quality, and minimum interruption of corporate functions.

Schedule and Cost Control Liaison
To efficiently provide a construction service to the Corporation by the management of and/or participation in all construction projects. Completely controlling costs, quality, manpower, and schedules.

Exhibit 1 (*Contd.*)
Quality Control Representative
Provide with efficient means to obtain quality construction services at a reasonable cost.

Site Manager 1
A solid construction team is our desired goal.
1. Our mission, as I see it, is to bring various groups within our team closer together.
2. It is my goal to understand the Construction Engineering Management job better.
3. A better working relationship between trades groups and engineers will guarantee a better overall work output.
4. Stop feeling that my job is the only important one and let's move out of isolation within groups.
5. More job-related discussions between Line Managers and Construction Engineering Managers.

Site Manager 2
To work together to get our jobs done.

To share our knowledge and specialities even though we have different areas of work and we are often on our own.

Site Manager 3
To coordinate the administration of the Construction Department Personnel and of construction efforts both inside and outside at the various sites.

Site Manager 4
Management of the facilities type construction needs of the Corporation.

This includes both the urgent or secret, small confidential or non-public needs to be performed by the in-house group as well as the public and large type of construction to be performed by contracting with outside contracting firms.

We are the construction expertise of. . . (the Corporation).

Employ minority contractors wherever possible.

Site Manager 5
Complete responsibility for the management of all new construction work connected with the Company's space needs and/or chemical requirements. Additionally, the Department makes its resources available as requested by the Machinery Construction Department.

Site Manager 6
To have a better and closer working relationship with the members in this room, to get their task done effectively. To make sure that each one of us understands his role and what the impact could have if we do not work with each other—understanding the real world that we have to work with is the key to our inprovement.

References

Aram, J. (1976) *Dilemmas of Administrative Behavior*, Englewood Cliffs, N. J.: Prentice-Hall.
Argyris, C. and Schön, D. (1974) *Theory in Practice: Increasing Professional Effectiveness*, San Francisco: Jossey-Bass.

Beckhard, R. (1972) 'Optimizing team-building efforts', *Journal of Contemporary Business*, **1**, 3, 23–32.

Beer, M. (1976) 'The technology of organization development', in M. Dunnette, ed., *Handbook of Industrial and Organizational Psychology*, Chicago: Rand McNally, pp. 955–61.

Berlew, D. and Harrison, R. (1977) *Positive Power and Influence Workshop*, Boston: Situation Management Systems, Inc.

Dyer, W. G. (1977) *Team Building: Issues and Alternatives*, Reading, Mass.: Addison-Wesley.

Kahn, R. L., Wolfe, D., Quinn, R., and Snoek, J. (1964) *Organization Stress: Studies in Role Conflict and Ambiguity*, New York: John Wiley & Sons.

Katz, D. and Kahn, R. L. (1978) *The Social Psychology of Organizations: Second Edition*, New York: John Wiley & Sons.

Likert, R. (1961) *New Patterns of Management*, New York: McGraw-Hill.

Mintzberg, H. (1979) *The Structuring of Organizations*, Englewood Cliffs, N. J.: Prentice-Hall.

Plovnick, M., Fry, R., and Rubin, I. (1975) 'New developments in O. D. technology', *Training and Development Journal*, **29**, 4, 19–28.

Rubin, I., and Beckhard, R. (1972) 'Factors influencing the effectiveness of health care teams', *Milbank Memorial Fund Quarterly*, **July**, 317–35.

Rubin, I., Plovnick, M., and Fry, R. (1978) *Task Oriented Team Development*, New York: McGraw-Hill.

Schein, E. (1978) *Career Dynamics: Matching Individual and Organizational Needs*, Reading, Mass.: Addison-Wesley.

Zander, A. (1979) *Groups at Work*, San Francisco: Jossey-Bass.

Groups at Work
Edited by R. Payne and C. Cooper
© 1981 John Wiley & Sons Ltd.

Chapter 3

Groups that Provide Specialist Services

Dan Gowler and Karen Legge

Introduction

This chapter deals with issues concerning the emergence, day-to-day behaviours, and development of 'groups that provide specialist services' in organizations, and stems from our research (supported by the Medical Research Council and Social Science Research Council) on the evaluation of planned and unplanned organizational change. In doing so, it focuses upon several interrelated questions. First, what is meant by a 'group that provides specialist services'? By what criteria may such groups by distinguished from other groups within an organization and how may these 'specialist' groups be distinguished one from another? Secondly, what factors lead to their emergence and how do such factors subsequently influence their behaviours? Thirdly, what are the characteristic problems, behaviours, and patterns of development experienced by such groups? It is to the first question that we now turn.

Identifying 'Groups that Provide Specialist Services'

Before embarking on the question of identifying 'groups that provide specialist services', it is necessary to clarify how the term 'group' will be used in this chapter. Obviously, the definition of what constitutes a 'group' is problematic. Suffice it to say that, rather than espousing a fully fledged social psychological definition, emphasizing psychological awareness, interaction and so on (Homans, 1950), we have chosen to treat as 'groups' those units within an organization that are formally and structurally differentiated from each other, and whose members are aware of the unit's 'separate' existence and unique identity. Thus, we have treated departments, functions, project teams, and committees equally as 'groups' irrespective of size, intensity of interaction, or whether they are temporary (certain project teams, working parties) or 'ongoing' (functions, departments). Because, therefore, our definition of 'groups' contains units too large to physically observe as one interacting entity, some of our discussion of 'group behaviour' involves consideration of how people behave in the roles that their group membership accords them. However, this approach we feel is justified since roles are not only conferred and confirmed by groups, but also symbolize their structures and meanings.

At first sight the problem may appear less one of identifying 'groups that provide specialist services' than of discovering any which do not. For it can be argued that most work groups are 'specialist' in some sense and most provide some sort of 'service'. To examine this assertion it is necessary to discuss briefly the concepts of 'specialization' and 'service'.

Organizations in industrialized societies rest very heavily on the principle of the division of labour (or, as Blau puts it, on specialization through developing 'homogeneity of tasks within units') in order to 'perform complex work better and with less skilled personnel' (Blau, 1974). As a result, virtually all formal work groups *specialize* in terms of task, and this task specialization is primarily based on either *hierarchy, function, product/service*, or *role*.

Specialization based on hierarchy is reflected in the differentiation in the types of decision making required at different organizational levels. For example, following Paterson (1972) it is senior management who specialize in policy making; middle management in planning how to carry out policies and in deciding how to implement the resultant plans ('programming' and 'interpreting' decisions); junior management in deciding which tasks need to be done to achieve the interpretation and in allocating the tasks and accompanying techniques to others ('routine' and 'automatic' decisions); while it is non-managerial employees who 'specialize' in following defined procedures to carry out a particular task, making decisions on how to follow the laid down procedure ('defined' decisions). The more senior the group in hierarchical terms, the more likely it is to specialize in long-term decisions, the effects of which are anticipated to be potentially far-reaching; the more junior the group, the more likely it is to specialize in short-term decisions, the effects of which are anticipated to be relatively narrow and bounded (see Jaques, 1961, on the time-span of discretion).

Specialization by function refers to task specialization on the basis of technical knowledge and competence required to perform the substance or core activities of a particular business function (for example, production, marketing, personnel, and finance). So that, for example, while members of the marketing function are likely to be differentiated individually by hierarchical level and so specialize in different levels of marketing decision-making, as a group of functional specialists they will share marketing knowledge and skills that differentiate them as a group from personnel, production, or finanacial specialists, each of whom have their own 'specialist' technical knowledge not shared by the other functions. Moreover, the group's perception of the organization as a whole will reflect a 'marketing' perspective for, as Lawrence and Lorsch (1967) suggest, members of a particular functional group tend to share common goal, time, and interpersonal orientations quite apart from the technical knowledge and skills that distinguish them from individuals in other functional specialisms. It is usually these distinctive technical competences that underpin claims to professional status and, thus, among other things are used to legitimize a given position in occupational and organizational hierarchies.

Task specialization may also be based on the product or service for which a group is responsible, so that the groups differentiated by hierarchy and function are further focused upon a specialized 'problem' area. For example, in a hospital not only are consultants and senior administrators hierarchically differentiated from junior registrars and junior administrators, just as all doctors are functionally differentiated from administrative and para-medical staff, but among doctors further differentiation occurs according to which problems their medical specialities address (for example, medical versus surgical, renal, gynaecological). This, in turn, is reflected in the hospital's differentiation of treatment units (surgical wards, renal units, etc.). The lines of product or service specialization cut across functional specialization, so that individuals divided by function may unite as a group specializing in that product or service (for example, the medical, para-medical, and ancillary staff on a ward; the production and marketing specialists responsible for a particular product; or working together in one product division or in one project team). Such patterns of differentiation, however, do provide a network of 'cross-cutting ties' that helps to maintain social cohesion in the face of the disruptive forces described below.

Task specialization by role refers to specialization in those 'management' activities that both occur within and transcend the boundaries of the forms of task specialization (hierarchical, function, product/service) already discussed. Our use of the concept 'role' has been influenced by the fact that, in its dynamic sense, it refers to a set of performances, expectations, norms, and related sanctions that are defined and manifested in *social interaction* (Goffman, 1959). In other words roles involve a specialization in social activities and relationships. Such activities would include information sharing and coordination, decision-making and problem-solving, monitoring and evaluation, negotiation and bargaining, and so on. Although these activities can be and often are undertaken by individuals working alone or in a dyadic relationship within one specialist group, specialist groups in the form of committees, negotiating teams or project working parties, which transcend the boundaries of other forms of task specialization, emerge as one strategy for coping with the problem of organizational integration.

At the beginning of this discussion it was suggested that it was difficult—at least in terms of task specialization—to identify groups which do *not* undertake specialist activities in organizations. Of course, this is not the same thing as saying that 'generalist' individuals do not exist for, given overlapping group memberships, individuals are often able and need to integrate a range of specialist skills and knowledge, derived from and legitimized by other group memberships, in order to perform one specialist task successfully (for example, to negotiate a development budget for a particular project requires the knowledge derived from membership of relevant hierarchical, functional, and product groups) (Mintzberg, 1973).

Turning from the concept of 'specialization' to that of 'service', groups conventionally receive this designation in two sets of circumstances: first, when they belong to an organization in the public or private service sector (a hospital or restaurant, for example), and secondly, when they are considered to provide a support service for the 'core' organizational activity, i.e. to be in a 'staff' relationship (providing advice and service) to the 'line' (which retains executive authority). We consider that both these distinctions are confused and frequently conflated. First, *irrespective of industrial sector*, while most specialist *workflow* groups are directly engaged in *transforming* some physical raw material into some tangible output, *all other* specialist groups are concerned with processing information that will lead indirectly to the successful accomplishment of the physical transformations. Secondly, as Fisch (1971, p. 235) points out, line/staff distinctions, in situations of increasing information processing, sophistication, and rapid product/service change, are proving irrelevant as so-called staff groups (e.g. engineering maintenance, materials management, R & D, personnel) 'are often of equal importance and, hence, require equal authority' with conventional line groups (for example, production and marketing). Yet, if we merely distinguish between 'specialist workflow groups' and 'specialist (non-workflow) service groups', we are left with some 'groups providing specialist services' (as conventionally understood), e.g. surgeons, teachers, and scientists, falling into the 'workflow' but out of the 'service' category. Furthermore, it could be said that every group which provides an input for another group is 'servicing' it. Even if this service takes the form of the physical output of the workflow group (for example, a sub-assembly, or a patient with a skin graft) it also provides an informational input for the receiving group—which blurs the distinction already made between 'workflow' and other specialist groups. Consequently, it appears that overall the problems surrounding the conceptualization of 'service' are more intractable than those surrounding 'specialization'. In this chapter then we choose to concentrate on the 'specialist' aspect of 'groups providing specialist services'. But if, as already suggested, most groups can be considered 'specialist' (as well as providing a 'service'!) what definition can be adopted that is not rendered meaningless by its degree of inclusivity?

We consider that the following distinction can be usefully, if somewhat arbitrarily, made: between groups whose specialist services are primarily *integrative* in function (i.e. which 'specialize' in developing cross-group(s) perspectives in mediating conflict and in coordinating the efforts of functional and product/service groups toward the achievement of common or compatible objectives) and those whose services are primarily *differentiative* (i.e. which emphasize the unique and individual nature of their group's problems, objectives, and achievements and also of the technical knowledge/skills required for their resolution). We say 'primarily' since this distinction is one of emphasis rather than 'either/or'. Groups specialized by product/service provide a case in point—particularly if organized on a project team or matrix principle (Kingdon, 1973; Knight, 1977). For such groups, depending on emphasis, may be regarded as either integrative, providing a common focus for different functional groups, or as prime examples of differentiation to cope with environmental complexity, in possible competition with and separated from other product/service groups within the organization, by resultant differences in priorities and perspectives (Lawrence and Lorsch, 1967). Similarly, while functional groups are conventionally regarded as epitomizing orgnizational differentiation, common membership of a functional group may serve to integrate groups differentiated by hierarchy. Furthermore, it could be argued that certain functional groups' (e.g. corporate planners) unique skills are aimed at an essentially integrative purpose.

The emphasis selected here, which will be elaborated in our subsequent discussion, is to treat groups specialized by hierarchy and role as primarily integrative and those specialized by function and product/service (somewhat controversially in the latter case) as primarily differentiative. One reason for this emphasis is that we consider that groups specialized by hierarchical level and by role require their members to act as 'generalists' (i.e. to integrate and use a *range* of skills and knowledge, in the sense discussed earlier), while functional and product/service groups above all require technical specialists (i.e. those expert in *one particular* skill/field of knowledge). Because differentiative groups, then, seem characterized by a more 'specialist', if not more 'specialized' perspective than the 'integrative' groups, it is upon the functional and product/service groups that we concentrate in this chapter. It should be noted here, however, that this integrative/differentiative dichotomy refers to the *purposes* in question. Obviously, such groups do not necessarily achieve integration or differentiation, which is in part due to the fact that these ends are also influenced by other powerful factors.

Group Emergence

What factors, apart from the rationality of the lateral and vertical division of labour, are associated with the emergence of specialist groups? Why do they come into being?

Research suggests that increasing size (in terms of numbers of employees) is associated, if at a decelerating rate, with increasing structural differentiation (Doreian and Hummon, 1976), 'as work is sub-divided into more specialized segments and assigned to separate units in an organization' (Aldrich, 1979, p. 205). Blau argues that size has a direct causal (apart from associative) effect here, as increasing size makes it increasingly difficult for an individual to become socially integrated into the organization, except through the mediation of some sub-unit, small enough to allow regular personal contacts among members. 'The larger an organization is, the more differentiation is required to produce the small sub-units in which regular personal contacts further social integration' (Blau, 1974, p. 336).

Equally, size has various indirect associative effects. First, there is the effect of the strategy chosen to achieve organizational growth. Growth via vertical integration is often a preferred strategy when environmental conditions are perceived as stable and predictable (when there is a continuing demand for a narrow range of products/services such that the search for a monopoly position and economies of scale is a viable long-term strategy) or when acquisition of suppliers or market outlets is perceived to reduce environmental variability. The emphasis of this strategy then is to capitalize upon or achieve environmental certainty. In contrast, growth via diversification enhances environmental complexity and, depending on the new markets/products/services entered, may enhance short-term variability and with it uncertainty, in the hope of reducing potential long-term uncertainties through over-reliance on one product/service. If the first strategy is adopted and the organization is basing its growth upon a single range of products/services, sold or dispensed almost exclusively in one market, the emphasis is likely to be on functional differentiation, coordination being achieved through a relatively flat hierarchy. If, on the other hand, the organization's growth is achieved through diversification, differentiation by product/service range is likely to be superimposed upon existing functional differentiation, while coordination may require further vertical differentiation and the setting up of integrative groups (for example, committees) spanning the boundaries of all the product/service groups (Child, 1977). The greater the degree to which organizational growth is accompanied by increased environmental complexity and variability, the greater the likelihood of specialist groups emerging, for product/service specialization will be imposed on functional specialization, and specialist boundary spanning groups are likely to multiply (Aldrich, 1979).

A second indirect effect of organizational size may be observed. As has been often stated (e.g. Cyert and March, 1963; Pfeffer, 1978; Thompson, 1967) organizations are coalitions, comprising at any time persons and groups with diverse preferences and interests which inevitably may conflict. One way of dealing with such potentially dysfunctional conflict is by attending to the various conflicting and possibly incompatible preferences and objectives sequentially (Cyert and March, 1963); another is by allowing the different interests 'unique domains in which they can control activity and obtain satisfaction of their interests' (Pfeffer, 1978, p. 239). Thus, for example, as Pfeffer points out, if there is conflict between those who wish priority in a university for either research or teaching, respectively, a structural solution is to develop groups or sub-units specializing in research, differentiated from those specializing in teaching. 'Such differentiation enables the various participants to act in isolation from those with whom they might be in conflict, while the organization retains the membership and action of all' (Pfeffer, 1978, p. 239). As organizations increase in size (especially if a strategy of diversification is employed) it is highly probable that the number of potentially conflicting preferences and interests will also increase. Additionally, the creation of specialist units, often only 'loosely-coupled' (Weick, 1976) to other potentially conflicting and competing groups is probably easier 'when the organization is large or has sufficient resources to permit many different activities to go on, which may account for the observed relationship between differentiation and size' (Pfeffer, 1978, p. 239). Gowler and Legge (1978, p. 171) have also discussed the emergence of specialized industrial relations departments and personnel during periods of organizational growth.

This brief discussion of group emergence points to several issues concerning groups' subsequent behaviours and development. The growth strategy an organization selects will not only influence the types of specialist groups to emerge (for example, whether conventional functional groups, or functional sub-groups within a larger product/service group, or fully-fledged project teams) but also the nature of their goals and primary tasks. It is suggested here that particularly if a specialist group is faced with uncertainties stemming from environmental complexity and variability, its members are likely to have difficulty in establishing consensus about goals and priorities, and the nature of 'proper' role performance. In these circumstances, is *role ambiguity* and *intra group conflict* likely to develop and, if so, will its incidence and nature vary as between different types if specialist group?

Secondly, if specialist groups emerge partly as a means of containing organizational conflict, to what extent and in what circumstances is this strategy likely to prove successful? Can we point to situations in which it is likely to fail and *conflict between specialist groups* develop?

Thirdly, entry into a new market/product/service may result in the groups concerned adopting practices perceived by the group as necessary to cope with new, unfamiliar demands, yet viewed as 'deviant' and illegitimate by the rest of the organization or by consumers, or the public at large. How do these practices develop, how are group members initiated into 'deviancy', how do other groups within the organization respond?

Task and Role Ambiguities

For any work group, ambiguity (a lack of clarity, certainty, and unequivocality) can surround *ends* (the objectives of its activity), *means* (ways of achieving the objectives), and the definition and measurement of that achievement (*success criteria*). It is sometimes assumed that 'differentiative' groups providing specialist services experience less task and role ambiguity than the less specialized 'integrative' groups because the bounded 'unique' nature of their contribution allows more precise task and role definition. While this may be true in conditions of environmental stability, when ends, means, and success criteria are likely to remain relatively stable, subject to clarification and refinement rather than to radical change, in conditions of environmental uncertainty, when there exists low clarity of information, uncertainty of cause and effect relationships, and long time spans of definitive feedback from the environment (Lawrence and Lorsch, 1967), the situation may be reversed. Here, it is likely that functional and product/service groups, through their own 'specialists' in boundary or interface roles, will act as initial mediators of that uncertainty for other groups less involved in the first stages of information search and processing. In adopting a 'filtering' function, these groups may absorb some of the potential uncertainties—and resultant ambiguities—that might otherwise have been experienced by other groups in the organization, but at the risk of exacerbating their own.

Ambiguity above Ends

Ambiguity about *ends* typically gives rise to highly abstracted and/or generalized statements about the nature of a group's goals, in order to accommodate 'changes in sentiment, new information and unforeseen problems and opportunities' (Sayles and Chandler, 1971), and, consequently, the likelihood of different and possibly conflicting interpretations of objectives either within a group or between groups. Thus, the conventional statement about a personnel function's objectives generally takes some form such as 'the optimum utilization of human resources in pursuit of organizational goals', while teachers subscribe to the goal of 'the development of students' intellectual and social skills', social work counsellors to that of 'helping individuals to develop meaningful and fulfilling relationships', and the police to 'the prevention of criminality and the repression of criminal activity, the protection of life and property, the preservation of peace, and public compliance with countless laws' (Wilson, 1962, p. 3). Such statements, particularly when groups operate in a very uncertain and politically charged environment, provide an umbrella to mask either their sequential changes in operational strategies, or members' simultaneous pursuit of essentially different strategies, which can only be reconciled at the highest level of abstraction. An example of this in the 1960s was NASA's stated objective that priority should be given to explorations that would reveal most about the origins of life and the solar system. This still left much ambiguity in the operational definition of this objective among the groups of scientists and engineers involved. Even if it was agreed that this would involve missions to the moon, Mars and Venus, 'how many and which ones should be manned, and what was the relative value of intensive exploration of the moon versus a one-slot landing on Mars or a fly-by?' (Sayles and Chandler, 1971).

Factors involved in the generation of ambiguity in ends, the nature of that ambiguity, and some of the effects of such ambiguity on group members' role definition may usefully be illustrated by reference to the position of one group of functional specialists—personnel managers. Personnel specialists may experience uncertainty generated in three environments: the economic environment, which can influence personnel policies indirectly through its effects on the organization's markets and corporate strategy *vis-à-vis* growth, investment, diversification, technological innovation, etc.; the political environment, which impinges directly through labour legislation and incomes policies; and the social environment, which affects the nature and level of employee expectations. Not only have these environments become increasingly complex, variable, and uncertain, but the fact that the pressures they generate often pull in opposite directions gives rise to a basic ambiguity in the ends a personnel function seeks to achieve. Although the statement of personnel specialists that their objective is 'the optimum utilization of human resources in the pursuit of organizational goals' (often by spokesmen for the 'profession') (Glueck, 1974; Megginson, 1972) which provides a face-saving, lofty formula to cover the ambiguities inherent in personnel work, ironically, it also points to what these might be. For, as indicated by this statement, ambiguity exists at two levels.

First, although flexibility *vis-à-vis* both achievement and action, necessary in coping with uncertainty, is afforded by the rhetorical use of the notions of 'optimization' and 'organizational goals', such concepts are highly problematic. It is generally recognized that, in reality, organizations do *not* seek to optimize, only to 'satisfice' (Cyert and March, 1963; Lindblom, 1959) nor, properly speaking, do they have goals at all. Rather, it is the dominant coalitions—and other groups within the organization—that compete to make or block potentially 'satisficing' choices perceived open to the organization at particular points in time (Child, 1972; Pfeffer and Salancik, 1978). In terms of what criteria, then, should personnel specialists interpret 'optimizing/satisfying', and in the case of competing coalitions, whose goals should they choose to support? These issues constitute a major source of ambiguity for personnel specialists, as for all specialist groups who combine the gatekeeper's role with that of an advisory or service function.

Secondly, the conceptualization of employees as 'human resources' adds a further dilemma. Should personnel specialists develop strategies on the assumption that employees are first and foremost fellow *human* beings, with an entitlement to a 'high' 'self-actualizing' quality of working life, or should they regard them as just one *resource* (labour), along with other inputs to production? Should personnel specialists emphasize the objective of 'developing resourceful humans' (Morris and Burgoyne, 1973) or of 'controlling human resources?' This dilemma, which lies in the three sets of environmental pressures to which personnel specialists have to respond, namely the economic constraints of capitalism on the one hand, and the often countervailing pressures of the political and social environments on the other, is neatly expressed by Thomason (1975, p. 26):

. . .if we see personnel management as having developed from two diverse origins, the one paternistically orientated towards the welfare of employees and the other rationally derived from corporate needs to control, we have a foundation for understanding the ambivalence so often associated with the function.

Watson (1977, p. 42) makes a related point:

The personnel function (is) now established with a role which (involves) both applying and furthering formally rational techniques in the sphere of labour utilization whilst, at the same time, having to cope with the contradictory or self-defeating aspects of these and other formally rational devices of human management. We can thus see an essential ambiguity underlying the personnel function itself.

In an attempt to cope with this underlying ambiguity in objectives, personnel specialists adopt a range of strategies which tend to be influenced by the nature of the environmental uncertainties which face them. When the economic environment is buoyant and the organization is growing, the potential conflict between what might be called an 'efficiency' perspective and a 'fairness' perspective can be avoided, as the road to efficiency is seen as requiring high salaries and good working conditions in order to attract labour of the appropriate quality and quantity. As one personnel manager, whom Watson (1977, p. 99) quotes, put it: 'There's no conflict if you can persuade people not to see things in conflict terms'. In situations of economic recession, however, when cost-cutting exercises may result in redundancies, this conflict between 'efficiency' and 'fairness' becomes very obvious. In these circumstances, personnel managers do their best to achieve a compromise, a balance between conflicting (i.e. economic versus political/social) interests (cf. Ritzer and Trice, 1969). As one personnel officer stated: 'Length of service must come in from the point of view of fairness. But from an efficiency point of view you'd have to look at the less able. You need to strike a balance' (Watson, 1977, p. 106). If, however, the economic climate is such that the organization's very survival is in question, personnel managers feel greater pressure to put efficiency criteria first. To quote a personnel manager with experience of carrying out redundancies:

The survival of the company is the prime concern. You then write the rules of L.I.F.O. (last in, first out) or whatever to suit the purpose . . . You therefore pay lip service, dishonestly, to L.I.F.O. You make it look like L.I.F.O. and you lose the right people (Watson, 1977, p. 106).

Ambiguity about ends has a direct influence upon personnel specialist's perceptions of the roles which they feel they should—or feel compelled—to adopt. Many personnel managers, irrespective of age or hierarchical position, see their role, in part, as being a 'man in the middle' mediating between the rest of management, to whom labour is a 'resource', and a workforce which no longer unquestioningly accepts management's right to treat it just as a means to an end (Watson, 1977).

One gets accused by employees of being a bosses' man and by the bosses of being the most militant shop steward. But this does mean that you can put over the shop-floor view to management and vice-versa.

There is sometimes an in-between role to play. We do have to protect employees from the worst excesses of capitalist oriented managers. We must represent to management the effect of decisions on people and defend these people (Watson, 1977, pp. 176, 177).

Although many personnel specialists choose to adopt this mediating role, some see it very much as a forced choice, regarding it less in proactive than in reactive terms. In their view, personnel specialists can get caught (rather than choosing to be) 'in the middle' as different interest groups place their own interpretation on the personnel function's ambiguously defined objective. Dryburgh, a Vice President of the (British) Institute of Personnel Management summarizes the problem:

Nearly always he (the personnel specialist) is the 'man in the middle'. For management, who pay his salary, he must argue the company case; from the union viewpoint he is expected to negotiate acceptable terms and conditions for the staff. If the personnel man adopts a progressive policy, management says 'slow down'. If he goes at the pace of many employers' associations, he is accused by the unions of 'lagging behind' (Dryburgh, 1972, p. 3).

However, it would appear that a minority of personnel specialists reject this role precisely because it may enhance the ambiguity they face while at the same time undermining their credibility with both management and workforce. In their words, a personnel specialist who adopts the role may find himself acting as a 'half-baked Dr. Kissinger . . .' (or) 'a bloody message boy' (Watson, 1977, p. 177).

This discussion of ambiguity of ends, though illustrated by specific reference to personnel specialists, does raise some general points about the behaviour of specialist groups. We would suggest, on the basis of this example, that when a specialist group has to cope with more than one sector of an uncertain environment, and when these sectors represent different interests and pull in potentially incompatible or conflicting directions, not only will the ends it seeks be ambiguous (and hence subject to compromise, negotiation, and bargaining) but, in an attempt to cope with this ambiguity, the group will tend to become involved in a wide range of mediating activities. Such specialist groups are then likely to become increasingly less 'specialist' (in the sense discussed earlier) but 'specialized' in integrative activities. For example, the personnel function that adopts a 'man in the middle' role is likely to emphasize and develop its 'generalist' skills—of negotiation, bargaining, monitoring, and evaluation—and place relatively less importance on specialist technical skills such as selection testing or mathematical manpower planning. At the same time, some specialist groups (or members within the group) when confronted with this environmental situation and ensuing ambiguity, may attempt to cope by denying that ambiguity does in fact exist. In other words, they may firmly ally themselves to one interest group in the organization, define their objective in that group's terms, and seek to achieve it through the use of their specialist technical skills. For example, a personnel function may define its objective as providing a service to line management, and operationalize it by seeking to provide the 'right' (managerially defined) quality and quantity of labour at the right price, using specialist rercruitment and selection techniques. A danger for groups that develop this strategy is that means tend to become ends in themselves and the purpose of their activity, unclear at best, may be lost from sight (Legge, 1978). In such circumstances the group's skills, while becoming increasingly specialist, may also become increasingly irrelevant to the real needs of the organization.

Ambiguity about Means

Ambiguity about *means* (ways of achieving objectives) is possibly even more prevalent among specialist groups. Even if a group has clarified its objective (to introduce a new computer system that will perform *X, Y, Z* functions, to design and develop a component that will achieve *Y*), it may be uncertain about how to achieve it, given a problematic knowledge base and problematic role relationships with other groups with whom it has to interact to achieve its objectives. We develop this theme in some detail below when discussing several sources of uncertainty, i.e. knowledge, relationships, and success criteria. But it is necessary to report here that recent commentators have pointed to the advantages of ambiguity. They suggest that it might be used, for example, to avoid evaluation (Goldner, 1970; Gowler and Legge, 1978); as an element in professional rhetoric (Gowler and Legge, 1980); as a means through which to create new organizational myths (Fletcher, Gowler, and Payne, 1979); or, in a 'positive' way, to re-negotiate meanings in complex and changing circumstances (Tyson, 1980).

Knowledge uncertainties. By definition, functionally specialist groups owe their existence to some form of task-related 'expert' knowledge. This knowledge may be problematic in three ways. First, it may be insufficient to achieve the task in hand. Doctors, for example, are obliged to practise even when their knowledge base cannot provide solutions to their clients' illnesses (for example, the treatment of presently incurable diseases). As Freidson (1970, p. 163) comments, 'Since its (the medical profession's) focus is on the practical solution of concrete problems, it is obliged to carry on when it lacks a scientific foundation for its activities: it is oriented toward intervention irrespective of the existence of reliable knowledge'. R & D teams working on advanced technical problems similarly may find the existing knowledge base to be inadequate for their solution, in which case the problem, and the scientists' objective itself, may have to be reformulated (Sayles and Chandler, 1971).

Secondly, the technical knowledge may exist to allow the achievement of a group's objective, but its volume and the rate at which new potentially relevant knowledge becomes available (and, conversely, earlier knowledge becomes obsolescent) may give rise to uncertainties in information processing. Mumford and Pettigrew (1975, pp. 86–94) cite an example of this problem in relation to computer specialists. The groups of computer specialists they studied (systems analysts, programmers) were clear about their overall objective (to develop an information processing system that would meet various specified organizational requirements) and about how this objective should be operationalized (through the purchase of new hardware and software). They had difficulties though in making relevant choices (for example, of data input equipment) due to the enormous amounts of technical data that successively had to be processed and evaluated, both individually and comparatively, at a point in time when decision-making criteria were implicit rather than explicit and weighed differently by the different computer specialist groups directly involved and those (for example, the Board) to whom they were reporting.

Thirdly, technical knowledge may be problematic less in its existence or processing than in its application, owing to opposition from other groups in the organization. For example, technically feasible ways of accomplishing objectives may have to be abandoned because they threaten the vested interests of existing powerful groups who can prevent their application. Mumford and Pettigrew (1975) show how different groups of computer specialists sought to block certain choices of computer equipment which on technical and economic criteria would have satisfied organizational requirements, because such choices would enhance the power of competing groups through their greater familiarity and expertise in that particular brand of hardware. Similarly, Fitzgerald (1980) has shown that while personnel departments can acquire the expert knowledge to develop theoretically workable and useful manpower forecasting techniques, their ability to make use of this knowledge is undermined by a lack of cooperation from line management in supplying data, since the latter tend to regard such manpower planning techniques as placing constraints around their own freedom to plan and manage their manpower as they think best.

Finally, group membership is often defined and confirmed by the possession of esoteric knowledge, which is not to be shared with 'outsiders'. Moreover, when such knowledge is released, it frequently takes the form of 'ambiguous presentation', 'calculated vagueness' (Gowler and Legge, 1980) or 'jargon' (Hudson, 1978). It is also well known (at least to anthropologists) that group boundaries are preserved with the aid of ritual languages and other forms of obscurantism.

Problematic relationships with other groups. These forms of knowledge un-certainty, in particular uncertainty in application, are associated with a second source of ambiguity experienced by specialist groups in seeking ways to achieve their objectives, namely problematic relationships with other groups. Leaving aside intergroup conflict for the moment (which will be considered in detail below), a major source of ambiguity here is what relationship specialist groups should have toward other groups within the organization. In theory, specialist groups as conventionally defined (that is, groups of specialists in 'staff' functions), are traditionally held to have a service or advisory relationship with core-task specialists (that is, the 'line'), whatever their respective levels in the hierarchy. Thus, a group of accountants may provide a service to production managers by providing financial feedback about their performance as against budget, and advise during the formulation of a production budget. However, particularly from the viewpoint of the provider, a service and advisory role can have major drawbacks. Not only is there pressure from line specialists that decisions about the nature, level, and timing of the service provided should rest largely with them, but if the service provided is considered good it is generally taken for granted, while if deemed inadequate, it tends to be highly criticized from a one-sided perspective. Similarly, useful advice has a habit of becoming the property of its recipients and, unlike 'bad' advice, its origins lost in the allocation of praise, while line groups can always seek to excuse their failures by attributing them to the 'bad' advice they received from specialist groups. Consequently, a danger specialist groups run if they become heavily involved in service and advisory relationships, is of becoming a cross between an organizational dogsbody and a scapegoat, while occupying a low power position.

Not surprisingly, then, functionally specialist groups have sought to restructure this traditional relationship in a variety of ways. The groups which have been most successful at this have been those which are recognized by other groups within the organization to play a major part in coping with environmentally or internally generated uncertainties which may impede the achievement of recognized organizational success criteria. These tend to be those specialist groups which, to use Hickson et al.(1971) terminology, are highly central (in the degree to which, or the speed and severity with which, their activities can affect those of other groups and the final outputs of the organization) and whose coping activities are seen as both highly expert and non-substitutable. In other words, these are often the boundary spanning groups, whether functional specialists (for example, the accounting functions, which tend to mediate environmentally general uncertainties) or specialists in integrative managerial activities (for example, bargaining and decision-making committees, which tend to mediate internally generated uncertainties). The question of which groups, among those in a boundary spanning position, are likely to achieve most power in any organization will depend on the nature of the uncertainties that are perceived salient to that organization in the light of its success criteria (Legge, 1978; Woodward, 1965, p. 128, Figure 28). Such groups are facilitated in achieving and maintaining a highly central, expert, non-substitutable and, hence, powerful position, by their ability to act as 'gatekeepers' (Kahn et al., 1964; Mechanic, 1962; Mumford and Pettigrew, 1975; Pettigrew, 1972, 1973) to information to which, in their boundary spanning position, they have privileged access and can therefore withhold, filter, and bias according to their own group's interests.

Restructuring the traditional service and advisory relationship into types of relationship which are expressive of the real power specialist groups often possess, may involve one or all of three strategies, which vary in their degree of formality. First, there is the most 'formal' strategy: specialist groups may encourage the development of a matrix organization. Secondly, and less formally, they may seek to develop 'auditing' and 'stabilization' (rather than 'advisory' or 'service') relationships with the line. Thirdly, and often unofficially, they may attempt to 'take over' line authority.

The advantage of a matrix structure for specialist groups is that their representatives in project teams have nominally equal decision-making status with their fellow members, drawn from other specialist groups, including the 'core' line specialism (production). Additionally, the project manager (the *primus inter pares*) may well be drawn from a specialist group that, in traditional terms, might be seen as a 'staff' function. As a member of a project team, the representative's standing in that group will depend upon the contribution his and his department's expertise makes to the success of the project, rather than on its (his) place in traditional 'line/staff' authority relationships. However, this strategy is not the most frequently adopted: it may be unnecessarily complex an arrangement in terms of general organizational requirements (Child, 1977, pp. 86–93), while the specialists themselves may be unhappy about the dual reporting relationships they have to maintain (to both their functional and project superior) and a perceived weakening of their specialist identity (Kingdon, 1973; Knight, 1977).

More popular are the attempts, often on an *ad hoc* basis, to develop 'auditing' and 'stabilization' relationships (Sayles, 1964). 'Auditing' relationships may be described as those that involve ascertaining whether the various functionally specialized (including the 'core' line specialism of production) group's activities are consistent with specified organizational rules or standards. 'Stabilization' relationships are those that involve granting prior approval to the critical decisions of these groups on the basis of a specialist expertise, that also takes into consideration the total organization's needs in this area. Both therefore assert specialized groups' control function in the organization, and are particularly prevalent in large, diversified organizations seeking coordination through uniform adherence to certain organization-wide rules and procedures.

Sayles (1979) provides a good illustration of how this may be done, with reference to a highly specialized group, the 'packaging design' department of a market oriented company. If such a department is to increase its power, Sayles argues, it should endeavour (a) to change its position in the workflow sequence and (b) to change its boundaries, in order to develop auditing and stabilization roles. Thus, Sayles suggests, the department should attempt to secure the following types of changes in its relationships with other departments:

1. To secure acceptance for (its) participation in early discussions concerning new

designs for company products, so that packaging needs can be considered with other requirements (change in workflow sequence)

2. To add designers who will draw up preliminary specifications for packaging, rather than have this function carried on in the industrial design department (change in boundaries)
3. To require all engineering managers to get approval from the department before changing the physical shape of the product (addition of stabilization role)
4. To establish a small group to do research on better packaging materials and maintaining durability at lower cost (addition of critical innovation responsibilities)
5. To evaluate existing product designs, shipment sizes, and routing policies and changes in them for their impact on packaging costs (addition of auditing)
6. To serve as a transmission link to connect the engineering design department to purchasing for the ordering of packaging materials (addition of new work flow sequence)
7. To request that the shipping department be shifted from the jurisdiction of packaging to production on the grounds that packaging does not handle routine business (change in boundaries)
8. To be available to assist cost reduction committees (addition of advisory role)
9. To eliminate the practice of the production department's requesting packaging studies by having such studies originate in the cost reduction committees (decrease in importance of service work)
10. To require that all contacts with outside testing laboratories which evaluate packaging materials be handled by packaging personnel (change in boundaries and shift of position in work flow) (Sayles, 1979, pp. 109–110).

Further accounts of specialist groups' attempts to develop 'auditing' and 'stabilization' relationships with other groups may be found, for example, in Goldner (1970), in reference to the I. R. function's relationships to production; in Strauss (1962), in reference to purchasing agents' relationships with engineering and production scheduling specialists; and in Stieglitz (1971), in reference to 'staff' groups generally.

The more a specialist group can develop its 'auditing' and 'stabilization' relationships vis-à-vis other groups, the more the question of who 'really' holds executive (line) authority is likely to be raised (Goldner, 1970, p. 130; Watson, 1977, p. 61). Thus, ambiguity about role relationships reaches its height when basic line/staff distinctions are not clear (for example, as in many public service organizations, in particular in voluntary associations) and two groups compete for 'line' authority, invoking different, but arguably equally legitimate, validating criteria. The authors observed a typical example of this form of ambiguity about role relationships within a voluntary service organization.

This organization, which was concerned with providing a specialist counselling service, had grown rapidly over recent years, while being aware that it competed almost directly for resources (private individuals' subscriptions and voluntary work, public support from government and local authorities) with other voluntary associations. In response to this situation it not only evolved a relatively sophisticated organizational structure (at national, area, and local levels), but had encouraged role specialization (both administrative and 'technical', that is, in counselling skills) at all levels in the organization.

One aspect of this role specialization was to introduce 'supports', that is, 'technical advisers' for the voluntary counsellors, and as time went on, to introduce similar supports for the 'technical advisers' themselves, that is, 'trainers'. These 'trainers' who, like the 'technical advisers' were organized at area level (the counsellors themselves being organized at local level), reported to a 'Head of Technical Services' at national level. Prior to the introduction of the 'trainer' role, such ongoing 'technical' support as the 'technical advisers' received had come from their area officers who, in a functionally non-specialist role, had combined largely administrative duties (for example, providing administrative support to local organizations, especially *vis-à-vis* fund-raising activities, keeping local organizations in touch with policy formulated at national level, arbitrating between disputing parties on local executive committees, allocating technical advisers to counsellors) with some technical ones (for example, being nominally responsible for the 'technical' standards/performance of counselling achieved by local organizations, occasionally running 'technical' discussion groups, or individual tutorials for technical advisers, offering them informal advice). The area officers reported directly to the 'Director of Services' of the national organization, to whom the 'Head of Technical Services' also reported.

When the trainers were appointed (generally one to each area, although occasionally one trainer would serve two areas) their duties were specified as 'being responsible for technical advisers' professional supervision and support. . . (and) for technical standards generally within the area'. In spite of the introduction of some confusion, due to overlapping role definitions as to who was to be ultimately responsible for technical standards within an area, there was no attempt to clarify this problem though instituting a clear-cut line/staff relationship (that is, the trainer role was *not* placed in a direct line relationship, reporting to the area officer to whom he logically might be accountable for the provision of support services in the area, but only in a functional relationship with the 'Head of Technical Services' to whom he was accountable for the technical content of his activities). Instead, the trainers were appointed as 'equal' within their area to the existing area officer; in theory they were to act as collaborative colleagues between whom a formal reporting relationship was deemed neither necessary nor appropriate.

In this vacuum both trainers and area officers then laid claim to line authority over the other. The argument of the trainer, supported by analogies to line/staff relationships within hospitals and universities, was that the focal task of the organization being counselling, the line responsibility was a 'technical' one (for the maintenance of the quality of counselling services), while the staff function was that of providing administrative support for those core technical services. They further supported their claim by arguing that the ultimate providers of the service (counsellors) reported to technical advisers (who had the power to 'stop' a counsellor practising, if considered technically inadequate) who, in turn, reported to them. This, they suggested, represented the 'true' line authority from local to area level, culminating in their own reporting at national level to the 'Head of Technical Services'.

The area officers presented a counter-claim. First, they argued that custom and practice gave them a prior claim to line authority, since they had enjoyed it undisputedly before the arrival of the trainers. Secondly, they maintained that they were still responsible for the technical *performance* of local organizations advised by the trainers, even if the latter could lay claim to responsibility for the technical *standards* of the individual technical advisers they supervised. However, their main argument was that the organization (and hence the basis of line authority) was defined not only by its focal task but equally by its voluntaristic structure and ideology. Although counsellors were validated by their training at the national headquarters, they were employed by their local voluntary organization's executive, which in theory could refuse to use a trained counsellor, if it so desired. Similarly, although a trainer was responsible for a technical adviser's 'technical' standards, the responsibility for employing a technical adviser (which, in practice, due to geographical constraints meant allocating him/her to one local organization rather than to counsellors scattered throughout the area) remained with the area officer, who tended to regard the technical advisers as his deputies within the local organizations they served. Hence, the area officers argued that it was in their direct relationship with the executives of the local organizations (a relationship the trainers lacked), linking local and national levels, rather than in their relationships with counsellors as such, that their chief claim to line authority lay. The legitimacy of this line relationship they claimed was symbolized by the fact that, unlike the trainers, they reported directly to the Director of Services, to whom the technical advisers' superordinate, the Head of Technical Services, also reported.

It is suggested that this form of ambiguity about role definitions and relationships is particularly prevalent during the early phases of organizational growth when, with increasing task specialization, 'generalist' line positions are being challenged, eroded, or usurped by specialists (Goldner, 1970), or when changes in the nature of the strategic contingencies perceived by an organization (Hickson *et al.*, 1971) greatly enhance the power of one specialist group, while diminishing that of previously powerful groups. In the former situation the 'generalists' tend to argue that the existing organization structure defines the nature of the task and of legitimate relationships, while the 'specialists' maintain that the logic of task specialization demands a re-examination of existing organizational structure and relationships. With increasing task specialization, however, all groups tend to pursue their relationship claims through the development of specialist skills, relevant to mediating salient organizational uncertainties, including specialist 'line' management groups and specialist 'integrative groups'.

Ambiguity about Success Criteria

Given the ambiguity that often surrounds their objectives and ways of achieving them, it is not surprising that specialist groups have problems in both defining and demonstrating successful performance. These problems, which stem largely from the goal, knowledge, and relationship uncertainties discussed above (and which certainly tend to exacerbate the latter) are interrelated. When success is difficult to demonstrate in terms of one set of success criteria, practical considerations, such as the need for performance appraisal, necessitate the development of a surrogate set. Equally, when it is difficult to define what constitutes success, it is, of course, doubly difficult to demonstrate it.

Given initial goal ambiguity, personnel specialists, for example, have difficulty in developing meaningful success criteria and in demonstrating success. First, they have difficulty in demonstrating the causal link between their activities and the employee behaviour that occurs in the workplace (such behaviour, whether deemed 'good' or 'bad' may be determined by many factors outside personnel specialists' control). Secondly, even where 'good' behaviours occur (low absenteeism and turnover, few strikes, high productivity) it occurs within other specialists' systems (production, R&D, marketing, etc.)—precisely because personnel specialists are chiefly concerned with providing efficient inputs for use within other functional systems—and is often seen to be the achievement of these other systems. The problem exists, as for many specialist service groups, that while the personnel department can itemize the number of activities undertaken, it can rarely, at present, demonstrate in quantifiable terms that X quantity and quality of these activities will have Y influence on employee behaviour, which in turn will contribute in Z degree to the achievement of a specific organizational end, such as profit, output, or market share (Goldner, 1970; Legge, 1978). It is often then purely the number and range of activities undertaken that have to serve as a success criterion for personnel specialists. But, as already discussed, when objectives are unclear (as they often are for personnel specialists) even the selection of activities to perform can be problematic, making the demonstration of success doubly difficult to achieve.

When, through goal or means ambiguity, problems in defining or demonstrating success exist, groups tend to evolve more 'achievable' and, hence, discriminating success criteria in order to facilitate performance appraisal. The strategies of police, doctors, and research scientists illustrate this dilemma well.

Concerning police groups in California (and analogies have been drawn with comparable police work in Britain) (Cox et al., 1977; Holdaway, 1979) Skolnick (1966), citing Goldstein (1960), argues their goal of 'full law enforcement' is recognized to be rhetorical rather than realistic, and points to:

ambiguities in the definitions of both substantive offences and due process boundaries, limitations of time, personnel, investigative devices, and pressures from within and without the department, as forces which generate selective enforcement (Skolnick, 1966, p. 165).

In these circumstances a surrogate measure of performance—for both individuals and groups—has been developed, namely the 'clearance rate' which is
the percentage of *actual offences known to the police* that have been solved.
Skolnick suggests that this measure in one sense heightens goal ambiguity rather
than diminishes it. For not only does the use of such a criterion lead to practices
that in turn attentuate its validity as a measure of quality control (that is, what to
a layman might be considered an actual offence may be recorded as an 'incident'
or a 'suspicious circumstance' and so not enter the 'actual offence' statistics) but
it may actually interfere with the legality and stated aims of law enforcement.
Thus, Skolnick reports that the easiest way for a detective to obtain a high rate of
'clearances' is to persuade a suspect to admit to having committed several prior
offences. But to gain such admissions the detective must provide the suspect with
either rewards or penalties to motivate self-incrimination. Use of rewards—such
as a reduction of charges and counts, concealment of actual criminality, and
freedom from further investigation of prior offences—seems the commonest
strategy. At worst, Skolnick argues, it is possible under this practice that
defendants who confess to a large number of crimes may be shown more leniency
in prosecution than those who are in fact less culpable—thus reversing the
hierarchy of penalties associated with substantive criminal law.

Doctors provide a comparable illustration of the development of surrogate
success criteria. Their ability to achieve their major public objective, to cure the
sick, is essentially problematic given the existing inadequate state of their
knowledge base, problems in its application (no two patients will respond
identically to the same treatment), and the condition of their patients. A trained,
skilled, and committed team of surgeons, irrespective of its competence, can fail
to cure a patient. In these circumstances, doctors have developed surrogate
success criteria, in that, among colleagues, they define successful performance,
not in terms of their public objective, but in terms of the 'proper' application of
accepted procedures of diagnosis and prognosis, which enables the achievement
of a surrogate goal, 'proper' prescription and treatment (Gowler and Legge,
1980; Stelling and Bucher, 1973). Similarly, a 'good' scientist or engineer is often
defined as one who follows experimental or design procedure correctly.

In general, it may be noted that whereas groups with highly developed
technical skills and/or a professional ethic tend to select qualitative surrogate
criteria (i.e. the manner in which an activity was performed, the adherence to
proper procedure), those with less highly developed skills and/or a managerial
orientation tend to select quantitative surrogate success criteria (number of
activities performed).

Ambiguity in success criteria and the consequent re-definition of success can
result in inter and intragroup conflict, as specialists often subtly shift their
objectives in directions that are not always clear to, or approved of, by other
groups, or even by their own colleagues. For example, doctors, when emphasizing
correct procedures, are implicitly placing a higher priority on the value of

technical expertise than on the 'old' professional value of altruism (which would place emphasis on the patient's final state rather than on the doctor's technical achievement), although to the public at large altruistic objectives might seem more important. Thus, the old joke 'the operation was successful, but the patient died', while precisely illustrating this re-definition of success criteria, also hints at the tensions it leaves unresolved. Ambiguity about which value should act as a determinant of success criteria not only underlies much doctor/patient conflict (for example, over the relevance of house visits, over the relationship between fee-paying and the standards of care in private health service) (Haug and Sussman, 1969), but may generate intragroup conflict as specialists themselves dispute which value should take precedence in defining success criteria. Such conflict is evidenced, for example, by the disputes between the new 'radical' professional (sub) groups, who argue that their more conventional colleagues place 'science' before 'patient care', or 'law' before 'justice', and these same colleagues, who counter with accusations of the radicals' charlatanism, unprofessional conduct, unprofessional lack of caution, and so on (Black, 1971; Gerstl and Jacobs, 1976; Gowler and Legge, 1980; Gowler and Parry, 1979).

Inter and Intragroup Conflict

Implicit in the preceding discussion of the task and role ambiguities that may confront specialist groups is the inference that such ambiguities may lead to both intra and intergroup conflict. If this is so, what types of specialist groups are most prone to conflict, over what issues, and what organizational circumstances are likely to contain or exacerbate its development?

Sources of Conflict

Conflict both within and between specialist groups tends to be over issues of scarce resource allocation, over 'who shall make the rules governing resource flows, what shall be the content of the rules, and who shall enforce them' (Aldrich, 1979, p. 91). As such, it is likely to arise from two major sources: divergent interests, values, and motives of group members, and ambiguities in the definition of organizational reality (Aldrich, 1979). Both these areas have been implicitly touched upon and illustrated in the discussion above, but a further point may be made here by way of elaboration. We suggest that while both intra and intergroup conflict may arise from either source, there is a tendency for intergroup conflict to arise mainly from the first source, i.e. divergent interests, and for intragroup conflict to arise from the second source, i.e. ambiguities in the definition of organizational reality. This point is perhaps best illustrated with reference to our 'differentiative' specialist groups, i.e. those specialized by function or product/service.

Different functional groups are well known to have mutually divergent interests, often expressed through their differing goal, time, and interpersonal orientations referred to earlier (Lawrence and Lorsch, 1967). Different technical and/or professional training and socialization gives specialist groups differing languages and world views. Thus, there arise such well-known examples of intergroup conflict as that between production specialists who want to limit their range of products in order to increase the volume of output for each one and reduce unit costs, and marketing specialists who want production to comply with the customer's exact specifications regardless of the case for standardization (Sykes and Bates, 1962). Conflict arising from such divergent interests is likely to be exacerbated if success criteria with a differential impact on the different groups exist (for example, a performance criterion of the marketing function, i.e. delivery speed, can cause problems for production). Criteria that are biased toward rewarding some groups, at the expense of others, provoke struggles to change the criteria or distort group performance to meet the criteria. Such divergent interests between functions tend to foster in-group solidarity within any one function. Similar processes occur both within and between specialist product/service groups. Those differences of interest that do occur *within* one function tend to develop between different hierarchical levels (or, within a specialist product/service group, between the different functions represented) and, therefore, in a sense, represent a form of inter (sub) group conflict. Where conflict is likely to occur within a specialist functional group is in the interpretation of organizational reality, as illustrated by our preceding discussions of personnel management, medical, and other specialist groups. Such conflict tends to be expressed in arguments about the definition of the group's true role in the organization(s) in which it operates, and in the adoption of different, potentially conflicting definitions of their own roles by group members, reflecting their adherence to different definitions of the group's role (Gowler and Legge, 1980; Gowler and Parry, 1979; Legge, 1978).

Generally speaking, it is probable that inter and intragroup conflict will increase with organizational size, particularly if organizational growth results from policies of diversification. This is for two reasons. First, the larger the organization the more specialist groups it is likely to have with potentially conflicting interests (see preceding discussion on group emergence). Secondly, the more diverse, complex, and uncertain the environments in which the organization operates, as discussed above, the more room there is for ambiguities in the definition of the organizational realities of objectives, ways of achieving them, and success criteria.

Conflict-prone Groups

Most intergroup conflict (both quantitatively and qualitatively speaking), is likely to occur between specialist groups experiencing task-related asymmetries (that is, where one group is 'unilaterally dependent upon another, or the flow of influence is decidedly one-way') (Aldrich, 1979, p. 93). Thompson (1967, p. 54) described this as a condition of 'sequential interdependence', in which one group must take some action before another can accomplish its tasks. A good example of such conflict is that which persists between production groups and specialist maintenance engineers, particularly in capital-intensive industries. In such situations, although nominally a line/staff relationship exists, with the production group theoretically in the position to demand and receive service, in practice the production group is heavily dependent upon the maintenance engineers to achieve efficient machine utilization and, hence, production targets. Not surprisingly, when the maintenance group seeks to exploit its power by deciding its own priorities rather than responding instantly to every production manager's demands, high levels of conflict are generated (Crozier, 1964; Goldner, 1970). This conflict is exacerbated by the fact that the production group is forced to recognize that the theoretical state of affairs (of line control over staff services) has been inverted by the maintenance group's real ability to cope with an important 'strategic contingency' (Hickson et al., 1971). (For further illustration of the intergroup conflict that is generated when a group tries to realign its relationships with other groups—and to its own advantage—readers are referred back to the previous section on 'means ambiguity'.) For the unilaterally dependant group, often its only means of assertion is through its use of 'negative' power (Handy, 1978), or vetoeing activities, when suitable occasions arise to retaliate against the dominant group in another arena (possibly in an 'integrative' group in which both groups are represented). Such activities, of course, serve only to heighten existing conflict.

Intergroup conflict, if to a lesser extent, is also prone to occur when groups are 'tightly' rather than 'loosely' coupled (Aldrich, 1979; Weick, 1976). 'Loose' coupling exists when groups in various parts of an organization are only weakly connected to each other and therefore are free to vary independently (for example, the personnel function and the marketing function, *totally* different product groups competing in different markets, new venture units). As mentioned above, 'loose' coupling is sometimes used as a deliberate strategy to contain potential conflict (Pfeffer, 1978). This is because loosely coupled groups interact rarely; therefore they have little effect on each other, their interests are unlikely to be highly salient to each other and, hence, few opportunities or issues for confrontation are likely to arise. 'Tightly' coupled groups, in contrast, are those which are *symmetrically* dependent upon each other, or which, in Thompson's (1967, p. 55) terminology, experience 'reciprocal interdependence', where the outputs of each group form the inputs for the others (for example, marketing and development functions). Tightly coupled groups not only interact frequently, but may compete to establish their own definition of common tasks and the nature of each group's contribution to success criteria. In situations where there is competition for scarce resources (or for a 'fair share' of free floating resources), this may lead to bargaining and conflict, as each group seeks to gain some measure of ascendancy in the process of 'mutual accommodation' (Thompson, 1967). At the same time, such groups have a strong incentive to contain their conflict within manageable limits, as their mutual interdependence necessitates cooperation, just as much as it may generate conflict. (Kahn *et al.*, 1964, make the same point, at the level of individual role analysis, in reference to the limited use of sanctions against each other, by mutually dependent, but conflicting, role incumbents).

The specialist groups in the voluntary service organization referred to earlier provide an illustration of this point. In spite of their conflict over the definition of appropriate accountabilities and reporting relationships, which was ultimately expressed in conflict over salary differentials, neither group, in prosecuting its respective claim, refused to work with, or cooperate with the other, although, at the height of the conflict this had been mooted—and rejected—as a possibility.

In discussing what may be termed 'competitor—colleague' relationships (Tunstall, 1971), reference should also be made to specialist 'integrative' groups, although, for reasons discussed earlier, such groups are not the prime focus of this chapter. By definition, integrative groups exist to bring together and coordinate actually and potentially conflicting interests and perspectives. To the extent that members of integrative groups (for example, executive board members, committee members, Cabinet ministers) enter that group as the representative of another specialist (that is, function, or product/service) group, which may be in conflict with other groups, whose representatives are also members to the integrative group, intragroup conflict is likely to emerge. Crossman's (1979) accounts of Cabinet meetings, for example, contain many vivid descriptions of such conflict, as the ministerial representatives of different government departments fought, within Cabinet, for as large a share of government revenue as possible. His account of his early battle to increase the housing department's budget (Thursday, 11 February 1965) is typical:

I spoke extremely moderately. I was followed by Callaghan (Chancellor of the Exchequer) who in a long, violent harangue said that we were going to crack up and crash unless the increase in public expenditure could be halted. He could not permit any increase in the housing programme because he was facing a budget situation in which even a neutral budget would fail to win the confidence of the bankers. . . . George Brown (First Secretary). . . replied . . . that the whole increase in the housing programme could be put through by expanding our industrialized building. This would not put a strain on our resources, but simply employ unused capital resources in which millions had been invested. So it was a straight conflict between the Chancellor and the First Secretary (for primacy in the economic planning process). . . . On my side I had George Brown, the Lord Chancellor, Frank Cousins, Fred Peart and Jim Griffiths, but very little other support. This was partly because the other Ministers were bound to support the Chancellor. Tony Crossland, for example, was obviously afraid that if housing got more money it would be taken from Education. Tom Fraser at Transport felt the same and so did the Minister of Power . . . (Crossman, 1979, pp. 76–77).

At the same time, however, such groups generally recognize that their major function is to agree a coordinated set of policies or strategies and that, this being the case, at worst, conflict must be contained and, at best, resolved. As Barbara Castle commented, referring to conflict over her (then) proposed industrial relations legislation:

I pointed out to them there were as many views about my Bill in the room as there were people. If we were the Cabinet, we would be disagreeing passionately. Yet, in the end we have to cohere around *some* view, even if we all marginally disagreed with it (Castle, Diary entry, Wednesday 7 May, 1969).

Indeed, the whole function of integrative groups is to transform competitors into colleagues through their acceptance of collective responsibility for jointly agreed strategies, aimed at the achievement of superordinate goals. The role of the Chairman (and his degree of patronage) in achieving consensus and cooperation and in containing conflict has frequently been commented upon (see, for example, Crossman, 1979; Janis, 1972).

'Deviant' Behaviour by Specialist Groups

'Work behaviour is subject to a variety of controls including legal codes, formalized expectations, customary standards, and informal social norms' (Bryant, 1974, p. 17). It is the violation of such codes, expectations, standards, and norms that constitutes 'deviant' behaviour on the part of the individual or group so acting, *in the eyes of those who institute or support such controls.* In other words, an individual or group which violates rules that the observer considers illegitimate or irrelevant is not deviant in that observer's eyes, but may be so in the eyes of those who regard the rules as both legitimate and relevant. For example, a 'ratebuster' who violates his workgroup's norms about 'appropriate' output levels may be labelled as 'deviant' in its eyes, but as 'a good worker—I wish we had more of them' in the eyes of management (Lupton, 1963; Roy, 1952, 1954). Similarly, a work group that ignores or 'bends' formal organizational, professional, or legal rules may be labelled as 'deviant' by other groups in its organization, profession, or by the general public, but not necessarily so by its immediate organizational milieu—unless pressurized by outside bodies. In this section, then, specialist groups' behaviours, which the general public most certainly, and the relevant employing organization, perhaps under pressure, might feel compelled to label as deviant, are considered.

As suggested earlier, 'differentiative' specialist groups often emerge in order to handle an organization's boundary spanning and innovative areas of activity. As such, to a greater extent than less specialist groups, they are likely to be called upon to cope with new, unfamiliar problems that may not combine readily with customary 'approved best practice' or 'due process', *particularly if traditional, often inappropriate criteria are retained for the evaluation of their success.* In these circumstances the groups involved may well feel compelled to ignore or break established rules about the *way* in which their work is to be done, in order to meet the traditional performance criteria. The more pressure there is for the groups to meet performance criteria, the more likely it is that 'deviant' behaviours will emerge. It should also be noted here that ambiguity and conflict contribute to the opportunity structures in which deviance and its attribution flourish.

To illustrate and develop this suggestion, the behaviours of two different types of product/service group, namely police narcotics law enforcement teams, and the project team in the B. F. Goodrich Co. involved in the design of the A7D aircraft break for the L.T.V. Aerospace Corporation, may be examined in some detail. Although operating in very different organizations and on different activities, the pressures on the groups to act 'deviantly' are conceptually very similar.

1. *Both groups emerged to cope with a new/non-traditional area of activity that was typified by uncertainties in its means/ends relationship.*

Police narcotics control squads are faced with a 'non-traditional' area of law enforcement—the 'victimless' crime (Schur, 1965). In contrast to 'traditional' crimes which typically take the pattern of assault, citizen accusation, identification, and defence (Skolnick, 1966) 'victimless' crimes are typified by lack of citizen complainant. The customer of a dealer in narcotics, a gambler, or a prostitute's client is usually not interested in having an arrest made. Hence, as Skolnick puts it '. . . vice control men (along with all those policing crimes against the state, such as espionage or counterfeiting) must, as it were, drum up their own business' (1966, p. 116).

In these circumstances, then, lacking citizen complaint and identification of the criminal, the narcotics squads are forced to abandon the traditional forms of detection, i.e. identifying and interviewing complainant witnesses, and resort to new tactics, i.e. the cultivation and use of informants and *agents provocateurs.* Because the uncertainties in this form of detection are potentially high (for example, problems in establishing crimes and identifying their perpetrators, reliance on questionably 'reliable' informants, protecting their identities and that of undercovermen) there is pressure upon the squads, given other factors which will be discussed shortly, to use 'deviant' practices in an effort to reduce this uncertainty.

Similarly, the project team developing the A7D brake was involved in a completely new design rather than in developing a modification to an existing brake. The uncertainties in the design were exacerbated by the fact that the contract had been won largely through the company's commitment to produce an extremely light weight brake, permitting little margin for error, under tight cost constraints. Again, this placed pressure on the project team when problems with the initial design were encountered (Vandivier, 1978).

2. *Both groups were confronted by success criteria which prioritized administrative/business values at the expense of legal/professional standards.*

As discussed earlier, the ambiguity surrounding police departments' ultimate objectives had given rise to a surrogate success criterion, the 'clearance rate' (see section on ambiguity about success criteria). Given that this criterion is used, in (American) police departments, as a measure of individual and group effectiveness—and is sold as such to consumer groups—there is pressure upon narcotics squads to perform well in terms of this administrative criterion (an 'end') at the expense of 'due process' or 'proper' means of job performance, as will be discussed below (Skolnick, 1966).

The project team at Goodrich was similarly faced with a clear-cut success criterion. The contract for the aircraft brake upon which it was working represented an important source of revenue to the company. First, it re-established relationships with a potentially major customer of the company's products, a relationship which had been broken off ten years previously, due to dissatisfaction on the part of the customer. Secondly, although the initial order was not large in cash terms, prospects for replacement parts, and contracts for updated modifications, which were likely to follow the initial order, would prove highly profitable. For the engineers working on the project the success criterion was that the company should keep to the deadlines and specifications of the customer, as a means of fulfilling the contract and so ensuring the profitable follow-up business. Ultimately, then, the success criterion for the project team could be expressed in terms of the business value of market share and profitability.

3. *Both groups, in attempting to satisfy their success criterion, were aware of external pressure underwriting its validity.*

As Skolnick (1966, chs. 8 and 11) reports, police departments are pressured into evolving such a surrogate success criterion as 'the clearance rate' by the public at large, who demand that 'crimes should be solved', that 'law and order should prevail', and that 'criminals should not get away with it'—almost irrespective of *how* criminals are caught. Similarly, at Goodrich the project engineers were aware that competition in the industry meant that keeping to deadlines and specifications was of crucial importance for survival and growth.

4. *Both groups, as a result of (1), were pressurized to 'bend' legal/professional rules about 'due processes' in order to satisfy their dominant success criteria.*

Police narcotics squads are faced with three major problems. First, their 'tip-offs' from informers tend to be general rather than specific (that is, X seems to be selling a lot to his friends' rather than 'I saw X rob Y type and amount of drugs from Z pharmacy). Yet searches of persons and premises, according to both British and American law (McBarnet, 1979; Skolnick, 1966) can only be made without a warrant in relation to a specific, arrestable offence. Exploratory searches, without a warrant, acting on the basis of some promising but non-specific (to an arrestable offence) information, are illegal. But the police know that drugs can very quickly and easily be disposed of. Therefore, if they apply for a warrant and, as is likely, 'the word gets around', the drugs can disappear hours before the police can legally commence their search. In such circumstances it is not surprising that the group norm of many narcotics squads is to ignore the 'due processes of the law' and conduct illegal exploratory searches. As one Scotland Yard detective made the general point:

Nearly always you have to act on his information (the informer's) so fast that there is no time to apply for search warrants. Even when you have the time you may not have the inclination because a certain amount of publicity is inevitable during the process of application . . . and if the word gets out it goes through the underworld . . . like a fire through a forest after a drought. (Cited in Gosling, 1959, p. 19).

The one constraint on this illegal activity—that evidence produced by illegal means is inadmissible in court—tends to be circumvented by three factors. First, narcotics squads' officers are informally taught how to write up their reports, after the event, so as to present a 'good account' (Skolnick, 1966, and cf. Chatterton, 1979). Secondly, the potential complainants of illegal searches, etc. often feel themselves to be in no position to make a formal complaint partly through problems of 'spoiled identity' (Skolnick, 1966, p. 130) and partly because, if legally caught at a later date, it might well be remembered, and held against them (Skolnick, 1966, pp. 146–147). Thirdly, if evidence is found, however illegally, courts often feel that they cannot totally ignore it (Skolnick, 1966, pp. 221–224; McBarnet, 1979).

The second major problem faced by narcotics squads which encourages deviant behaviour is the use of the informer system. As Skolnick points out, to gain informants' cooperation, police have to employ sanctions which may involve gifts of money but, more importantly, charge reductions and, in certain cases, the licensing of crime. Hence, 'burglary detectives permit informants to commit narcotics offences, while narcotics detectives allow informants to steal' (Skolnick, 1966, p. 129). This, of course, may represent a further consequence of the use of the 'clearance rate' as a surrogate success criterion—the recording and clearance of burglary offences are of no administrative concern to narcotics squads—only the clearance of narcotics offences (and vice versa as far as burglary detectives are concerned). If condoning informants' burglaries faci-litates the achievements of a high clearance rate of narcotics offences, burglaries are likely to be condoned. (In other words, this represents an unusual example of a common occurrence—two groups' attempts to optimize on their own success criterion without the control of superordinate success criteria may result in overall sub-optimization.) Although Skolnick (1966, p. 124) discounts suggestions that narcotics squads actually licence certain informants to commit narcotics offences (counter-productive if the 'clearance rate' criterion is employed), in situations where the surrogate success criterion is the *arrest* rate, as it was for the (British) Scotland Yard drugs squad, it has been claimed that this practice did develop.

A system (was) created whereby certain dealers were in effect licensed by the Drugs Squad to deal without much fear of prosecution, in return for providing a number of their customers as 'bodies' for the police. These favoured dealers could set up deals specially for the Drugs Squad: or, if approached themselves in a genuine deal, they could choose to call in Pilcher's men, see the other parties to the deal arrested, and get back part of the drugs involved as a reward. The Home Office, once they discovered what was happening, had a name for this technique: they called it 're-cycling' (Cox *et al.*, 1977, pp. 86–7).

This quotation hints at a third major source of potentially deviant behaviour on the part of narcotics squads, i.e. in their role as *agents provocateurs*. This occurs when, in order to gain the conviction of a known 'primary source' dealer, the police themselves become major purchasers of narcotics and, in a sense, 'create' the evidence which will form the basis of a conviction. The squads perceive this as a necessary strategy, since the big dealer, working through 'employees', may be difficult to implicate, unless this is done directly by undercovermen. However, not only does this result in the fact that 'narcotics police inevitably are part of the "dope rings" they themselves help to create' (Skolnick, 1966, p. 161), but it may lead to even more questionable practices such as the 'planting' of evidence (Cox *et al.*, 1977, p. 94). While the role of *agent provocateur* may or may not be officially condoned by the police hierarchy (cf. Cox *et al.*, 1977; Skolnick, 1966), the general public certainly appear uneasy about the practices involved—especially when 'legitimate' enterprises contain such deviant behaviour as 'planting', 'phone tapping', and so forth.

Turning to the R&D team at the Goodrich Company, deviant behaviour again resulted from attempts to succeed in terms of business success criteria in a situation of high means/ends uncertainty. The brake as initially designed was discovered by a junior engineer, on testing, to be far too small for the job intended, 'there simply was not enough surface area on the discs to stop the aircraft without generating the excessive heat that caused the linings to fail' (Vandivier, 1978, p. 84). However, on the strength of the chief design engineer's reputation, not only had the projects manager, a technically less qualified man, assured the customer, L.T.V., that 'all there was left to do on the brake was pack it in a crate and ship it out of the back door' (Vandivier, 1978, p. 84) but the four-disk-brake sub-assemblies had already been ordered. In these circumstances, aware of the cost in money and time of re-designing the brake—not to mention loss of credibility with an already wary customer—the projects manager decided that the team should press ahead, experimenting with new linings and 'nursing' the brake through its tests, in the hope that it would 'come right'. Still the brake proved inadequate.

At this point the project team was faced with a major constraint. The brake's final destination was as part of a military aircraft. As such, the brake assembly was required to undergo a series of 'qualification' tests, the content, method, and success criteria of which being tightly specified by the military. Given that such qualification tests were generally considered to set extremely high 'professional' standards, in the light of business values, some 'nursing through' was considered legitimate, even under normal circumstances. Even with 'conventional' nursing through the brake failed the tests.

In the interests of the long-term credibility of the company, in terms of business as well as professional success criteria, the brake should now have been scrapped. But, costs in money and time had risen even higher and the projects manager, his superordinate, the manager of the whole design engineering section, and the manager of the technical services section (of which the test lab was a part) were alarmed at the possible repercussions on their careers if they admitted they had pressed on in the light of earlier negative test results. As a result, pressure was placed on the project team and test lab to 'fudge' the results of the qualification tests, in blatant disregard of the military specifications about test content and procedure. Two types of deviant behaviour resulted. First, the test engineers deliberately broke test procedure. For example:

Fans were set up to provide special cooling. Instead of maintaining pressure on the brake until the test wheel had come to a complete stop, the pressure was reduced when the wheel had decelerated to about 15 mph, allowing it to 'coast' to a stop. After each stop, the brake was disassembled and carefully cleaned, and after some of the stops, internal brake parts were machined in order to remove warp and other disfigurations caused by high heat . . . for some of the stops, the instrument which recorded the brake pressure (was) deliberately miscalibrated so that, while the brake pressure used during the stops was recorded as 1000 psi (the maximum pressure that would be available on the A7D aircraft), the pressure had actually been 1100 psi! (Vandivier, 1978, pp. 87–88).

Secondly, the project team in writing up the qualification report deliberately falsified data:

Resorting to the actual data only on occasion, Lawson and I proceeded to prepare page after page of elaborate, detailed engineering curves, charts and test logs, which purported to show what had happened during the formal qualification tests. When temperatures were too high, we deliberately chopped them down a few hundred degrees, and where they were too low, we raised them to a value that would appear reasonable to the L.T.V. and military engineers. Brake pressure, torque values, distances, times—everything of consequence was tailored to fit the occasion . . . . Occasionally, we would find that some test either hadn't been performed at all or had been conducted improperly. On these occasions, we 'conducted' the test—successfully, of course—on paper (Vandivier, 1978, p. 93).

The sequel to this 'deviant' episode was that on flight testing a serious accident was narrowly averted and, following members of the project team's voluntary confessions to the F.B.I., the company was forced to withdraw the brake and qualification report and to make restitution to L.T.V. At a governmental hearing, however, the company scapegoated the junior members of the project team and 'the four-hour hearing was adjourned, with no real conclusion reached by the committee' (Vandivier, 1978, p. 100).

Although these two examples of specialist groups have been used to illustrate the general points made in some detail, other cases of innovative or boundary spanning groups drifting into deviant behaviour through a similar set of pressures may be cited, for example, the 'Watergate conspirators' and those marketing specialists involved in the price-fixing agreements that resulted in the heavy electrical equipment anti-trust cases of 1961 (Dean, 1977; Geis, 1978; Reichley, 1978).

Recognition of Deviance

The behaviour reported here is 'deviant' in the sense that consumer groups recognize it to be so, whether or not the participants do. In the case of the narcotics squads, the participants and their immediate superordinates do not, as a rule, consider most of the behaviour outlined as deviant, although the general public as well as more traditional police units, tend to label it as such. Narcotics squads consider such behaviour to be morally right and necessary in order to get the job done, arguing that the distinction between 'legal' and 'factual' guilt places a constraint on their ability to control crime (Packer, 1964). The junior members of the project team at Goodrich, however, recognized that their behaviour deviated from professional standards and attempted to resist the pressures placed upon them to engage in such behaviour. Fears for their security of tenure and future in the company led to their ultimate compliance.

This raises two related points about the development of deviance in specialist groups. First, deviant behaviour may be embarked upon solely to perform a task successfully, without any consideration of personal gain. Yet, such practices may present *opportunities* for gain which are later exploited, resulting in behaviours recognized by the participants to be deviant, even while maintaining validity of the 'deviant' core of their activities. Thus, Drugs Squad members may not consider their actions as *agents provocateurs* to be deviant, but recognize that to under-report the amount of drugs seized in order to retain the rest for personal profit, to be so. The problem is that condoned deviance for 'legitimate' organizational purposes can very easily present opportunities for deviance that the organization does not condone.

Secondly, participation in deviant activities often involves the participants in taking a series of downward steps in a 'moral career' (Sherman, 1974; Ditton, 1977). In other words, having taken a first step which may appear to be only on the borderline of legitimacy (for example, attempting, by dubious 'tinkering', to get a brake containing a recognized design fault to work) individuals may find subsequent steps easier, as they feel increasingly disqualified to put up strong resistance to ever more serious acts, having once deviated (for example, having broken test procedure, what does it matter if test data are misrepresented?; if false data have been compiled, is it any worse to write the report based on the data?). Sherman (1974) reports how police can graduate from increasingly serious *passive* acts of deviance (from accepting seemingly legitimate perks, such as free meals, to accepting increasing sums for turning a blind eye to successively more serious 'victimless' crimes) to *proactive* acts (such as committing planned burglary on a regular basis). The moral career of a corrupt policeman from a 'grass eater' to a 'meat eater' is vividly documented in the Knapp Commission Report (1972). The group member's initiation into such deviant acts is generally by his work group, on the pain of ostricization if he does not comply with the group norm about appropriate (deviant) behaviour (Knapp, 1972; Sherman, 1974).

Conclusions

In this Chapter it has been suggested that 'differentiative' specialist groups—possibly to a greater extent than some other work groups—typically experience problems of task and role ambiguity, intra and intergroup conflict, and pressures towards 'deviant' behaviour. Although these issues have been treated separately, they are linked by a common theme: *the role specialist groups play in information processing for effective task performance.* As Galbraith (1973) argues, the amount of information an organization has to process is a function of its size, the degree of uncertainty concerning task requirements (itself a function of degree of market complexity and variability), the number of elements (for example, departments, clients, products) relevant for decision-making, and their degree of interdependence. As has been discussed in this chapter, size and market complexity and variability appear associated with the emergence of differentiative specialist groups; uncertainty, with task and role ambiguity, and with deviant behaviours; and interdependence with the nature and degree of intergroup conflict. It should be noted too that, although this chapter has concentrated on what we have termed 'differentiative' specialist groups, the behaviours of *all* specialist groups are highly influenced by the information processing role they adopt. Hence, the role played by integrative specialist groups generally reflects the coordinative requirements deriving from the degree of interconnectedness—whether 'pooled', 'sequential', or 'reciprocal', to use Thompson's terms—between organizational activities.

We suggest then that a fruitful approach to the analysis of work group behaviour is through the study of organizational information processing requirements, groups' interpretations, negotiations and perceptions of these requirements, and their development and adaptation of customary patterns of behaviour to meet these requirements as definitions emerge.

References

Aldrich, H. E. (1979) *Organizations and Environments*, Englewood Cliffs, N. J.: Prentice-Hall.

Black, J. (ed.) (1971) *Radical Lawyers*, New York: Avon.

Blau, P. M. (1974) *On the Nature of Organizations*, New York: Wiley–Interscience.

Bryant, C. D. (ed.) (1974) *Deviant Behavior, Occupational and Organizational Bases*, Chicago: Rand McNally.

Castle, B. (1980) *Diaries*, London: Weidenfeld and Nicolson. (First serialized in the *Sunday Times*, January and February 1980.)

Chatterton, M. R. (1979) 'The supervision of patrol work under the fixed points system', in S. Holdaway, ed., *The British Police*, London: Arnold.

Child, J. (1972) 'Organization structure, environment and performance—the role of strategic choice', *Sociology*, **6**, 1, 1–22.

Child, J. (1977) *Organization*, London: Harper and Row.

Cow, B., Shirley, J., and Short, M. (1977) *The Fall of Scotland Yard*, Harmondsworth: Penguin.

Crossman, R. (1979) *The Crossman Diaries* (condensed version). London: Magnum Books. (First published in three volumes under the title, *The Diaries of a Cabinet Minister*, 1975, 1976, 1977, by Hamish Hamilton and Jonathan Cape.)

Crozier, M. (1964) *The Bureaucratic Phenomenon*, Chicago: University of Chicago Press.

Cyert, R. M. and March, J. G. (1963) *A Behavioral Theory of the Firm*, Englewood Cliffs, N. J.: Prentice-Hall.

Dean, J. (1977) *Blind Ambition*, London: Star. (First published in U.S.A., 1976.)

Ditton, J. (1977) *Part-Time Crime*, London: Macmillan.

Doreian, P. and Hummon, N. P. (1976) *Modeling Social Processes*, New York: Elsevier.

Dryburgh, G. D. M. (1972) 'The man in the middle', *Personnel Management*, **May**.

Fisch, G. G. (1971) 'Line staff is obsolete . . . and should be replaced by the functional team-work concept', in H. E. Frank, ed., *Organization Structuring*, London. McGraw-Hill. (First published in *Harvard Business Review*, September/October, 1961.)

Fitzgerald, A. P. (1980) 'Manpower planning at the company level', Doctoral Thesis, University of Bradford.

Fletcher, B., Gowler, D., and Payne, R. (1979) 'Exploding the myth of executive stress', *Personnel Management*, **May**, 31–34.

Freidson, E. (1970) *The Profession of Medicine*, New York: Dodd, Mead.

Galbraith, J. R. (1973) *Designing Complex Organizations*, Reading, Mass.: Addison-Wesley.

Geis, G. (1978) 'White collar crime: the heavy electrical equipment anti-trust cases of 1961', in M. D. Ermann and R. J. Lundman, eds., *Corporate and Governmental Deviance*, New York: Oxford University Press. (First published in Clinard, M. B. and Quinney, R. (eds.) (1967) *Criminal Behavior Systems: A Typology*, New York: Holt, Rinehart and Winston.

Gerstl, J. and Jacobs, G. (eds.) (1976) *Professions for the People: The Politics of Skill*, New York: Schenkman.

Glueck, W. F. (1974) *Personnel, a Diagnostic Approach*, Dallas, Taxas: Business Publications.

Goffman, E. (1959) *The Presentation of Self in Everyday Life*, Harmondsworth: Penguin.

Goldner, F. H. (1970) 'The division of labor: process and power', in M. N. Zald, ed., *Power in Organizations*, Nashville, Tenn.: Vanderbilt University Press.

Goldstein, J. (1960) 'Police discretion not to invoke the criminal process: low visibility decisions in the administration of justice', *Yale Law Journal*, **69**, 559–60.

Gosling, J. (1959) *The Ghost Squad*, New York: Doubleday.

Gowler, D. and Legge, K. (1978) 'Participation in context: towards a synthesis of the theory and practice of organizatonal change', Part 1, *Journal of Management Studies*, **15**, 149–75.

Gowler, D. and Legge, K. (1980) 'Evaluative practices as stressors in occupational settings', in C. L. Cooper and R. L. Payne, eds., *Current Concerns in Occupational Stress*, London: Wiley.

Gowler, D. and Parry, G. (1979) 'Professionalism and its discontents', *New Forum*, **5**, 54–56.

Handy, C. (1976) *Understanding Organizations*, Harmondsworth: Penguin.

Haug, M. R. and Sussman, M. B. (1969) 'Professional autonomy and the revolt of the client', *Social Problems*, **17**, 3, 153–61.

Hickson, D. J., Hinings, C. R., Lee, C. A., Schneck, R. E., and Pennings, J. M. (1971) 'A "strategic continencies" theory of intraorganizational power', *Administrative Science Quarterly*, **16**, 2, 216–29.

Holdaway, S. (ed.) (1979) *The British Police*, London: Arnold.

Homans, G. C. (1950) *The Human Group*, New York: Harcourt Brace and World.

Hudson, K. (1978) *The Jargon of the Professions*, London: Macmillan.

Janis, I. L. (1972) *Victims of Groupthink*, Boston: Houghton Miff lin.

Jaques, E. (1961) *Equitable Payment*, London: Heinemann Educational Books.

Kahn, R. L., Wolfe, D. M., Snoek, R. P., Diedrick, J., and Rosenthal, R. A. (1964) *Organizational Stress*, New York: Wiley.

Kingdon, D. R. (1973) *Matrix Organization*, London: Tavistock.

Knapp, W. (1972) *The Knapp Commission Report on Police Corruption*, New York: George Braziller.

Knight, K. (ed.) (1977) *Matrix Management*, Farnborough: Gower Press.

Lawrence, P. R. and Lorsch, J. W. (1967) *Organization and Environment: Managing Differentiation and Integration*, Cambridge, Mass.: Harvard Graduate School of Business Administration.

Legge, K. (1978) *Power, Innovation and Problem-Solving in Personnel Management*, London: McGraw-Hill.

Lindblom, C. E. (1959) 'The science of "muddling through" ', *Public Administration Review*, **Spring**.

Lupton, T. (1963) *On the Shop Floor*, Oxford: Pergamon.

McBarnet, D. J. (1979) 'Arrest: the legal context of policing', in S. Holdaway, ed., *The British Police*, London: Arnold.

Mechanic, D. (1962) 'Sources of power of lower participants in complex organizations', *Administrative Science Quarterly*, **7**, 349–64.

Megginson, L. C. (1972) *Personnel—A Behavioral Approach to Administration* (Revised eds.), Homewood, Ill.: Irwin.

Mintzberg, H. (1973) *The Nature of Managerial Work*, New York: Harper and Row.

Morris, J. and Burgoyne, J. G. (1973) *Developing Resourceful Managers*, London: I.P.M.

Mumford, E. and Pettigrew, A. M. (1975) *Implementing Strategic Decisions*, London: Longman.

Packer, H. L. (1964) 'Two models of the criminal process', *University of Pennsylvania Law Review*, **113**, November, 1–68.

Paterson, T. T. (1972) *Job Evaluation*, London: Business Books.

Pettigrew, A. M. (1972) 'Information control as a power resource', *Sociology*, **6**, 187–204.

Pettigrew, A. M. (1973) *The Politics of Organizational Decision-Making*, London: Tavistock.

Pfeffer, J. (1978) *Organization Design*, Reading, Mass.: Addison-Wesley.

Pfeffer, J. and Salancik, G. R. (1978) *The External Control of Organizations*, New York: Harper and Row.

Reichley, A. J. (1978) 'Getting at the roots of Watergate', in M. D. Ermann and R. J. Lundman, eds., *Corporate and Governmental Deviance*, New York: Oxford University Press. (First published in *Fortune Magazine*, **88**, 1, 1973, 90–93, 170–74.)

Ritzer, G. and Trice, H. M. (1969) *An Occupation in Conflict*, Ithaca, N. Y.: Cornell University Press.

Roy, D. (1952) 'Quota restriction and goldbricking in a machine shop', *American Journal of Sociology*, **57**, 2, 427–42.

Roy, D. (1954) 'Efficiency and "the fix": informal intergroup relations in a piecework machine shop', *American Journal of Sociology*, **60**, 3, 255–66.

Sayles, L. R. (1964) *Managerial Behavior*, New York: McGraw-Hill.

Sayles, L. R. (1979) *Leadership*, New York: McGraw-Hill.

Sayles, L. R. and Chandler, M. (1971) *Managing Large Systems*, New York: Harper and Row.

Schur, E. M. (1965) *Crimes Without Victims*, Englewood Cliffs, N. J.: Prentice-Hall.

Sherman, L. (1974) *Police Corruption*, New York: Doubleday.

Skolnick, J. H. (1966) *Justice Without Trial*, New York: Wiley.

Stelling, J. G. and Bucher, R. (1973) 'Vocabularies of realism in professional socialization', *Social Science and Medicine*, 7, 661–75.

Stieglitz, H. (1971) 'Staff–staff relationships', in H. E. Frank, ed., *Organization Structuring*, London: McGraw-Hill. (First published in *Management Record*, February 1962, by the National Industrial Conference Board, New York.)

Strauss, G. (1962) 'Tactics of lateral relationship: the purchasing agent', *Administrative Science Quarterly*, 7, 2, 161–86.

Sykes, A. J. M. and Bates, J. (1962) 'Study of conflict between formal company policy and the interests of informal groups', *Sociological Review*, **November**, 313–27.

Thomason, G. F. (1975) *A Textbook of Personnel Management*, London: I.P.M.

Thompson, J. A. (1967) *Organizations in Action*, New York: McGraw-Hill.

Tunstall, J. (1971) *Journalists at Work*, London: Constable.

Tyson, S. (1980) 'Taking advantage of ambiguity', *Personnel Management*, **February**, 45–48.

Vandivier, K. (1978) 'Why should my conscience bother me?', In M. D. Ermann and R. J. Lundman, eds., *Corporate and Governmental Deviance*, New York: Oxford University Press. (Extract originally published in Heilbroner, R. L. *et al.* (1972) *In the Name of Profit*, New York: Doubleday.)

Watson, T. J. (1977) *The Personnel Managers*, London: Routledge and Kegan Paul.

Weick, K. (1976) 'Educational organizations as loosely coupled systems', *Administrative Science Quarterly*, **21**, 1, 1–19.

Wilson, O. W. (1962) *Police Planning*, Springfield: Charles C. Thomas.

Woodward, J. (1965) *Industrial Organization: Theory and Practice*, London: Oxford University Press.

Groups at Work
Edited by R. Payne and C. Cooper
© 1981 John Wiley & Sons Ltd.

Chapter 4

Groups and the Informal Organization

George F. Farris

Since the early 1960s I have been fortunate in that I have been able to study group functioning in a number of different contexts. These have included laboratory experiments involving ad hoc groups (e.g. Farris and Lim, 1969), laboratory training groups (e.g. Rubin, Kolb, McIntyre, and Farris, 1969), and groups at work (e.g. Farris and Butterfield, 1973; Andrews and Farris, 1976; Farris, 1979). The groups at work have involved a variety of persons engaged in a diversity of activities. They have included both blue and white collar workers, groups headed by first-line-supervisors, and groups headed by company presidents, group tasks ranging from creative research to loading trucks. The individuals involved have worked in many countries throughout the world.

In observing all these groups and in attempting to help some of them to function better, one conclusion has become patently clear: groups at work cannot be fully understood without reference to the organizations and environments in which they are located. Groups are embedded in an organizational context and an organizational history. Individual members belong to a number of groups in addition to the one under study. Some of these are located within the focal organization, while others are outside it.

Consequently, studies of ad hoc laboratory groups or groups of strangers in laboratory training can provide only partial insight into the functioning of groups at work. Important as this insight is, it is also necessary to understand the ways in which groups and their members relate to other parts of the organization and its environment. In concluding their landmark book, *The Social Psychology of Organizations*, Katz and Kahn (1966) warned against the 'sociological error', a tendency to explain organizational behavior without reference to the individuals involved and the 'psychological error', a tendency to explain organizational behavior in terms of the individuals involved without reference to the organizational constraints under which they are working. To the sociological and psychological errors we can add the 'social psychological error', a tendency to focus on internal group dynamics to explain organizational behavior, without reference to its organizational context. Any theory of groups at work based upon studies of groups outside their organizational context, such as laboratory groups or training groups, is especially prone to such a social psychological error.

In the present chapter an approach will be described to help understand the functioning of groups in the organizational context. The chapter is divided into three parts. The first describes empirical examples of groups functioning in the organization. The second develops an approach to help understand the functioning of groups in organizations. It is based upon a series of studies of informal groups and organizations. In the third part applied work using the informal organization approach is described.

Groups in the Organization

Groups working in organizations are influenced not only by their internal dynamics but also by their positions in the formal and informal organization structures. Two cases of groups at work illustrate this point. The first involves a management committee making a strategic decision for approval by the corporation. The second is concerned with a project team seeking resources to implement a decision already made.

Organizational Decision Making

Consider the following situation. As part of the lengthy agenda of their regular board meeting, the management committee of a major subsidiary of a large multinational corporation is considering a pricing agreement for purchase of a large supply of raw materials. The eleven-person management committee is chaired by the president of the subsidiary and includes the executive vice president, the other vice presidents, and heads of the company's major departments. Two alternatives are under consideration: a proposed new pricing agreement and continuation of terms reflected in the current contract. The management committee is to make a recommendation to the parent corporation the next day as to the appropriate price to pay the supplier.

The discussion opens with the president proposing the new pricing agreement. He states that he will have to present the management committee's recommendation to the corporation the next day. His purpose in presenting the item to the management committee is to get their views on the new pricing proposal. The president then spends about two or three minutes describing the new pricing agreement proposal.

Almost interrupting, the executive vice president injects, 'I strongly recommend that we proceed on the basis of the present contract'. He raises two questions critical of the proposed new agreement. The president responds, but apparently not comprehensively enough. After the president speaks for two or three more minutes, the executive vice president repeats one of his critical questions.

The discussion proceeds for some time. The president makes statements in favour of the agreement. The executive vice president makes several statements against it. The other management committee members' comments are limited almost exclusively to raising points for clarification. A senior vice president raises the majority of these points. At one juncture in the discussion he suggests considering the situation in terms of corporate goals as stated in the long-range plan. The executive vice president responds, 'I don't quite follow you. The highest cost is with the new agreement, not the present agreement. I'm not trying to criticize your division's investments'.

Late in the discussion the president points out that there would be a chance for a substantial discount with the new agreement. The executive vice president soon suggests a compromise of sorts—a long-term contract if the new proposal is recommended. Another vice president asks how much money will be lost by a delay in settling the issue.

After close to an hour of discussion, the president suggests that perhaps the committee is spending too much time on the agenda item. Then he adds, 'But one thing. . .', and makes another point in favour of his position. Finally he summarizes the discussion. 'We'll argue from the point of view of the new proposal, but we'll point out the economics of the other arrangement. Personally, I don't strongly prefer either'.

Another vice president makes a further suggestion. Then the president says, 'Well, I will say that we favourably consider this new pricing agreement proposal'.

A student of group dynamics, a practitioner of team building, or an expert in process consultation would find much to comment upon in this example. The conflict between the president and executive vice president over this issue is obvious. So is the unwillingness of other members of the management committee to take sides overtly in this conflict between the two highest ranking members of the group. Only a senior vice president spoke frequently, and his comments were aimed at mediating the dispute by finding common ground for a compromise. The other members of the management committee had little or nothing to say. The decision which emerged from the meeting was clearly not the result of a consensus having been reached in the discussion. The issue had not been fully resolved.

A practitioner of team building approaches to organization development would be apt to try to improve the situation described by helping the group members to become aware of the manifest and latent conflicts apparent in the group. Approaches to conflict resolution would be tried. Common interests of the group members would be stressed. An expert in process consultation would probably intervene in a similar manner, depending on his or her preferred approaches to organization development. Heavy reliance would probably be placed on the management committee members themselves to discover and report their feelings about the group and its functioning. Both these approaches could clearly achieve a great deal in this situation. However, to the extent that they concentrated on internal group dynamics while excluding the organizational context, they would fall short of fully diagnosing the problems faced by the management committee and taking appropriate actions to solve them. To illustrate, let us consider subsequent events in the case of the pricing agreement decision.

As the president pointed out at the beginning of the meeting, the management committee is to make a recommendation to the parent company the next day as to the appropriate price. The decision by the management committee, as summarized by the president, is to 'favourably consider the new pricing proposal'.

The next day a presentation was made to the parent company. The recommendation to favourably consider the new pricing proposal was rejected.

Knowledge of the dynamics of the management committee as a group is insufficient by itself to explain the rejection of the recommendation by the parent company. Nor is knowledge of the dynamics of the executive committee of the parent which rejected the recommendation sufficient to explain what happened. To explain the decision by the parent company it is necessary to move outside the boundaries of the two management committees involved to consider the organizational structures which connect them. Two structures are relevant: the formal structure and the informal structure. The former refers to the explicitly stated procedures for connecting the relevant offices in the parent and subsidiary. The latter is concerned with the relationships which evolve among relevant members of the parent and subsidiary at their individual discretion, regardless of the relationships mandated by the formal organization structure. Let us first examine the formal organization.

The by-laws of the corporation state that the office of the president of the subsidiary is responsible for coordinating decisions of the subsidiary with the goals of the parent corporation. As a consequence, the incumbent in the office of the president is responsible for presenting recommendations by the management committee of the subsidiary to the parent for consideration and approval. If the president is unable to represent the subsidiary, then the responsibility is to be carried out by the incumbent of the next highest office in the subsidiary, that of the executive vice president. This situation occurred in the case of the pricing decision.

On the evening after the meeting of the management committee the president became ill and was unable to present the recommendation of the subsidiary. Therefore, the responsibility fell upon the executive vice president.

Does this knowledge of the formal organization explain the decision by the parent company? Not by itself. The formally stated responsibilities of the president and the executive president in his absence include representing the position of the management committee of the subsidiary to the parent. Indeed, when queried after the meeting with the parent company as to whether he had had any difficulty recommending a position against which he had argued in the meeting of the management committee the previous day, the executive vice president smiled knowingly and replied, 'No problem. . .'.

Knowledge of the formal organization together with knowledge of the content (but not necessarily the process) of the discussion of the management committee helps explain the decision by the parent company. Certainly the executive vice president would be less apt to argue persuasively for a management committee position he personally opposes than for one which he supports. He may have met the letter but not the spirit of the formal organization's procedures. Of course then, the 'No problem' comment of the executive vice president cannot be taken at face value. According to this line of thinking, the recommendation of the management committee would have been approved if the president had been able to present it to the parent company himself.

Yet there are strong indications that the new pricing proposal would not have been approved by the parent company even if the president himself had been able to make the presentation. These indications are not apparent from the internal group dynamics of the management committee or the executive committee of the parent. Nor are they apparent from detailed knowledge of the structure of the formal organization. Rather, a thorough understanding of the informal relationships among members of the key executive groups of the parent and subsidiary suggest that the new pricing proposal was doomed to failure. Without going into excessive detail, salient aspects of these informal relationships may be summarized.

The subsidiary had recently been formed by means of a reorganization and consolidation of many of the parent company's worldwide operations. A few members of the management committee were new to the company, but most of them had previously worked closely with officers of the parent. Often they had suffered the common fate of living abroad in a 'company ghetto' where they had had to fend off two major adversaries who were not wholly sympathetic with their situations: corporate executives from headquarters and people from the host country. Relationships developed from such common experiences tend to persist. Moreover, many executives of the subsidiary were in close informal contact with their functional counterparts at headquarters. Although the formal organization indicated no reporting relationships along functional lines (recall that the subsidiary reports to the parent through its president alone), members of the management committee found it necessary to coordinate activities in their functional areas with their counterparts at headquarters. Moreover, career advancement for many members of the management committee had been and would continue to be heavily dependent upon the support and sponsorship of their functional counterparts at the parent company.

These informal relationships established over time among members of the management committee and executives of the parent had a great impact upon the decision-making behaviour of the management committee and the rejection of their recommendation by the parent company. Through their informal contacts, members of the management committee were able to sense the mood of parent company executives concerning the pricing proposal. Moreover, those in the parent and subsidiary who felt strongly about the proposal one way or the other were able to utilize these informal relationships to persuade key decision makers to agree with their positions. Thus, many members of the management committee had their minds made up before the lengthy discussion at their regular meeting. Similarly, members of the executive committee of the parent had also formed their opinions, and many members of the management committee of the subsidiary were aware of these opinions. Their behaviour in the management committee meeting was affected by this knowledge, causing many of them to withdraw from the conflict which emerged secure in the knowledge that their participation would not substantially influence a decision already made. The small benefits from active participation were strongly outweighed by the high costs of alienating either the president or the executive vice president.

Thus, it is apparent that the informal organization had an important impact upon the meeting of the management committee and the events which followed. Efforts at organization development through team building or process consultation would have to proceed very successfully to identify let alone change the important informal relationships involved. Moreover, the change in the formal structure had failed to change many of the informal relationships which had developed. Later in this chapter approaches for developing and changing the informal organization will be considered. Knowledge of the informal structure of the organization is a prerequisite to influencing its development or using it to help achieve the goals of a given individual or group. The next example, which deals with the implementation of a decision, illustrates this point.

Decision Implementation

Once a decision has been made by the formal organization, its implementation is not automatic. This situation is particularly so when turnover of key personnel occurs. Despite formal commitment to a course of action, the new executives often can delay allocation of resources so that implementation of the decision is badly crippled. Such was the situation in the case of the project team.

After several months of negotiation, a five-year system development project was agreed upon among the parties involved. Resources were allocated for the first two years, with the understanding that the project would be renewed for the final three years unless major problems occurred.

Three parties were involved in the negotiations, but the emphasis here in this case will be on one of them, a large federal government agency. Shortly after the project was approved by all three parties, the chief executive of this agency was forced to resign due to unexpected health problems. He was succeeded by one of the agency directors, a man who had opposed the development project when it had been presented to him for comments.

Meanwhile, work began on the project. A team of full- and part-time personnel was formed to work on it. It included all those persons originally agreed to, with one critical omission. Two full-time professional staff were to have been assigned by the government agency, but neither was assigned initially. Given the change in top management of the agency, the other project personnel were not especially concerned at first, but their concern increased as several weeks elapsed without agency personnel being assigned. Written requests were passed to the chief executive but no one was assigned.

Next, several personal requests were made by members of the project team, including both those employed by the government agency and those who were not. Still no one was assigned. However, after several entreaties the chief executive finally agreed that he could spare one professional staff person full time in addition to the several agency managerial personnel who were already working part time on the project. Although this represented a 50 per cent reduction in the commitment of full-time personnel, project members felt that 'a bird in the hand is worth two in the bush', since by this time the project was over half way to its renewal deadline. Progress had been made toward achieving project goals, but the pace was much slower than anticipated owing to the absence of full-time agency personnel.

Yet more weeks and months elapsed, and still no one was assigned. By this time all obvious approaches through formal organization routes had been attempted, without success. Each member of the project team had at one time or another personally requested the chief executive to provide the promised resources. The request had been made by section heads, department heads, division directors, and members of the project team not employed by the government agency.

Finally, one of the project team members had an insight. By this time he had become familiar with many of the informal relationships in the government agency. A number of these were work related, while still others were purely social. Several sources had convinced him that one of the agency employees was the mistress of the chief executive. Armed with this knowledge of the informal organization, the team member began establishing friendly social relations with her. After some time, he shared the project team's resource problem with her. Finally, when the occasion presented itself, he sent her flowers. The following week, a full-time professional was assigned to the project.

Assuming that the efforts of the project team member had indeed led to the assignment of the full-time professional, this case illustrates an insightful use of the informal organization to facilitate achievement of a group's objectives. Faced with the failure of all formal channels to achieve the desired results, and confronted with only meagre outcomes from personal entreaties by team members formally related to the chief executive, the team member sought an 'idea advocate' to support his team's request for the needed resource. His knowledge of the informal organization allowed him to identify an individual uniquely qualified to advocate an idea to the chief executive. The effectiveness of this group at work was substantially enhanced by use of the informal organization. Reliance upon the formal organization and internal group dynamics alone had failed to produce such a favourable outcome.

Informal Organizations

The two cases of groups at work just described demonstrate how groups are intimately bound up in their organizational contexts. The group behaviour of the management committee could not be fully understood without reference to the informal organizations to which members of that committee belonged. The project team was unable to acquire a promised resource until a member understood and utilized the informal organization of the government agency.

Although case examples such as these are useful for illustrating the impact of informal organizations upon groups at work, they are no substitute for a comprehensive theory of groups and the informal organization. Ultimately, it will be necessary to go beyond a series of case studies and anecdotes to develop a comprehensive set of propositions based upon precise definitions of key theoretical concepts. In this section a step is taken toward that objective. First, an excerpt from a systematic study of groups at work is described in order to show how studies of informal organizations can move from relatively qualitative to more quantitative approaches and to introduce concepts relevant to the proposed theory. Next, the theory is described through a series of propositions. Finally, informal organizations as conceived here are contrasted with groups and formal organizations.

A Sociometric Study

A common theme ran through the two case examples: idea support. In each situation a group at work was attempting to obtain support from a higher level in the organization. Informal relationships established by the management committee sometimes led to support of the committee decision but, on balance, they led to its rejection. An informal relationship established by a member of the project team led to the allocation of a long delayed resource. Idea support was therefore a critical element in each case.

It is possible to study a function of the informal organization such as idea support systematically through sociometric methods. One simply asks members of an organization to name colleagues who have been especially useful to them for supporting or advocating their ideas—for making sure that their ideas receive a fair hearing so that other ideas do not win out prematurely. Based upon answers to this question, it is possible to map the idea support aspect of an informal organization, connecting individuals diagramatically with those who support their ideas. Such a sociometric map appears in Figure 1. It is an excerpt from a series of studies of the role of the informal organization in research and development (Farris, 1971, 1972, 1974, 1976, 1978, 1979, 1980).

Figure 1 shows one department of a research and development laboratory as well as the laboratory management to which it reports. Each circle represents an individual. An arrow from one individual to another indicates that the first person reported that the second was especially helpful to him for supporting his ideas. The solid lines indicate the boundaries of the department, and the dashed lines indicate the boundaries of the two technical groups in the department.

Several aspects of the informal structure for idea support should be noted. First, not all individuals in the department participate. Some do not name anyone as especially helpful. Several others are not named by any colleagues as helpful. A number of individuals are neither givers nor recipients of idea support. Those individuals who do not participate in a given informal structure may be called 'isolates' with regard to that structure. The research to date cited above indicates that on the average isolates are lower performers and feel less involved in their technical work. Some isolates prefer to work as 'lone wolves', but others do not. They seem to drift into a situation of isolation.

Secondly, a few individuals are named frequently by their colleagues as helpful for idea support. These individuals are called 'sociometric stars' or 'key persons' in the informal organization. A number of these are supervisors or managers, but others are not. These key persons tend to be higher technical performers who are more involved in their work.

Thirdly, for this department only one instance of a reciprocal choice occurs for the role of idea support. Reciprocal choices refer to situations where person A names person B as especially helpful and person B in turn names person A. Several reciprocal choices were found in the larger research study, however. One

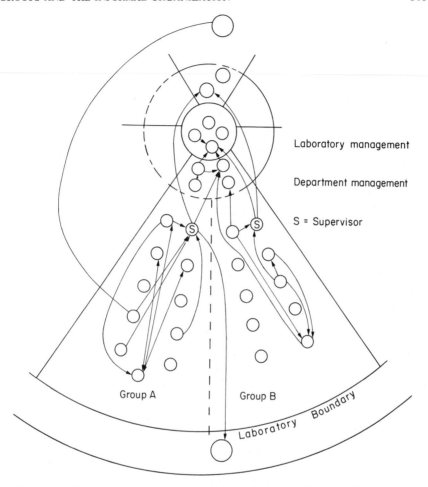

Figure 1. Ideas support in a research and development laboratory department

fruitful combination, as indicated by higher performance for those involved, was the pairing of idea support with idea origination. When person A named person B as especially helpful for idea support, and person B named person A as especially helpful for original ideas, the technical performance of the pair was significantly higher than average.

Finally, most of the choices for idea support took place either within the person's own work group or went to department management. Occasionally, laboratory management was chosen, as were members or managers from other departments within the laboratory. On the whole, considering the entire laboratory, it was found that for idea support 42 per cent of the choices were within one's own group, 29 per cent in the department but outside the group, 19 per cent in the laboratory outside the department, and 10 per cent outside the laboratory (Farris, 1980). Seventy-two per cent of those named were managers, confirming the expectation that those with formal authority have substantial influence through functions such as idea support.

To obtain a complete picture of the informal organization of this laboratory, it would be necessary to repeat the sociometric mapping shown in Figure 1 for the other departments in the laboratory and for all functions, in addition to idea support, which theory or observation suggest to be important to the informal structure. The research studies cited above have done just that. Similarly, a quantitative sociometric mapping for all relevant functions could facilitate understanding of the informal structure of the management committee's organization or that of the government agency in which the project team was located. The input to this mapping can be self-reports, as in the case of the laboratory, observations by a researcher, or unobtrusive measures such as logs of telephone conversations. Whatever the input, a picture of the informal structure and the place of a given group in it is the end result. Isolates, key persons, reciprocal choices, and the relationship between informal and formal structures can all be determined.

Toward a Theory of Informal Organizations

With reference to the two case studies and the sociometric study, a theory of informal organizations can now be described. At this stage of its development it is more a theoretical approach than a complete theory. Yet several propositions can be specified. They are outlined below.

1. *The basic unit of the informal organization is the individual role.* As defined by Katz and Kahn (1966, p. 174), a role 'reflects the essentially persisting features of recurring actions of an individual appropriately interrelated with the repetitive activities of others so as to yield a predictable outcome'. In this sense idea support is an example of a role. To the extent that she repeated her entreaties to the chief executive of the government agency, his mistress was playing the role of idea support. Similarly, members of the management committee of the subsidiary and the executive committee were playing the role of idea support in the case of the pricing decision. The sociometric study identified individuals who played the role of idea support in the research and development laboratory.

Numerous other roles are possible in an informal organization. They include such diverse activities as spreading rumours, providing technical information, providing critical evaluation, or providing comic relief. The essential requirements are that these behaviours are repeated and that they are related to the activities of other persons. Since so many roles are theoretically possible, one characteristic of a parsimonious theory of informal organization is that it identifies a relatively small number of roles especially important to the informal organizations under study. For example, Farris (1971) studied seven roles in the investigation of a research and development laboratory.

Of course, many roles are also performed within groups, whether they are groups at work, laboratory training groups, or the laboratory groups of the social psychologist. Bales (1958), for example, names several. Some of these may also be roles played in the informal organization. The critical difference, however, is that a given role in the informal organization involves individuals who are not necessarily members of the same group. The second proposition emphasizes this point.

2. *Connections between role players and role receivers constitute role networks.* A role player is the individual who performs the role for another person, while a role receiver is the person for whom the role is performed. For example, the insightful project team member was the role receiver and the chief executive's mistress was the role player in the case of idea support in the government agency. In Figure 1 above, the role players are those individuals with arrows pointing to them, and the role receivers are those persons from whom the arrows emanate. Figure 1 itself depicts the role network for the role—idea support—in a department of a research and development laboratory.

Note that the minimal size of a role network is two persons, a dyad. Connections between these dyads taken together create the total role network structure for an organization. Thus, a role network may be contrasted to a clique. In the former, individuals are connected to others through a pairing process often involving third parties. In the latter, individuals interact directly with one another, often conspiring to meet common objectives. All members of a clique are apt to be members of the same role network; however, all members of the same role network are unlikely to be members of the same clique.

3. *The structure of an informal organization is the sum total of all its role networks.* In other words, all the relationships between people in which one person plays a role for another are the structure of an informal organization. To map this structure it is necessary to identify all the roles which are played and who plays these roles for whom. Having mapped this structure, one can identify individuals who are isolates and key persons in the overall informal organization.

4. *The structure of an informal organization is hierarchical.* Some individuals are more influential than others in the informal organization. Sometimes more and less influential individuals in the informal organization hold the same formal status, as did several of the vice presidents on the management committee. Sometimes individuals with less formal status have more informal influence than do others with more formal status. For example, the mistress of the chief executive of the government agency had more informal influence and less formal status than the division director who was a member of the project team. The hierarchy in the informal organization may be called a 'lateral hierarchy', in contrast to the vertical hierarchy of the formal organization. Some individuals attain higher degrees of influence in the informal organization than others who have the same status in the formal organization.

Participation in informal organizations is highly skewed, creating sociometric stars and isolates. A considerable amount of empirical research has been devoted to identifying characteristics of very influential individuals in the informal organization. Depending upon the roles they play, they have been called key persons (Farris, 1971), gatekeepers (Allen, 1977), high information potentials (Holland, 1972), and grapevine liaisons (Davis, 1953). Sometimes organizations become extremely dependent upon these very influential individuals. When one of them leaves, role networks must be re-built for the organization to begin to resume its previous level of functioning.

5. *The basis for communication in an informal organization is proximity.* Individuals are more apt to interact informally when they are closer to one another in any one of several ways. At least five types of proximity can be identified: physical, professional, task, social, and formal-organization-created. Let us examine each in turn.

Physical proximity means that individuals are more apt to interact informally if they are situated close to one another physically. An engineer in a development laboratory is more apt to discuss a technical question with his office mate than with someone across the hall. He is more apt to discuss it with someone across the hall than with someone else on another floor or in another building.

Other things being equal, active participants in the informal organization are more apt to be located near a high-traffic area such as coffee room, an entrance, a rest room, or a water cooler. Inactive participants are more apt to be situated far out of the normal traffic pattern. When discussing isolates with supervisors in the research and development laboratory mentioned above, I was invited by them to visit an isolate in their department. To find him, we walked for about two minutes until we reached the end of a long, dead-end corridor. Reaching the last office, we opened the door only to find an inner office with a door which was also closed. We knocked, but received no answer. Finally we opened the door to the inner office and found that the isolate was not at his desk!

Physical proximity was important in the other two organizations mentioned above. As previously pointed out, many of the strong informal bonds between members of the management committee of the subsidiary and members of the parent company executive committee were formed when the individuals had been working together in close physical proximity on international assignments. In the government agency an inefficient elevator system in their high-rise office building frequently caused groups of people on each floor to congregate in front of the elevators for several minutes at a time. A great deal of social and some business interactions occurred in these circumstances.

Some attempts have been made to take account of physical proximity in the architectural designs of work spaces. For example, Morton (1971) reports on efforts to create geographical barriers and bonds among engineers at Bell Laboratories and Western Electric, and Allen (1977) reports an experiment to create a non-territorial office among production engineers.

Professional proximity means that people of similar professional backgrounds are more apt to interact informally than people with different professional backgrounds. It has been my observation, for example, that geologists in oil companies often create informal groups which exclude others with different backgrounds. It is easier to discuss matters with others who share similar approaches to work, have similar cognitive styles, or share interests in similar problems. The work on 'invisible colleges' (e.g. Crane, 1969) indicates that scientists, at least, maintain contact with colleagues of similar backgrounds despite barriers of great physical distance which separate them.

Task proximity means that people working on the same task are more apt to interact informally than people working on different tasks. This informal interaction may be concerned with the task at hand, or it may deal with another issue. As March and Simon (1958, p. 167) point out, 'Channel usage tends to be self-reinforcing. When a channel is frequently used for one purpose, its use for unrelated purposes is encouraged'. For example, members of the project team in the government agency found it easier to discuss non-project matters after they had worked together for a period of time on the system development project. It is not uncommon for managers to form administrative task forces partly to create a situation in which certain individuals will interact with one another. Their hope is that the channel of interaction created by the administrative task force will continue to be used for other matters important to the organization.

Social proximity means that individuals who have social contact with one another are more apt to interact informally regarding work-related matters. The effect of the social relationship between the chief executive of the government agency and his mistress on the project team is an obvious example. Even less intimate social contact can create a basis for friendship which makes it easier for individuals to collaborate informally concerning work problems. The members of the management committee of the subsidiary who were friendly on a social basis tended to support one another's positions quite frequently in the management committee meetings.

Formal-organization-created proximity means that individuals in the same formal organization unit are more apt to interact informally than those in different units. A major purpose of formal organization design is to enhance communications among particular subsets of its members. Certainly the role network for idea support shown in Figure 1 indicates more contact within formal units than between them.

Another way in which the formal organization enhances informal or discretionary interaction is by assigning some individuals to offices or positions which require interaction with several other individuals. Supervisory positions and liaison offices are examples. Empirical research has found that supervisors are often key persons or technological gatekeepers in technical organizations (Farris, 1974; Allen, 1977) and that others in formally created 'boundary spanning' positions are central figures in communications networks (Keller and Holland, 1975).

6. *The structure of informal organizations develops through role episodes.*

Informal organizations are built from roles which individuals play for one another. Roles, in turn, are the persisting features of activities in certain interpersonal transactions called 'role episodes' (Katz and Kahn, 1966). Informal organizations develop according to events which occur in these role episodes. If an episode has a favourable outcome, then a further transaction between the same individuals is more apt to occur in the future. For example, if person A seeks technical information from person B and receives it, he will be apt to return to person B in the future when he needs similar information. Moreover, person B may be more apt to seek assistance from person A, for whom he has just done a 'favour'. As persons A and B experience successful transactions about technical information, they may begin to interact informally about other matters as well. Recall March and Simon's (1958, p. 167) statement that, 'Channel usage tends to be self-reinforcing. When a channel is frequently used for one purpose, its use for unrelated purposes is encouraged'. In this manner, a series of interpersonal relationships develops among members of a formal organization, and an informal organization is formed.

Sayles and Strauss (1966, p. 89) suggest additional consequences of these interpersonal relationships.

Brought together by the formal organization, employees interact with one another. Increasing interaction builds favourable sentiments toward fellow group members. In turn, these sentiments become the foundation for an increased variety of activities, many not specified by the job description. . .And these increased opportunities for interaction build stronger bonds of identification. Then the group becomes something more than a mere collection of people. It develops a customary way of doing things—a set of stable characteristics that are hard to change. It becomes an organization in itself.

Thus, a series of interpersonal transactions develops over time into an informal organization which can be characterized by strong bonds of identification. A model describing these interpersonal transactions and their consequences is shown in Figure 2. It expands Katz and Kahn's (1966) concept of a role episode in a formal organization to describe the development of informal organizations.

As shown in Figure 2, person A sends information to person B (e.g. I would like technical information about topic X). Person B receives A's message, possibly not exactly as A sent it, and processes it. Two factors affecting B's processing of A's message are the causal attributions he makes about it (i.e. why is A asking me for this information) and his judgement under uncertainty as to the type of information which would be most responsive to A's request.

Person B then responds to A's request. His action in responding to A, if it recurs, may be termed a 'colleague role': recurring behaviour by one person in an interpersonal relationship with a colleague. Person A then receives information from person B's behaviour, processes it, and provides feedback to person B (for example, the information you provided is very helpful). The role episode has been completed. If person A were to be asked, through sociometric measure-

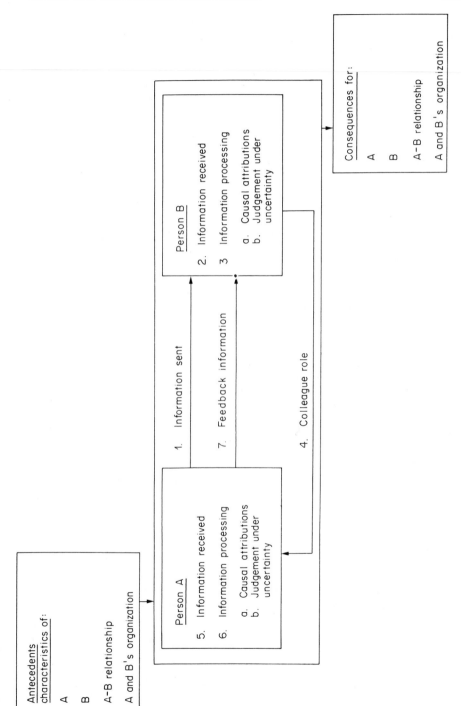

Figure 2. General model for examining a role episode

ment, who has provided him with technical information, he would be apt to name person B in this example.

This role episode is apt to be affected by certain antecedent conditions, and it is apt to have consequences extending beyond the role episode itself. Generically, these antecedents and consequences are apt to be characteristic of person A, person B, the relationship between A and B, and A and B's organization. Two empirical studies will help to illustrate these antecedents and consequences.

In one study Farris (1976) examined idea origination and evaluation in an R&D laboratory as a function of person A and person B's preferred working styles (antecedent conditions). Idea origination and evaluation were also related to consequences for A and B such as rewards, reciprocal help, and technical performance. In brief, the study found that idea evaluators, but not originators, preferred a collaborative working style. Idea evaluators were better rewarded and received reciprocal help from more colleagues. Although idea originators themselves were more innovative and productive technical performers, recipients of idea evaluation from more sources were higher performers.

Another study proposed that advancement in an R&D organization is contingent upon having a 'good' work assignment. Since there is typically a scarcity of such assignments, and

a will on the part of the work assigner to favour those he knows and likes, or who are recommended by persons he knows and likes. . .the ambitious and resourceful individual finds it expedient to approach others ostensibly in order to get functionally necessary information and advice, but actually to make contacts and establish relationships which may be helpful when it comes time to manoeuver himself into a position to get a choice work assignment (Howton, 1963, p. 505).

The author's participant observation was consistent with this proposition. Clearly, the information processing by the participants in the role episodes in this example would strongly affect the success of the manipulative attempt. The emerging literature on causal attribution and judgement under uncertainty should be useful in helping to understand the dynamics of such role episodes.

Thus, informal organizations develop from role episodes. The model presented in this section should provide a start in understanding the dynamics through which this process occurs.

7. *An important basis for power in informal organizations is the capacity to help a colleague achieve important goals.* Role episodes occur when one individual interacts with another in order to help achieve a personal goal. If the goal is achieved, the same person is apt to be sought out in the future. If this person is able to help a number of colleagues achieve their goals, he or she will acquire increasing power in the informal organization. Such was the case for the chief executive's mistress in the government agency.

Two of French and Raven's (1960) sources of power are apt to be especially important in informal organizations: expert and referent power. If an individual seeks advice from someone else, the latter's expertise is an important basis for power. If someone seeks a favour from another, the degree to which the latter likes him is a source of referent power. In short, expert power enables one to give assistance, and referent power increases the likelihood that assistance will be offered once it is sought.

8. *Norms are an important basis for control in informal organizations.* Common themes or patterns of behaviour run through some informal organizations but not others. These themes represent norms or accepted ways of doing things. These norms may be described in terms of the roles related to them. For example, critically evaluating a colleague's ideas is a role which some individuals may play in a given informal organization. If this role is played frequently in this informal organization, it may be said to be a norm in this organization. Other norms may include behaviour which results from a series of role episodes, for example coming to work late, leaving late, having lunch at one's desk, or attending a committee meeting only after having thoroughly studied the relevant documents. A norm of the management committee of the subsidiary was to refrain from publicly criticizing the activities of another executive's department. Norms control behaviour in the informal organization. Those who do not conform to the norms may find themselves isolated from important parts of the informal organization.

9. *The underlying reason for the creation of informal organizations is the achievement of individual goals.* According to the theoretical approach being advanced here, individuals enter into interpersonal transactions in order to help achieve personal goals. If the transaction or role episode is successful, and if it is repeated, a role has been played and the basis for a role network has been formed. Thus, the achievement of individual goals is at the heart of the informal organization. The informal organization is congruent with the formal organization to the extent that individuals can achieve their goals through the formal organization. Thus, informal organizations may support or oppose the formal organization depending on the degree of congruence between individual and organizational goals.

To summarize, informal organizations are interpersonal relationships collateral with the formal organization which develop to help achieve individual goals. Organizational and individual goals may be congruent or in conflict; so may the formal and informal organization. The structure of informal organizations consists of overlapping role networks; the basic structural unit is the individual role. This structure is hierarchical; lateral hierarchies form when unequal status creates isolates and a few very influential individuals. The structure of informal organizations is determined by several proximities—physical, professional, task, social, and formal-organization-created. The structure develops through a series of role episodes over time. In these interpersonal transactions an important basis for power is the capacity to satisfy a colleague's important needs.

Informal Organizations, Formal Groups, and Formal Organizations

In order to put the above theoretical approach in perspective, some contrasts may be made between informal organizations, formal groups, and formal organizations. These contrasts are shown in Table 1, where informal organization refers to the concept being employed in this chapter. Formal group refers to any group at work created as a unit by the formal organization. An 'informal group' would share characteristics of formal groups and informal organizations. Formal organization refers to the common usage of the term in the literature.

The basic structural unit of an informal organization is a role—a repeated pattern of activities in an interpersonal transaction. In the formal group the unit is the individual, and in the formal organization it is the office or position which 'locates the individual in relation to his fellows with respect to the job to be done and the giving and taking of orders' (Katz and Kahn, 1966, p. 180).

The basis for communication also differs. In the informal organization it is proximity—physical, professional, task, social, or formal. In the group it is membership, while in the formal organization it is the formal relationship between offices.

In the informal organization the basis for power is the capacity to help achieve individual goals. This is often achieved through expert or referent power. In the formal group all of French and Raven's (1950) bases of power may come into play: legitimate, expert, referent, coercive, and reward. In formal organizations, legitimate authority is the basis for power.

Norms serve as an important control mechanism in the informal organization and in formal groups. Rules are also important control mechanisms in formal groups and serve as the sole control mechanism in formal organizations.

The hierarchy in informal organizations is lateral, with people of the same formal status having different degrees of informal power. In formal organizations the hierarchy is vertical, while formal groups have both lateral and vertical hierarchies.

Finally, the salient goals in informal organizations are the individual's. In formal groups they are the group's goals, and in formal organizations the organization's goals are salient.

Thus, informal organizations as depicted in this section share some qualities with formal groups and formal organizations. Yet they differ in many important respects, as the cases of the management committee, the government agency, and the research and development laboratory have illustrated. Table 1 should help clarify the differences.

Applying the Informal Organization Approach

In order to illustrate applications of the informal organization approach to groups at work, two studies will be discussed briefly. The first describes the

Table 1. Some contrasts among informal organizations, formal groups, and formal organizations

Element	Informal organization	Formal group	Formal organization
Structure unit	Role	Individual	Office
Basis for communication	Proximity	Membership	Offices formally related
Basis for power	Capacity to help achieve individual goals (often through expert or referent power)	Legitimate, expert, referent, coercive, and reward power	Legitimate authority
Control mechanisms	Norms	Rules and norms	Rules
Type of hierarchy	Lateral	Lateral and vertical	Vertical
Salient goals	Individual	Group	Organizational

informal organization of innovative technical groups. The second study describes some interventions and their outcomes with the management committee discussed at the beginning of the chapter.

Innovative Groups

A number of studies of scientists and engineers have indicated that interaction with colleagues is associated with innovation, but the exact nature of interaction which stimulates innovative work is poorly understood. To attempt to determine aspects of colleague interaction which may foster innovation, the informal organizations of more and less innovative groups were contrasted. All groups were doing advanced development or applied research work, but the work of the members of some groups was more innovative according to an expert panel of judges. Through a sociometric study, members of all groups named colleagues who were especially helpful to them for seven roles which could potentially help in technical problem solving. Role networks were then drawn for the more and less innovative groups.

Although the findings are based on a small number of groups and should be regarded as tentative, a consistent pattern of results did emerge. In the more innovative groups members collaborated more actively with one another than in the less innovative groups. Moreover, the more innovative groups received relatively little help from outside the group. On the other hand, members of the less innovative groups relied quite heavily on outsiders for technical and administrative help.

The roles played by the supervisors of the more and less innovative groups bear special attention. Several sources suggest that the supervisors of the more innovative groups were *less* creative than the supervisors of the less creative groups. The latter scored higher on a test of creative ability, were named more frequently by group members as helpful for original ideas, and were named more frequently by outsiders as helpful for original ideas. The supervisors of the more innovative groups, on the other hand, were named more often by group members as helpful for three other roles: critical evaluation of ideas, help in thinking about technical problems, and administrative help. They were acting as catalysts and facilitators, whereas in the less innovative groups the supervisors may possibly have been imposing their own ideas on the group members. If these findings can be replicated in other organizations, they will have considerable implications for the appropriate role behavior of supervisors of groups striving to be innovative.

The Management Committee

In addition to the observations of the management committee described at the beginning of this chapter, efforts were made to improve the committee's functioning. According to before–after self-report measures, these interventions had considerable impact. More interaction was seen as occurring between departments and there was increased satisfaction with the interaction. All members of the management committee, especially the more reserved ones, felt that they had more influence on strategic decisions than before. These changes occurred in the absence of any alterations in the structure of the formal organization or changes in personnel serving on the management committee. Thus, interventions in the informal organization may have been the cause of the perceived changes in communications and influence.

The interventions were of two general types: role negotiations and influencing proximities. After several individual and group sessions in which feedback was given on the process of decision making by the management committee, a retreat of the committee was held to negotiate the role most appropriate for the group members. It was decided that everyone should influence the decisions of the management committee, both at the meetings and outside. The committee's role was to be one of decision making, not simply giving advice to the president. Committee members' loyalties should be to both the company as a whole and their individual departments. Thus, the roles negotiated were concerned both with individual roles in the management committee meetings and with roles played in the informal organization outside the meetings.

Attempts were also made to affect proximities. International travel schedules were coordinated to increase attendance at management committee meetings. Even the shape of the meeting table was made more circular to facilitate interaction. Thus, physical proximities were addressed. In addition, task forces including committee members were established, thereby creating greater task proximity. Finally, social proximity was increased as management committee members from the same suburbs formed car pools for riding to work, and all management committee members agreed to have more meetings and lunches together outside the office.

These role negotiations and changes in proximities apparently paid off for the company. Although they dealt with only a subset of the problems identified, their impact was evident on a before–after questionnaire. The results were consistent with expectations derived from the above approach to informal organizations.

Conclusions

In this chapter it has been asserted that groups at work operate in an organizational context, and a theoretical approach to informal organizations was proposed to help understand relationships between groups and the informal organization. Empirical studies were described illustrating the importance of considering the informal organization as well as the formal group and the formal organization. The chapter concluded by summarizing two applications of the informal organization approach to improve the functioning of groups at work.

In closing it should be reiterated that knowledge of the informal organization should help in understanding groups at work. Group members participate in multiple role networks, and this participation affects their behaviour in their work groups. Sometimes the result helps the group to function better, as in the case of the government agency, and sometimes it inhibits group effectiveness, as in the example of the management committee. Whatever their effects, informal organizations are with us so long as individuals collaborate to achieve their personal goals. As Simon (1976, pp. 148–49) pointed out, 'It would probably be fair to say that no formal organization will operate effectively without an accompanying informal organization'.

References

Allen, T. J. (1977) *Managing the flow of Technology*, Cambridge, Mass.: M.I.T. Press.

Andrews, F. M. and Farris, G. F. (1976) 'Supervisory practices', in D. C. Pelz and F. M. Andrews, *Scientists in Organizations* (Rev. edn.), Ann Arbor, Michigan: Institute for Social Research Press, pp. 383–401.

Bales, R. F. (1958) 'Task role and social roles in problem-solving groups', in E. Maccoby, T. M. Newcomb, and E. L. Hartley, eds., *Readings in Social Psychology* (3rd edn.), New York: Holt, Rinehart and Winston, pp. 437–47.

Crane, D. (1969) 'Social structure in a group of scientists: a test of the "invisible college" hypothesis', *American Sociological Review* 34, 335–51.

Davis, K. (1953) 'A method of studying communication patterns in organizations', *Personnel Psychology* 6, 43–49.

Farris, G. F. (1971) 'Organizing your informal organization'. *Innovation* 25, 2–11.

Farris, G. F. (1972). 'The effect of individual roles on performance in innovative groups'. *R & D Management* 3, 23–28.

Farris, G. F. (1974) 'Leadership and supervision in the informal organization'. In J. G. Hunt and L. L. Larson, eds., *Contingency Approaches to Leadership*, Carbondale, Illinois: Southern Illinois University Press, pp. 63–86.

Farris, G. F., (1976) 'Idea origination and evaluation in the informal organization of a research and development laboratory', Brussels, Belgium: European Institute for Advanced Studies in Management, Working Paper no. 76–34.

Farris, G. F. (1978) 'Informal organizations in research and development', Paper presented at the Joint National Meeting of The Institute of Management Sciences and Operations Research Society of America, New York.

Farris, G. F. (1979) 'The informal organization in strategic decision making', *International Studies of Management and Organization* 9, 4, 37–62.

Farris, G. F. (1980) 'Problem solving structures in research and development organizations', Paper presented at the Joint National Meeting of the Institute of Management Sciences and Operations Research Society of America, Washington, D.C.

Farris, G. F. and Butterfield, D. A. (1973) 'Are current theories of leadership culture-bound? An empirical test in Brazil', in E. A. Fleishman and J. G. Hunt, eds., *Current Development in the Study of Leadership*, Carbondale, Illinois: Southern Illinois University Press, 105–40.

Farris, G. F. and Lim, Jr. F. (1969) 'Effects of performance on leadership, cohesiveness, influence, satisfaction, and subsequent performance', *Journal of Applied Psychology* 53, 6, 490–97.

French, J. R. P. and Raven, B. (1960) 'The bases of social power', in D. Cartwright and A. Zander, eds., *Group Dynamics*, Evanston, Ill.: Row, Peterson, pp. 607–22.

Holland, W. E. (1972) 'Characteristics of individuals with high information potential in Government R&D organizations', *IEEE Transactions on Engineering Management* **EM-19**, 38–44.

Howton, F. W. (1963) Work assignments and interpersonal relations in a research organization: some participant observations *Administrative Science Quarterly*, **7**, 502–520.

Katz, D. and Kahn, R. L. (1966) *The Social Psychology of Organizations*. New York: Wiley.

Keller, R. and Holland, W. E. (1975). 'Boundary spanning roles in R&D organizations: an empirical investigation', *Academy of Management Journal* **18**, 2, 388–93.

March, J. G. and Simon, H. A. (1958) *Organizations*, New York: Wiley.

Morton, J. A. (1971) *Organizing For Innovation: A Systems Approach to Technical Management*, New York: McGraw-Hill.

Rubin, I., Kolb, D., McIntyre, J., and Farris, G. F. (1969) 'Individuals and organizations: the process of joining-up', in *New York Educational Opportunities Forum*, Fall.

Sayles, L. R. and Strauss, G. (1966) *Human Behaviour in Organizations*, Englewood Cliffs, New Jersey: Prentice-Hall.

Simon, H. A. (1976). *Administrative Behavior* (3rd edn.), New York: Free Press.

Temporary Groups in Organizations

Chapter 5

Temporary Committees as Ad Hoc Groups

David L. Bradford and Leland P. Bradford

Committees are a pervasive part of modern organizational life. Staff groups, project teams, standing committees, work groups, task forces, and executive committees are just a few of the forms such groupings take. Some of these are intrinsic parts of the formal system whereas others are as temporary as the sub-group formed at the end of one week's meeting to prepare for the next. But whatever the form or function, as harried managers can attest to, meetings and committees are a constant part of their world. In fact, Mintzberg (1973) in his observational study of chief executives found that over half of their time was spent in scheduled meetings.

This paper cannot do justice to so wide an area. Rather than covering committees in general, we will focus on ad hoc groups. These are groupings not part of the formal structure, that have a limited life, and which comprise a secondary task for the members. Focusing on such groups does not reduce the domain to insignificant proportions because task forces, project teams, and temporary committees are a frequent occurrence in most organizations. This is particularly true of those coping with turbulent environments caused by changes in external conditions, technology, personnel, or organizational goals (Bennis and Slater, 1968).

We are focusing on ad hoc groups for several reasons. First, an adequate literature already exists for established groups; much has been written about team building, developing staff groups, and running meetings (Bradford, 1976; Golembiewski, 1965; Maier, 1963). Secondly, certain unique problems exist for temporary groups that are not as frequent for standing committees. And thirdly, and most importantly, ad hoc groups offer great potential for the practising manager. The manager who knows how and when to use such groups can increase task accomplishment while at the same time developing individuals and changing the organization.

This chapter will explore the domain of ad hoc groups both from the view point of the person who initiates such a group and of the chairperson who actually leads the committee. Our exploration of project teams and temporary committees will discuss what the initiator and the chairperson can do to realize the potential while minimizing the problems of this organizational format.

Perhaps the major reason why managers consider establishing an ad hoc group is due to new problems that cannot be adequately handled by the existing departments and standing committees. These include changes in the external environment such as breakthroughs in technology, product innovation by a competitor, changes in market conditions, new government regulations, and upturns or downturns in the economy. Or the impetus may be changes needed in the internal environment such as deciding how to decentralize the organization or modifying the compensation system. Finally, task forces may be established in response to anticipated changes in internal or external conditions. For example, a school decides to evaluate its curriculum to see whether or not it has kept abreast of current knowledge and student needs. In all these cases problems arise that may not fall within an existing department's or committee's jurisdiction. Thus, establishing an ad hoc group may be more appropriate than adding still another department.

A second reason for the use of committees is to provide horizontal integration in what is basically a vertical organization. With the traditional notions of division of responsibility and chain of command, the formal system encourages communication flow up and down the organization. Horizontal communication either does not occur or takes place through informal relationships. But as Galbraith (1973) has pointed out, lateral forms of problem solving have to be developed given the massive increase in the amount of information that has to be processed in an organization. Such forms can be parts of the formal systems (as standing committees) but ad hoc groups give the manager much greater flexibility in bringing together just those parts of the organization that are needed for the specific problem at hand.

An ad hoc group is thus a deviation from the existing organizational structure. It is a different response than changing the formal system by reorganization, establishing a new department or division, or setting up a standing committee. But saying that the ad hoc group is a deviation is not saying that it is inappropriate or that it necessarily represents a failure in the existing system. No manager can be effective and totally work within the organization's structure. Likewise, no organization could afford to encumber itself with the great variety of structures to meet all possible problems. Even if one could foresee the future, any attempt to create a structure that can handle all contingencies would produce a system so cumbersome, so rigid, and so resistant to change that it would soon be obsolete. Thus, even if ad hoc groups are a deviation of the formal organization, they are frequently a necessary deviation. But by recognizing that ad hoc groups are separate from the existing system allows us to understand that it is this very separateness which is the source of many of its problems (as well as its strengths).

Thus, the decision to establish an ad hoc group should be made after careful consideration of such costs and benefits. Too frequently, initiators jump to this alternative under the pressure of a crisis without weighing the alternatives. Even if such consideration leads to establishing an ad hoc group, the manager, by being aware that this option is a violation of the existing structure and process, can foresee and prevent many of the problems that might otherwise occur. Such a stance allows the initiator to take full advantage of the opportunities that temporary groups can provide.

Advantages of Ad Hoc Groups

Better Solutions Because the Membership Comes From Different Areas

Some issues can best be solved if members come from different departments, divisions, or regions. Even though an existing department could make a passable stab at the problem, the solution would be decidedly superior if diverse view points were brought together in a task force. For example, organization X has embarked on a new hiring procedure which will require new supervisory skills, a modification of the performance appraisal system, and the establishing of a career development system. Certainly, Personnel could deal with these issues but it might be that the various operating divisions have information based on their experience that would lead to superior decision.*

A superior decision may arise not because of new information that different departments would bring but because the department normally responsible for resolving that issue is unable to do an adequate job. A fresh look at the problem is needed and assigning the problem to Engineering would produce Engineering's standard response. Or the department is viewed as having a vested interest in a certain outcome thus precluding an objective assessment of the situation. Similarly, the department may be so torn with internal conflict that giving them the task will further polarize the members. But even when such internal difficulties are not present, the initiator may still choose to go the task-force route. The relevant department may not have the time for an in-depth analysis of the situation, or the problem solution is so delicate (e.g. which plants to close down) that the department faced with the decision wants another external group to give it support.

A third reason why involving different departments in the group is beneficial has less to do with the quality of the decision as it does with acceptance of the solution. Even if the solution is basically the same as would be produced if sent to Personnel, there will be greater ownership if the areas that have to implement the decision can develop it to meet their specific situations.

The Problem may be More Quickly Solved

Depending upon how the committee is established, it is possible for quicker problem resolution with an ad hoc committee than with an existing department. The establishment of the committee itself can be a signal that this problem is

---

* Another advantage of such groups is that it can keep decision making at the appropriate level in the organization. As Jackson and Morgan (1978) point out, there is a tendency for decisions to be pushed up (at least) one level higher than they should be. It is the *superior* of the people who have the relevant information who is the only individual with access to all the information and has the integrative perspective. But a committee (ad hoc or standing) that is composed of members who collectively have the information can together provide the needed integration which keeps the decision making at the desired level.

being given priority consideration. That, plus extra resources and special powers which, when coupled with an energized committee, can produce quick results.

Another reason why ad hoc groups can work more quickly is that they frequently have greater freedom to move across organizational lines (and cut through procedures) to obtain the information they need. This is particularly likely if they have a powerful initiator who provides a strong mandate.

Ad Hoc Committees Frequently Create Less Resistance than Forming a New Steering Committee

A major advantage of a temporary group is that it is temporary! Because such an arrangement does not mean a permanent shift in power within the organization, others are more likely to allow the structure to be temporarily modified and procedures violated than if such an arrangement were to be permanent. The temporary nature of this arrangement also allows the executive to try out an approach without fully committing the organization's resources or his personal credibility to the project. The temporary nature of this arrangement also gives the group greater freedom to use new methods and procedures since it is less restricted by tradition or past practices.

Since it is temporary, the ad hoc committee is not concerned with establishing a permanent power base. Thus, such groups can frequently be more task focused than a new department which often is worried about jurisdictional issues. Ad hoc groups more frequently work *with* others is such a way that *includes* them as contrasted to permanent groups where concerns about boundaries lead them to act *exclusionary* and seek influence *over* others.

Ad Hoc Groups may be More Economical

When the problem is episodic in nature, it obviously makes no sense to go through the trouble of establishing a permanent committee (e.g. a curriculum review that occurs only every seven years)! But even when the problem is more likely to be ongoing (and/or recurring) forming a task force may be financially preferable since establishing a new department can require extensive overheads. Also, if there are permanent personnel to do the work, work has to be found for such personnel to do! What happens when the group has outlived its usefulness? It is easier to give birth to a standing committee than to kill it off. The statement may be made that 'we will evaluate the usefulness of this program after three years' but such a pronouncement will only guarantee that the department will expend energy to publicize its importance.

Ad Hoc Groups can Develop Individuals and the Organization

In addition to accomplishing a needed task, a temporary committee can be a way to assess and develop subordinates. Those who have been locked into narrow jobs can develop new skill and learn about other aspects of the organization if assigned to a wide-ranging task force. Young managers who appear to have great potential gain visibility to wider areas in the organization without incurring the risk of a permanent assignment if they do not live up to their promise.

In addition to developing individuals, a temporary committee or task force can develop the organization. Representatives from different departments that have interdependent functions but few previous working relationships can be brought together in the same group. Not only will their different view points lead to a potentially more creative task solution, but relationships can be developed that will prove useful in future interactions.

We have listed five major advantages to using ad hoc groups. But these advantages are not without potential costs. As we will explore in the next section, many of these disadvantages are just the reciprocal of the benefits just discussed!

Potential Problems of Ad Hoc Groups

Weakening the Organizational Structure and Process

The obverse of the temporary group's advantage in cutting across departmental boundaries and violating standard/traditional organizational processes is that such actions can subvert the system. One way that the establishment of an ad hoc group can weaken an organization is by compensating for a flaw rather than correcting it. Is the reason for setting up an ad hoc group the failure of an organizational unit to do its job adequately? Is the formation of a task force to explore new products and new market conditions a sign that strategic planning is lacking in the organization? In such a case, it might be best for the manager to correct the deficiencies in the delinquent department because establishing a temporary committee may just perpetuate an inadequate organizational system by compensating for its deficiencies.

But even when establishing an ad hoc group does not reflect failure in the existing system, it can still weaken the organization. The fact that this group is outside the formal structure may encourage others to violate standard procedures. The task force could make it difficult for established departments to fulfil their normal function in the future. For example, setting up a task force to explore new compensation systems may be interpreted by the rest of the organization as a sign that the Personnel Department is incompetent and should be by-passed when other issues arise.

Leading to a Lower Quality Solution

Bringing together people from different sections of the organization who hold divergent viewpoints does not necessarily lead to a higher quality solution. Interdepartmental rivalries might be so high and the value and attitude gulfs so wide that the diversity cannot be utilized for a creative solution. Instead, a compromise solution evolves and the effort to please everybody satisfies nobody.

Even when the difficulty is not a major conflict between areas or among values, there are other factors that can mitigate against the successful working of ad hoc groups. Given that the committee's assignment is in addition to the member's primary jobs, the latter can take precedence over the former. (This can be the case particularly if there are no clear rewards for serving on the committee—the rewards at performance appraisal time being based on the primary job.) There also may be problems of work overload or demands by each member's superior to give the department's task priority over the committee's.

Personal Needs Rather than Organizational Needs are Primary

We said that one of the advantages of an ad hoc group is that members could be selected for their competence and the group can be mandated to work just on this assigned task (and not for its own aggrandizement). But what if the initiator had covert, personal reasons for establishing the committee? Feelings, ambitions, fears, worries, likes, and dislikes play a part in all individual behaviour, no matter how 'objective' people believe they are. But what if these motivations play a major part in the formation and composition of the committee? What if the private reason to 'send it to committee' was to block the normal operations of the executive group? What if the task force is a pawn in an ongoing power struggle with another department? What if the selection of the committee chairperson and member serves to pay of old debts, reward friends, or punish enemies? When such covert reasons exist to a significant extent, then the formation of a temporary committee can be at the expense of organizational effectiveness.

Among the numerous hidden motives that could be present in the decision to establish a temporary committee, the following are probably the most general.

(a) *To prevent a larger group from making an immediate decision.* The initiator may feel that the decision the larger group is leaning toward is one that is undesirable because: it may discredit the initiator; it may upset other plans the initiator has in mind; or it may decrease his/her power and prestige. The reasons do not even have to be so Machiavellian. The initiator may feel that the larger group is moving in undue haste, that it has not considered all the relevant information, and is being swept along by the passion of the moment.

There may be many reasons why the initiator is not able to confront directly the larger group. For example, his role may prevent him from expressing his point of view on a divided issue; even if he expressed it, his opinion would not stop the tide; or even if he could decide the issue, such an action would antagonize the losers. Instead, establishing a task force to study the issue gives time to diffuse emotional pressure, disperse the strength of a clique within the larger group, and allow marshalling of counter-forces. The initiator can use delaying tactics to serve personal motives while appearing to use stateman-like caution to arrive at a judicious decision.

(b) *To deflect blame away from onself.* The task force composed of impartial and valued employees may come up with the same (unpleasant) recommendation that the initiator would have, but now the latter can implement the solution as the committee's idea. Or the problem may be so difficult that no feasible solution exists. The failure of the committee to solve the problem takes some of the onus for previous failure off of the manager.

(c) *To develop alternatives without commitment.* The organization may be at a crucial decision point; which of many paths should top management take? The answer may become clear only after several alternatives have been explored and tentative steps taken. For the executive to make a premature decision raises the possibility of being blamed for the wrong choice. But a temporary committee can serve as a trial balloon and the manager can wait for a recommendation that gains a favorable reception and then accept the credit.

In another situation the task force's report creates conflict and disagreement within the organization. The initiator now steps in, King Solomon-like, and offers the compromise that gains the approval of both camps.

Such personal motivations probably exist in varying degrees in most situations. Some of these reasons might actually be for the betterment of the organization; not all are for personal aggrandizement and empire building. But they have been labelled 'covert' because for any one of a number of reasons, the initiator cannot make them public.

When such covert reasons are a major determinant for establishing a temporary committee, certain problems are likely to arise. If these reasons sabotage a task force's efforts, then frustration and disillusionment can result. Not only will morale and commitment likely decrease for members of that particular group but future groups can be affected as well. The next task-force leader will find it that much more difficult to build commitment and motivation if there is a feeling among members that 'this is all a sham; it does not make any difference what we turn out'.

To Summarize

The judicious use of ad hoc groups can be a powerful management tool. It allows the executive quickly to establish a problem-solving mechanism with hand-picked membership which has authority to cut across organizational boundaries and procedures. Such a tool can explore possibilities without forcing the executive to make a permanent commitment in terms of organizational direction. Finally, it can be used to develop (and assess) potential key subordinates and build important integrative ties across organizational units.

On the other hand, forming a structure outside the formal system, even if it is only temporary, potentially can cause problems. Is the establishment of a task force an indication that the regular department is unwilling to make tough choices? Will dragging out the process, even if a higher quality solution is produced, really warrant the stress produced by the greater time required? Is the temporary group a sign that there are inadequacies in that department which should be corrected? Will the decisions of the temporary committee change the power distribution in the organization (as would be the case when the ad hoc group is deciding on a new organizational structure or new markets to enter), and will other departments see this as a threat to their security and respond with attack rather than with assistance?

These are just some of the dimensions that the initiator(s) should consider. Unfortunately, an exact contingency model cannot be developed which would say 'under these conditions always use (or never use) an adhoc group'. Each situation is to some extent unique. The most this chapter can do is lay out the general dimensions and leave it to the practising manager to weigh the relevance of each variable in that particular situation. Since any decision always has a cost, the question is whether the benefit of establishing an ad hoc group is worth the cost.

But even when forming an ad hoc group appears to be the appropriate decision, there are steps the initiator (and the chairperson) can take to capitalize on the potential benefits and minimize the costs. The next section will look at the following six key questions that are important for task-group success.

(1) What exactly is the purpose of this group? What should the charge to the committee be?

(2) What criteria should be used for selection of the chairperson and committee members?

(3) What should be the relationship between the initiator and chairperson committee?

(4) How can one build group cohesiveness and member commitment while operating under time limitations?

(5) What ties should the committee form with other parts of the organization?

(6) How should the committee report its conclusions to the initiating group?

Establishing and Managing the Committee

Determining the Purpose

In some cases the charge to the committee may be clear in the minds of the initiator(s). Furthermore, the purpose may be non-political in content so that it can be publicly announced. But in other cases the situation may not be quite as clear. It could be that the decision to form a task force resulted from confusion or disagreement either in the original decision-making group or in the mind of the initiator(s). To further compound this situation, some of the reasons may be of a political or personal nature and cannot be publicly announced.

One of the major dangers in the latter situation is that the charge to the chairperson and committee is given in more definitive terms that is warranted.

Thus, the assignment does not reflect the actual confusion, political infighting, or conflicting forces inherent in the problem being tackled. If the committee is not informed of all these factors, members will be misdirected and operate as if there is certainty in that world of ambiguity.

When there are covert reasons behind the formation of the temporary committee, then one of the important criteria for selection of the chairperson is that he/she can be trusted to be privy to these reasons. In the best of all possible worlds these reasons could also be shared with the committee members, but, at least to the extent the chairperson is informed, the greater the chance that wasted effort, error in direction, and frustration will be reduced.

It is inappropriate to lay total responsibility for clarifying the charge on the doorstep of the initiator. As we mentioned, there is a tendency for the initiating persons to express the assignment as more clear-cut than is actually the case. The reciprocal trap is for the chairperson, perhaps wishing to show enthusiasm for the task, to accept such a charge without question. An important initial action by the chairperson is to question the initiator(s) as to the exact reasons for forming the committee. Were there conflicting reasons? Dissention among members of the original decision-making group? Any skeletons the chairperson ought to be aware of? Political interests that the committee's solution should take into account?

The need for a joint clarification of the charge is required, not just at the beginning, but often at different points in the committee's life. As the group gets into the problem, new dimensions may arise. It could be that what the initiator(s) thought was the problem is only a symptom of a more underlying difficulty, or that the general direction the executive preferred is unfeasible. Thus, at these times a re-negotiation of the charge to the committee is necessary. The chairperson and the initiator(s) have to see clarification of the task as an ongoing process. It may be that the greatest benefit the temporary committee can provide is helping the initiator(s) recognize what the core problems are (rather than just going along and coming up with a solution to the initial but irrelevant issue).

Directions to the chairperson and committee include more than *what* has to be done but also *how*. One aspect of the *how* is the final form the committee's work is to take. Is it a report (written or oral), a series of interim presentations, or a prototype or demonstration? Does the initiator want just one outcome, or two or more options from which to select? Another aspect of the *how* is the jurisdiction of the committee. Will members have access to all relevant information? Can they contact and query others in the organization? Or are they only to cogitate in the meeting room dependant solely on their own resources?

Selecting the Chairperson and Committee Members

The choice of committee composition rests on many factors. Some are mundane (such as who is available) and some are more important (such as responding to the political realities of the organization). Obviously, competence should be the central dimension but competence refers to more than just technical ability. There are two other major dimensions of competence: (1) competence in relating to the initiator and other organizational members, and (2) competence in working in a temporary group. The relative importance of these three will be somewhat different depending on whether one is selecting the chairperson or the committee members.

Technical competence. There is frequently the (erroneous) belief that the chairperson should be the individual with the greatest technical competence. The job of the chairperson is not to come up with the answer, but to *establish conditions where the answer can be developed.* The leader needs only enough technical expertise so that he/she: (1) knows the major blind avenues to avoid and promising routes to follow in order to provide general direction to the committee; (2) knows enough about the subject matter to assess the validity of points being made by the committee; and (3) has enough of a reputation in the technical area to lend credibility to the committee's deliberation and conclusions.

These reasons for technical competence on the part of the chairperson are based not on the notion of knowledge to solve the problem, but knowledge as a *source of power.* If that person is technically unskilled, then others with expertise have an undue amount of influence which can interfere with the chairperson's ability to lead. Thus, the group leader does not have to 'have all the answers' but has to be sufficiently knowledgeable about the topic being considered to know whether or not the committee is finding the answers! Given that the leader has a minimum level of technical ability, then members can be selected to provide the additional expertise.

Relational competence. Even though the task force is outside the formal organizational structure, it is still part of that larger system. Thus, a crucial role for the chairperson is the external liaison role. As we mentioned, one important aspect of this liaison function is with the initiator. The latter needs to select somebody with whom a good working relationship is possible. The chairperson has to be a person that the initiator can trust (so he/she will not constantly be breathing down the chairperson's neck) and can communicate openly with (including sharing many, of not all, if the covert reasons that the initiator has for establishing the task force).

But such a working relationship can have its own complications. Sometimes the initiator is caught between two opposite pressures. One is to select a person who can be relied upon to 'do the job' (which may mean coming up with a solution the initiator can live with). The other pressure relates to a particular situation in which the committee's assignment demands total independence from the initiator. The latter situation is particularly important in cases where the initiator may receive improper benefits from a certain committee decision (for example, where the group's task is to determine blame for a failure, or to make a decision about the organization's structure, direction or products—all decisions which could favour the initiator). In those situations, independence of the chairperson may be required if the committee's recommendations are to have credibility.

But in both cases the chairperson has to have the relational competence to gain maximum freedom for the committee's activities without jeopardizing the relationship with the powers that be. In the first situation mentioned above where there is no danger of potential conflict of interests the problem facing the task force might be having such close ties that they become a rubber-stamp group. In that case the chairperson has to work to gain independence, whereas in the second situation where independence is built in through the selection of an impartial chairperson, there is frequently the need to build a working relationship with the initiator (so there is sufficient support for the committee's activities).

Picking a chairperson with relational skills carries beyond the ability to have a working relationship with the initiator. The committee will need information and cooperation from the organization. In this case the relational competencies of committee membership often play an important part. Not infrequently, members are selected because of their ties with key organizational members. Although appropriate, this can be a double-edged sword. Such relationships can be invaluable in opening up access to information that is necessary if a successful solution is to be reached and accepted in the organization, but such ties can also allow external members to have undue influence over the committee's deliberations. The problem relates to the flow of influence; is it primarily from the committee member to the key external member or primarily from the latter to the committee member? The former tends to lead to greater task success.

Group process competence. The chairperson (and members) need skills in managing the group development and decision-making process. A temporary group with no previous history has unique problems not found in established departments. For example, members come to the committee with a high commitment to the task (since they were probably selected primarily for their interest and expertise) but they also may feel ambivalent about the assignment. This task is in addition to their normal work load; will the group's efforts lead to any beneficial change or personal rewards that compensate for the extra work? Members frequently join a task force as representatives from their own areas. Not only is it likely that they have a particular point of view to champion but they have stereotypes about what the other areas represented on the committee are like. How can these differing viewpoints be expressed and utilized without polarizing the group to the point that a viable solution is blocked?

In addition to such issues which may or may not occur, there are some that can be expected to arise in all temporary groups. From a collection of separate individuals there has to be built: cohesiveness and commitment; norms and procedures; and an openness of communication. Equally important is the ability of members to surface and effectively utilize conflict and disagreement; the pressure to build a cohesive team cannot be at the expense of smothering individual viewpoints and differences. And all of these group-process issues need to be dealt with in a relatively short period of time.

Thus, an important criterion for chairperson and member selection is competence in working together and building a high-performance group. At times it is necessary to sacrifice technical competence or connections with key organizational members for interpersonal and group skills. In most cases it is impossible to maximize all three types of competence so the person selecting the group (the initiator and/or the chairperson) has to make trade-offs in achieving the appropriate combination of these three variables.

Determining the Relationship between the Committee and Initiator

As mentioned in the previous section, there are some situations in which the chairperson and committee must preserve independence from the initiator (as was the case with the Watergate Investigations *vis-à-vis* the relationship of the Chief Investigator and Nixon). But in most cases the task force is not investigating the initiator but fulfilling a task for that individual. In that situation the initiator and chairperson need to work out the two central issues of support and of control.

Support includes the amount the initiator will back the committee through the use of personal and position power. If there is controversy and conflict, can the committee count on the initiator to provide appropriate defence? If it is necessary to obtain information or cooperation from others in the organization, will the initiator help them achieve it? But support also includes such tangible forms as release time from other activities, a budget, and secretarial assistance. Although these may appear mundane, they can play an important role in facilitating the group's operations (as well as signalling to the committee the importance of their task).

Control refers to the limitations placed on the scope of the committee's activities. This includes not only the content areas that the group can explore but the extent the group has access to other people in the organization. Control is more than a set of restrictions laid down initially, but also refers to the ongoing control the initiator imposes as the task force progresses. Does he/she want to attend all meetings (or to drop in whenever desired)? Does the initiator want frequent interim reports? The amount of latitude the task force is given will be determined by the nature of the task, the perceived competence of the chairperson/members, and the initiator's personal comfort with letting go of control.

Control and support are not opposite ends of the same scale but rather are independent dimensions. That is to say, there can be conditions of high control and high support as well as low control and low support (as well as high on one dimension and low on the other). It is likely that greater control is needed the more important the task and the greater the range of types of outcome. If the task is relatively unimportant then few people will care what the outcome will be. Likewise, if the focus is highly specified and there are few possible outcomes (so that the control emanates from the assignment), then external control is less necessary. High support is needed the more controversial the issue and therefore the greater the chance of opposition and attack.

As with achieving clarity of the committee's charge, working out relationships of support and autonomy must be continuously dealt with over the life of the committee. Even though the chairperson needs initially to negotiate an acceptable amount of backing and freedom (and may not want to accept the committee assignment unless a successful agreement is reached), the amount will vary at different points in time. When first established, the committee may need public support to gain legitimacy and cooperation from other departments but, later on, more freedom is required if the committee is to adequately do its work. But the crucial point is that the chairperson (and initiator) must realize that negotiating issues of support and autonomy is an ongoing process and appropriate for either party to bring up for reconsideration.

Leading the Committee: Building Cohesiveness and Commitment

Even if all of this pre-work has been adequately accomplished, the job of the chairperson has barely begun. In order for the committee to accomplish its task, the chairperson needs to help build a cohesive, high-performing team in a relatively short period of time. Time may be of the essence when the ad hoc group was formed to deal with a (real or perceived) emergency. Not only does the initiating group quickly want an answer, but the support for the temporary committee may dwindle as months pass. Often the organization is most receptive to change under these crises conditions.

The emergency itself can increase member commitment. The issues can mobilize members to set aside other tasks and throw themselves into this project. But such involvement will continue only as long as they feel the committee is successfully grappling with the issue. Thus, the chairperson's meeting/management skills are crucial not only for task attainment but also to sustain the initial enthusiasm.

Ware (1977) describes some of the specific areas the chairperson must attend to in managing a task force. His recommendations to the chairperson are:

1. 'Hold full task force meetings frequently enough to keep all members informed about group progress.'
2. 'Unless the task force is very small (fewer than 5–7 members), dividing up into groups will be virtually mandatory.'

3. 'Be careful not to align yourself too closely with one position or subgroup too early.'
4. 'Set interim project deadlines and demand adherence to them.'
5. 'Be sensitive to the conflicting loyalties created by belonging to the task force.'
6. 'Your most important leadership role is that of communicating information among task force members and between the task force and the rest of the organization.'

Since Ware has covered the specifics in running such a group, this chapter will focus on the underlying problem of how the chairperson can build and sustain commitment when the group has an ongoing task and does not have involvement from responding to an emergency. If members have been selected on the basis of their competence and interest in the topic (and not to appease political factions), their commitment to the group will be largely determined by the extent to which the group is seen as an important vehicle, not a barrier, for task attainment. The job of the chairperson is to deal with those factors which could be a barrier.

One of the initial hesitancies members have about being committed to the group concerns their question as to whether the group's efforts will have any impact. 'Is the initiator(s) really committed to having the task force work or is this a ploy to appease a certain faction or derail an impending decision?' A related issue is 'does the group have the power-authority to do the task adequately?' Some of this hesitancy may come from suspicion as to the initiator's motives or it may come from a history of the organization's use of temporary committees to bury undesired proposals. When such suspicion is unfounded, it may require the chairperson to seek tangible signs from the initiator as to that person's investment. These signals may be the initiator allocating scarce resources for the committee's work, publicly backing the committee, or even just being willing to come to a meeting to be questioned. But when the members' suspicion is grounded in reality, the chairperson is faced with the problem of how much to reveal. Sometimes the issue can be dealt with openly by the chairperson sharing with the group that members should not expect much from their work or put much effort into the task, but more frequently the initiator and chairperson can subtly convey the message of 'do not take this too seriously; go through the motions'. This includes such signals as missed deadlines, meetings that are called off, and lack of adequate support. Such an (unspoken) agreement has the virtue or not raising expectations which would otherwise cause frustration and greater cynicism.

Another factor that can lower commitment to the group is the perception that the different values and viewpoints of other members are blocks to one's own view of successful task accomplishment. 'If Joe from Finance gets his way, this new computer system will not be able to meet our needs.' This viewpoint leads the task force to be seen as a battleground to vanquish enemies, not as a place to utilize the richness of diversity. The task of the chairperson is to value and use these differences without splintering and polarizing the group. After all, one of the advantages of a temporary group is to bring people from diverse areas together. Not only is the eventual solution likely to be more creative if the group can utilize different perspectives, but it is more likely to fit the unique requirements of various departments in the organization.

A crucial determinant of how this issue will be resolved is the chairperson's attitude toward conflict. If the leader views conflict and disagreements as undesirable and something to avoid or suppress, then the quality of the solution goes down and battles are fought underground. On the other hand, if the leader values disagreements as a method for surfacing differences, then the solution is likely to be more creative and of a higher calibre. Hence, the task of the chairperson is to help members see disagreements as valuable inputs to goal attainment by helping them struggle with and work through their differences.

But commitment to the group also comes from members' personal needs being fulfilled by task-force membership. Members agree to serve not only to further task attainment but also to develop their skills, make contacts, gain visibility, learn about new areas and so forth. Some of these personal motives can be counter-productive to task attainment (e.g. the desire to block another individual or another unit) but others may not be. The task of the chairperson is to find out such personal needs of the members and attempt to integrate them with the group's efforts. Some of these 'hidden agendas' may not be very hidden; members are often quite willing to share what they personally want to gain. Others will be shared only with informal contact between the chairperson and individual members. But if the chairperson knows 'that Mary has the professional goal to find out more about Finance', putting Mary in charge of that aspect of the project can increase her involvement and commitment to task success.

Thus, an important function of the initial meetings of the committee is to build the cohesiveness of the team. Frequently there is too rapid movement into sub-group assignments without finding out what members' personal goals are, without making sure that members feel committed to the group, and without seeing that differences are valued as an important resource. On the other hand, members can feel frustrated with initial meetings which appear to be 'all talking and no progress'. They need to see such activities as crucial in developing a common view of the problem. The skill of the chairperson is knowing how to balance these conflicting pressures.

Relations with Other Individuals and Departments

One of the issues that the chairperson (and group) will have to struggle with is how isolated they want to be from other people in the organization. On the one hand, close ties may be important to gain information and to make sure there is support for the committee. But such ties can also be a source of pressure. The last thing a committee may need in its attempts to objectively examine the pros and cons of various alternatives is to be harassed by different interest groups. Instead, they may decide to have closed meetings, not issue any progress reports, and not share the content of their deliberations.

But there can be other occasions when such a stance would be counter-productive. It is likely that once into exploring the task, the committee finds that, in order to deliver on their assignment, other aspects of the organization have to be modified (e.g. a new hiring practice to attract better managers will not work until the appraisal and promotion system is overhauled). This may require going back to the original decision-making group to ask for a re-definition of their charge or to go to the relevant department (Personnel in this case) and gain their support. Otherwise, if the committee were to remain isolated and unilaterally take on this added assignment, there might be no support for their final conclusions.

At this stage in the committee's work their activities may well begin to produce reactions from other parts of the organization. The task force is pursuing a line of inquiry that is causing concern in a certain department, or with a powerful member of the executive committee. Group members see that there are certain key individuals or departments whose support they need if the solution is to be accepted and implemented. All of these factors are likely to pull the chairperson away from the task-force meetings and towards spending an increasing amount of time dealing with these other individuals and departments. These activities may involve re-negotiating the original assignment, modifying the relationship of the committee with the initiator, meeting informally with key individuals in the organization, or visiting staff meetings of certain departments to give them a progress report.

Acceptance of the Committee's Solution

Too frequently, the committee sees its end-product as a report (the longer the better) that is delivered cold to the decision-making group. Not only is there the blind hope that the report will be thoroughly read beforehand but also that the logic of the arguments will carry the day. What is ignored is that the decision-making group is back where the task force started in terms of understanding the complexities of the problem. If the distance the committee has travelled is far, the decision-making body may have difficulty understanding the reasoning that led to the final conclusions.

There are various methods the committee can use to report to a larger group. One is bringing the initiator and/or decision-making group along during the committee's deliberations through preliminary reports or briefing sessions. A second method is for the chairperson to meet with each of the members of the decision-making group on a one-to-one basis before the final report is written to see that the conclusions are compatible with what they want. Thirdly, some sub-set of that group could be invited to attend one of the committee's meetings to react to the proposal.

This type of preparatory work by the chairperson before the final presentation should be welcomed by the initiator and decision-making group. If they only see the product at the end, they are faced with the options of either acceptance or rejection and 'sending it back to committee' can be demoralizing for every body involved. Much more preferable would be discussions during the developmental stage when modifications can be made without such comments being experienced as failure by the committee.

Another aspect of the group's solution is the question of what form should their conclusions take. There is nothing sacrosant about total reliance on written reports. Engineering has the tradition of developing prototypes; 'softer' areas can do the same. For example, if the charge to the task force has been to develop an executive training programme, perhaps one aspect of the 'final report' would be to have the decision-making group personally go through their model programme.

A third aspect has to do with the timing of the presentation or report. Usually that decision is determined by the completion of the committee's work; sometimes it is decided by the running agenda of the decision-making group. But the pressure of other events can increase or decrease the receptiveness of that group to the committee's recommendations.

A fourth aspect has to do with the extent to which the final proposal is, in fact, final. There is a tendency for people to assume that a quality job is defined by having the definitive answer. This leads to conclusions which lock the organization into a course of action far into the future. But the 'final report' of a task force could contain provisions for a period of experimentation and then reassessment. This requires, of course, that the committee has thought through how that assessment is to be done and the dimensions on which the project is to be evaluated.

Conclusion

This chapter has attempted to lay out various issues that need to be considered for the successful operation of a temporary committee. As stated initially, a task force or temporary committee can be a very powerful management tool. It can provide flexibility for the executive to explore new options, bring together disparate areas, and develop and test promising subordinates. When not used excessively, a temporary committee can provide a useful alternative to the formal structure without weakening it. But the power of a temporary committee can be realized only if careful thought is given to the purpose, composition, and charge. Furthermore, the chairperson is not a passive part of this process but can also influence the committee's area of responsibility. Hopefully, by being aware of the various dimensions explored in this chapter, the initiator and the chairperson can structure the process so that the potential of such groups can be fulfilled.

Acknowledgements

We would like to thank Allan Cohen and James Shultz for their helpful comments on an earlier draft of this chapter.

References

Bennis, W. G. and Slater, P. (1968) *The Temporary Society*, New York: Harper & Row.

Bradford, L. P. (1976) *Making Meetings Work*, La Jolla, California: University Associates.

Galbraith, J. (1974) *Designing Complex Organizations*, New York: Harper & Row.

Golembiewski, R. T. (1965) 'Small groups and large organizations', in J. G. March, ed., *Handbook of Organizations*, Chicago: Rand McNally.

Jackson, H. H. and Morgan, C. P. (1978) *Organization Theory: A Macro Perspective for Management*, Eaglewood Cliffs, New Jersey: Prentice-Hall.

Maier, N. R. F. (1973) *Problem-Solving Discussions and Conferences*, New York: McGraw-Hill.

Mintzberg, H. (1963) *The nature of Managerial Work*, New York: Harper & Row.

Ware, J. (1977) 'Managing a task force', Intercollegiate Case Clearing House (1–478–002).

Groups at Work
Edited by R. Payne and C. Cooper
© 1981 John Wiley & Sons Ltd.

Chapter 6

Project Groups

Alan W. Pearson and Hugh P. Gunz

Introduction

In her classic study of industrial management, Joan Woodward (1965) delivered the *coup de grâce* to the notion that there is one best way of organizing. Firms with differing technologies, she found, tended to adopt *inter alia* differing structures so that, for instance, one making single units to a customer's order was likely to look quite different from a mass-production plant.

Like all of the best ideas this was, no doubt, blindingly obvious after the event and yet it remains a curious observation that many organizations, for much of the time, struggle to cope with many different kinds of work using a structure which is suited perhaps to only a small proportion of what is going on. If one then considers the problems of organizing not just for a mixture of activities, but a changing mixture, one is describing the situation of managing project groups. A hypothetical—but not atypical—illustration may bring out some of the difficulties to which we allude.

Consider the workload of a Research and Development (R&D) department. It is likely to include many, if not all, of the items from the following list:

basic research
product development
process development
product testing
customer service
production support
technical information and consultancy.

Each kind of activity not only varies greatly in character from industry to industry, perhaps even from firm to firm, but also is very different from the other activities. There are many ways in which this variation between activities could be classified, but we only focus on two: time-scale and repetitiveness.

Some (perhaps customer service, product testing, technical information) have a routine, repetitive side to them, the workload typically consisting of a series of similar, short jobs which mean that things will be much the same this year as they were last year, assuming the firm is making much the same kind of product. Other activities (especially development work) will have longer time-scales, perhaps a year or more, one activity in the same class may differ markedly from the next both in technical nature and in the mix of skills needed, the nature of its goals (technical, budgetary, time, market), and so on. These are the activities we shall define as projects.

It is as if the organization has to cope with two strikingly different technologies, to use Woodward's terms. The first (service, etc.) bears some resemblance to large batch or even mass production, while the second (development, etc.) is far more similar to the unit production business. The final twist in the tail, however, is that not only may all these activities be going on in the same part of the firm, but the same people may be involved in several of them.

We are not arguing here that R&D is necessarily unique in this respect, nor that a mixture of activities is bad for people (there is evidence that the opposite can be the case; see Pelz and Andrews, 1966). Our point is that in organizations like this the workload means that whichever form of organizational structure is chosen, it is quite likely to be wrong for something or someone. There are many different ways in which this strain can be accommodated. It may well be the case that the problems are not all that severe and that they can be handled by allowing a certain amount of fuzziness in the definition of people's roles. Job descriptions with such phrases as 'to liaise with such-and-such a group' are prime instances of this. A second, and fashionable, approach is to institutionalize ambiguities by structuring the organization as a matrix. A third is to adopt the classic behaviour identified by the Carnegie school of organization theorists among others, focusing on each most pressing problem in turn. This can easily mean regular re-structuring of the organization as the nature of the problems change. Studies of practice show that all of these ways are adopted whether by design or by default. Unfortunately the evidence is that the net effect is not always that desired and in particular is not always in the best interests of the project leader and the team members.

In this chapter discussion is focused on the different types of temporary group which are commonly encountered within, and alongside, the more permanent structures found in any organization. An examination of some the factors which influence the performance of such groups leads us to suggest that it is clearly important to recognize explicitly the variety and to ensure that project leaders are provided with the necessary skills to assist them in identifying and managing the particular problem area for which they are responsible. However, it is equally important to realize that there are advantages to be gained from paying more attention to the area of team development.

The Temporary Project Group

A number of writers have been concerned with the problem of what happens in organizations when things get complicated and the communication channels necessary to their operation get overloaded. A particularly useful analysis is due to Galbraith (1973), who argues that there are four possible strategies that can be adopted. The organization can invest in slack resources—inventories, queues—which may well happen anyway simply by doing nothing. It can increase the capacity of its vertical (line) communication channels perhaps by installing computer-based information systems. It can split up the organization into self-contained parts, each coping with a distinct problem area (such as a major project) and incurring the cost of duplicated resources. Finally, it can off-load the information processing to lower levels of the organization where the work is done. This last strategy can involve anything from simple liaison roles to complex matrices, and incurs the obvious cost of time spent in meetings and discussions.

It is the last approach that best describes the kind of project groups typically found, for example, in technical organizations. Projects tend not to involve many people: a group of thirty is large by these standards, and the active core of the group is often less than half a dozen at any one time. The workload involved is such that individual members are not likely to be fully occupied with work on one project, but combine their roles as group members with that of many others, perhaps including membership of other project groups. Times-scales vary enormously, but a very large proportion are of less than a year's duration.

There are obvious exceptions to these generalizations, for instance in aerospace, but on the whole they describe a situation which is inimical to the kind of organizational structure described by Galbraith's third strategy. It is one thing to set up a project organization to design a Boeing 747 or a Ford Fiesta, but quite another to create a self-contained group whose membership does not need to be full time and to work on a project of relatively short duration. In such situations we are in the area of temporary groups, with all of the problems of divided loyalties and conflicting objectives that this implies.

Project groups may be formed for an enormous variety of purposes, but it is this temporary nature that they share. They are constituted in order to achieve a particular objective, and once having achieved it their rationale no longer exists. Unlike, for instance, business functional groups, policy groups such as top management teams or shop stewards' committees, in principle they are disbanded at the end of the project. Of course, this is a simplistic view which overlooks the need to keep a specialist group together because of the skills it has developed, the need for someone to continue to service the product of the project after the objective has been achieved, even the natural tendency of groups and organizations to change their goals in order to survive as entities (see Perrow, 1972). Much of what we have to say, particularly when we discuss the nature of the linkage between the project group and the organizational decision makers who set the rules of the game, is relevant also to these non-temporary groups.

Organization and Control

In so far as a project group is set up to work to achieve specific objectives, it is a kind of organizational sub-contractor. From the overall organization's point of

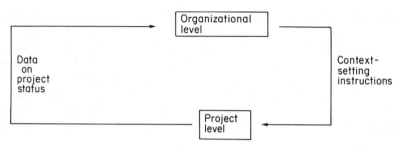

Figure 1

view, a particular problem is isolated from the general continuum of activities. It is packaged and sub-contracted to a department, an individual, a group of people from several departments, perhaps even groups from quite a separate part of the firm or another firm altogether. The problem that arises as a result is the classic managerial one of managing autonomy; how does one devolve control, and what mechanisms are needed in order to:

(a) convey new information into the project or

(b) monitor potentially important deviations, bearing in mind that one wants to encourage initiative through some autonomy in decision making?

However it is done, project management involves decision making at two levels. In considering this issue we have taken a very simplistic view through the use of a two-level model, as shown in Figure 1. The levels are (a) the organizational level, that which defines and subcontracts the problem, and (b) the project level, involving the project group itself (Gunz and Pearson, 1979). The two are connected by information channels which form the control links in the system. The first, from the organization to the project level, defines the context of the project group, setting the rules of the game that the project team must play, so to speak. The return link from the project team reports on progress against plan and on any potentially significant information which might not only affect the attitude of the organizational level decision makers to this project but which may have wider and longer-term impacts. We introduce this highly schematic model in order to identify two major problem areas facing project groups. These are first to do with agreeing which kind of problem belongs at which level in the organization, and second what kind of information needs to pass along the channels connecting the two levels.

It is vital to recognize that we are not really dealing with a who-does-what issue but a which-role-does-what. This is why we have not drawn Figure 1 on an organization chart. Some examples of the kinds of decisions which belong at each level may make this point clearer.

Organizational-level Decisions

At least two important classes of decision can be identified as belonging to this level: project selection and termination, and resource allocation between projects. We are, of course, ignoring for the moment large areas of organizational life which in practice can play important parts in the way in which project groups work, in particular those concerned with the needs and motivations of the people making up the organization.

Project selection and termination are part of the strategic questions the organizational decision makers have to be concerned with, for example what business are we in? Once the decision has been taken to set up a particular project an investment has been made which will take some time to show results, and which will stop the organization from moving in other directions, since it cannot do everything. Equally, the decision to terminate a project is part of the same strategic question. From a purely practical point of view both kinds of decision have to be based on information from as wide a range of sources as the organization has available to it. In short, project selection and termination decisions in principle affect all members of the organization in their capacities either as information providers or as people affected by the decisions, or both, and are therefore organizational-level decisions.

There is always a limit to resources, so that at some stage someone has to allocate that which is available between those who want it. Clearly this class of decision belongs at the organizational level since it is in a sense a follow-up decision of the same kind as the original strategic one to initiate the project. Typically the decision is implemented by assigning a priority to the project. Later we shall be discussing the way in which this can affect the operation of the project group, but for the moment it should be pointed out that there are many ways in which it can happen. Formal devices are for example based on economic or financial analysis coupled to a predetermined ranking system, using a form of ratio analysis. These form one end of a kind of spectrum at the other end of which is the free market. Here projects compete with each other for resources, the latter going to the groups either with the most persuasive or senior leaders, or the projects which interest the resource providers most, and so on. It is important to realize, however, that as with Galbraith's first design strategy (slack resources) the decision to do nothing about allocating resources still represents a decision on resource allocation. Intermediate cases are, of course, possible, such as the 'assisted free market' in which important projects are given to particularly influential, persuasive people to manage.

Project-level Decisions

In any project a constant stream of situations will crop up in which things do not turn out quite as expected. Perhaps more tests than planned are needed, delays have cropped up in some crucial phase of the work, something which everybody had thought feasible turns out to have hidden snags, and so on.

There is a great deal of evidence from studies of how organizations go about making decisions (for instance, Bower, 1970) that much of the control effectively rests at the level of the people doing the basic work, by feeding organization-level decision makers with heavily filtered information. Not only is the project group, if involved in project design, capable of influencing future directions through the alternatives it considers, but, once the plan has been authorized (the organization-level decision) it has great discretion over how it chooses to cope with deviations from plan. The nature of the control links between the two levels of the organization, therefore, is a crucial part of the way the system works.

In broad terms, our point is that decisions of this kind may have hidden snags, and so are project-level to the extent that the actions that flow from them do not really affect the organization as a whole. If, for instance, the problem in question can be solved without affecting the planned completion date or upsetting any other work since it is not going to make excessive demands on anyone else's time, we class the decision as project-level and well within the sub-contractor's discretion to deal with. There are, of course, many situations which are far less clear-cut. Perhaps the completion date will be affected or resources from elsewhere will be needed in greater quantities, or this particular problem is likely to crop up in other work around the organization, or the project team has simply reached an impasse and needs help from someone else.

Control Links

Obvious limitations on the amount of variety the organizational-level decision makers can cope with from the many projects they are responsible for mean that routine information passing along the information links has to be highly abstracted, i.e. formalized and coded. Most project planning and monitoring techniques are attempts to set out context-setting instructions defining both the limits of descretion of the project team and the way in which the project team reports on its activities to the organizational level. The difficulty is in providing sufficient information for decision making at the appropriate level.

For instance, if the message that the project team passes up the line is that completion will be delayed by three months, that by itself is not enough for the organizational level to decide what, if any, action is needed. Equally clearly, if they ask for too much information they are not likely to have the time properly to evaluate it. What we are outlining is one of the great problem areas of managing and coordinating project groups, and one which causes a great many difficulties in practice. It is a special case of the general problem of the allocation of responsibility. This is why we emphasized that the two-level model is concerned with which-role-decides-what. For instance, an alternative solution to the problem of supplying organizational-level decision makers with adequate information is to involve members of the project group in the organizational-level decision. In many organizations, and in some project management structures, this does in fact happen, in particular in those which are based on hierarchical principles with the project leader being a senior person who is part of another management structure which crosses project boundaries (see, for example, Likert, 1961), as shown in Figure 2a. In some cases there will also be projects which have overlaps in team membership, as shown in Figure 2b.

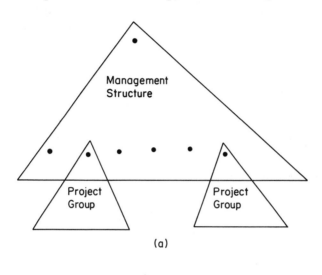

(a)

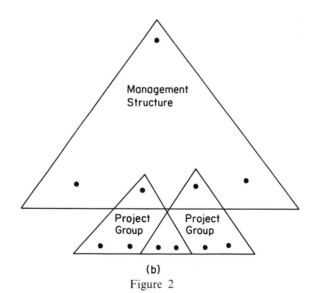

(b)

Figure 2

Such arrangements allow the normal organizational structures to play an important part in the information processing particularly at the organizational level. At the same time, we must not forget that there may be a very powerful informal structure which is likely to play a major part in satisfying the communication and information processing needs of both the project and organizational levels. Farris (1978), in examining the literature on this subject, concluded that five factors had an important influence on the patterns of interaction in informal organizations, namely physical proximity, professional proximity, task-created proximity, social proximity, and formal-organization-created proximity.

A further discussion of the negative and positive effects the informal organization can have on the workings of the formal is beyond the scope of this chapter. Nevertheless, it underlies much of what we have to say, and is particularly important in discussions of matrix management. At this point, however, we need to focus more on project groups and the variety of tasks which they have to face.

Characteristics of Project Tasks

Our starting point in beginning to focus on the group itself is to consider the kind of problem the project has been set up to handle. These can vary in many ways, and in order to try to maintain some kind of coherence to the discussion we shall concentrate on the projects typically found in technical organizations. Technical project groups are those most commonly written about in the literature, and the nature of technical work places a heavy premium on effective project management. Further more, the nature of the problems and the output of technical projects is often more tangible than for many other kinds of project, making the processes taking place easier to illustrate.

It is important to understand the nature of the task in order to be able to begin to describe how the group works. A useful contribution has been made by Gordon (1966) who, in analysing the performance of technical groups, was concerned to move away from a texonomy based on the common research–development axis. He argued that these are somewhat indefinite concepts, and that what seemed more relevant were two characteristics which he called urgency and predictability.

Urgent projects are those from which someone wanted an answer yesterday. They are not necessarily high priority projects: *priority is a concept relevant to the organizational level which has no meaning at the level of the project.* So, for instance, a project team may be told that they are working on a very urgent project, only to discover that there are a lot of other very urgent projects going on, making it difficult for them to get at what they need. There is no inconsistency here, however frustrating the situation, since two distinct logics are in action. The first, the 'urgent' message, is in project-level language and the second, the 'you

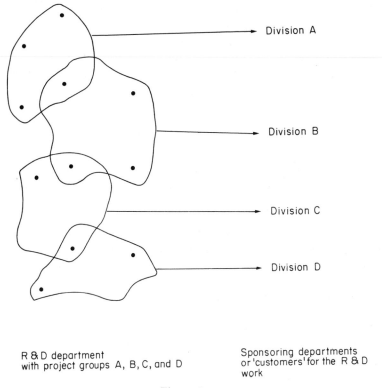

Division A

Division B

Division C

Division D

R & D department
with project groups A, B, C, and D

Sponsoring departments
or 'customers' for the R & D
work

Figure 3

don't have the only urgent project' message, is in a language which only has meaning in terms of the organization as a whole. This distinction becomes even more important when industrial projects have different sponsors or there are people outside the immediate working group who have a concern for the output. This happens frequently in research and development where a central facility is often set up to serve a number of different functional departments and in some cases, outside departments. Figure 3 is a simple illustration of a typical situation. In such cases it may be that all projects are of high urgency when seen from the sponsoring department's point of view. If so, then almost inevitably constraints will be met in the availability of resources, so that the question of allocating priorities arises. At this point it becomes necessary to question the extent to which each department has any concern for the interests of the others, and the higher level question arises of the way in which departmental goals are related to organizational goals.

Whatever the urgency of the project it is also necessary to consider the extent to which it is possible to predict the outcome. An urgent project for which it is easy to determine the solution and time-scale will need quite different handling from one for which no one is sure how to go about it or how long it will take. Different kinds of people will probably be picked to work on these two projects, different progress reporting systems will be involved, the relationships between the team members will differ, and so on. Predictability, therefore, is a characteristic of a project which is independent of its urgency, so that one can classify projects on a simple 2 × 2 matrix assigning them to one of four cells (see Figure 4). Cell 2, for instance, describes a situation in which no one is in a hurry for results, nor is it expected that anything unusual will happen. Cell 3, by contrast, is the high-adrenalin case where the team is heading into the unknown but is expected to have a solution by midnight.

The urgency–predictability typology enables one to make some useful predictions about the pressures acting on a project group and the way in which the group might organize itself to respond to them. For example, box 1 (high urgency, high predictability) suggests the need for a very precise plan, perhaps a critical path network form of presentation. This approach allows for the option of identifying in advance areas where additional resources can be applied if there is increasing pressure on deadlines. It also suggests the need for a strong project leader with the ability to motivate people towards completing tasks which essentially they know they can perform and which in some cases may not be so exciting. A commitment of all individuals to their part of the work is essential.

In contrast, box 2, the low urgency, high predictability one, suggests a project in which it is going to be very difficult to get commitment and motivation. People will tend to do other things first if they have the option and such projects will drag on often with the end result being a much lower level of performance than should be expected. Because of this there is a good case for eliminating such projects or at least for postponing the start until the urgency increases (i.e. until the organizational need and hence priority is seen to be higher). An alternative approach, which has been encountered in practice, is to give all such projects to more junior people with the net effect that they get even lower priority. An unfortunate additional consequence can be a setback to the career development of the individuals concerned.

Urgency

1		2
High U High P		Low U High P
3		4
High U Low P		Low U Low P

Predict-
ability

Figure 4

To complete this brief look at the urgency–predictability typology, box 4 (low urgency, low predictability) suggests a more research-type project requiring a variety of approaches and some intermediate rethinking. Box 3 requires little explanation. High urgency, low predictability is invariably a high risk situation for any project leader and must be recognized. This simple classification then provides useful insights into two sets of characteristics of a project which must be taken into account when groups are established.

However useful the urgency–predictability typology may be in analysing the project group, it neglects another dimension which is important in defining the nature of the group processes. We shall call it here the modular–integrated dimension.

Modular problems are those which can in practice be dissected into relatively self-contained sections which can then be farmed out to separate project team members. In a sense, a project itself represents a module of a larger problem which could be anything from a larger-scale project (as might be the case in the aerospace industry) to keeping a business going (if the project is, say, concerned with developing a new product). If a project is dealing with a modular problem it could well be the case that the team consists of a group of heads of groups, each concerned with a particular aspect of the overall problem, and project group meetings are mainly times at which position reports are exchanged.

Modular problems may well be those in which there is a high proportion of routine, predictable work; but this is not necessarily the case. One oil refinery, for instance is much like another and the work of designing one consists of coordinating the activities of a variety of different engineering groups, each with a distinct task which can be pursued relatively independently of the others. The length of time each stage takes, including constructing and commissioning the unit, is predictable. By contrast, developing a new drug must count as one of the world's more unpredictable businesses, even when one has started with a compound (a 'product candidate') which has some proven therapeutic activity. There are innumerable hurdles it must clear before it can be launched on the domestic market, let alone markets foreign to the drug company's home base. As with designing a chemical plant, the work is highly modular, and each specialist group's contribution may be very routinized. A two-year toxicity test, for instance, not only takes two years, but must be carried out under very carefully controlled conditions. However, while designing pipework runs for a refinery may also be highly routinized (especially if computerized) the output is certain; no one knows what the toxicity test will show until the results are available.

There are other problems which are very difficult to sub-contract in this modular form. Such problems may well need a variety of disciplines and approaches brought to bear on them, each person's contribution being interdependent upon those of the others. Progress meetings are simply not enough to coordinate the work adequately and the problem must in a sense be jointly shared by all members of the team. Examples of this type of project often fall within the area of the development of new products and processes. We have designated these as 'integrated' problems because the direction they take will often depend upon the information generated to date and the way this is integrated into the overall plan. They are characterized by project groups consisting of people from different disciplines but with a shared interest in a common, and agreed, goal.

Examples of such problems also arise during the kinds of crises which demand all hands to the pumps to put right. A task force may well be assembled consisting of anyone who has experience of the problem area and goes to work as a group, perhaps using problem-solving techniques such as brainstorming and concentrating on the project to the exclusion of anything else. Urgency, in other words, may well be associated with integrated projects, simply because there is no time to follow normal procedures based on conventional divisions of labour. The boundary spanning activity this involves (Katz and Kahn, 1966; Organ and Greene, 1972) can be exhilerating for those taking part (Keller, *et al.*, 1977), as they learn about how the other half of the world lives and bureaucratic stereotypes crumble. In a sense an island of 'task culture' (Handy, 1976) is created in the midst of what may well be a 'role culture'.

Similarly, unpredictability may well be a characteristic of integrated problems; if no one knows quite how each step is going to turn out, there may be much to be said for working closely together on a continuous basis. (We must be careful, however, to distinguish between different types of uncertainty. In particular, different management issues are raised by projects in which the uncertainty lies (a) in the outcome, and (b) in the process of making progress towards the outcome.)

The three dimensions discussed so far, therefore, may well not be strictly orthogonal (it would be most surprising if they were). In the $2 \times 2 \times 2$ cube they define (see figure 5) we expect some boxes to be more thickly populated than

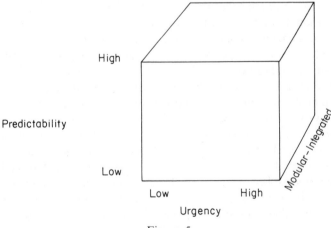

Figure 5

others for the kinds of reasons we have outlined, although there do not seem *a priori* reasons for expecting any boxes to be forbidden. What is important to note is that the nature of the problem, as defined by the box to which it can be assigned, will have a major impact on the composition of the project team and the way in which it operates.

For example, a high urgency, high predictability project which fits into our category of 'modular' is likely to be most effectively managed through an experienced project leader and the assistance of structured planning aids, regular action-oriented meetings, and formal communication links. The opportunity for individuals to learn on the job and gain experience relevant to their specialist career development is likely to be limited. The motivation for participants on such a project is less towards the work challenge derived from professional requests and more towards the challenge to meet predetermined and agreed goals.

On the other hand a high urgency, high unpredictability integrated project is going to be very difficult to manage and in fact it is obvious that the expectation of meeting any predetermined deadline is likely to be low. Such cases can arise in situations where pressures are high, or external threats, e.g. potential government legislation, are imminent. Drawing upon the innovation literature mentioned earlier it can be argued that it is vital to have support from the top management, a product champion, priority, resource availability, etc., and even then the risk is high.

An alternative way of looking at the modular–integrated distinction is to concentrate on the way in which boundaries between the disciplines of the team members are handled. We distinguish here between what we choose to call multidisciplinary and interdisciplinary work. The former implies the ability to break down the project into work packages which can each be managed independently and without requiring any interaction with the work going on in other packages. Interdisciplinary work implies the opposite of this, i.e. the need to have a close working relationship between each individual in order to progress the project in the best possible way.

Again the dimensions of urgency and predictability must be considered. For instance, in the more basic areas of research where there is a high degree of uncertainty and where, in general, time-scales are relatively long, there should be plenty of opportunity for individuals to acquire information from the literature and to exchange it amongst interested parties so that the necessary interdisciplinarity is built up as the needs of the project or area develop. However, the evidence is that there are some significant additional factors to be considered. One of these is communication, but communication based on understanding and motivation (Pearson, 1978). There is evidence that people from different disciplines find it difficult to understand each other's way of thinking, and also have difficulty in understanding their specialist technology and jargon (Bärmark and Wallen, 1979).

A detailed discussion of the nature of cognitive boundaries and the ways in which these become institutionalized is beyond the scope of this chapter, although it is clearly important to a full understanding of the operation of groups drawn from several disciplines. For instance, in institutional settings, e.g. universities, where rewards are not given to those prepared to put aside the time to overcome these barriers, the amount of interdisciplinary work which is successfully undertaken is very low in comparison to the potential. It is therefore important to consider the way in which personal goals are compatible with the goals of the project. In situations where this is not the case it is vital that agreement is reached between all parties about which goals are going to be given preference during the course of a particular project. If this is not done then individuals may choose to pursue their own goals—a distinct possibility in temporary groups and more particularly in groups which involve people who are asked to make contributions to more than one project simultaneously. The net result of not clarifying these goal differences is likely to be the situation we referred to earlier in which important decisions which will affect the progress of a project are made at the wrong level in the organization. For instance, a key individual may choose to allocate priority between the different projects with which he is associated on the basis of the contribution they make to his personal development rather than to organizational needs. We shall return to this point when we come to consider team development issues.

The dimensions discussed so far clearly do not complete the picture as far as the project leader is concerned. An important factor which must be taken into account in understanding the issues facing temporary groups is the structure adopted by the organization and alongside this the overall level of resources which is available to service individual projects. In the next section we turn to this aspect, focusing particularly on matrix organizations.

Organizational Structure

Considerable interest has been shown recently in the management of interdisciplinary groups, this interest being generated, we believe, because organizations are finding more of their work falling into categories which require a combination of specialist skills and at the same time are finding that such specialists do not always work together easily. Some of the literature suggests that difficulties of communication and interaction are inevitable in any work in which people from different backgrounds and with different educational and work experiences are required to cooperate. We accept this, but we also believe that many of the difficulties arise because of a lack of clear definition of what is required, where particular responsibilities lie, and how the interaction should be managed.

In a study of forty R&D organizations (Gunz and Pearson, 1977a) we attempted to identify how different types of structures assist (or otherwise) people to manage their activities. The organizations operated in a wide range of industries in both public and private sectors, including chemicals, foods, textiles, engineering, metallurgy, construction, and packaging. They varied greatly in size from a formulation laboratory for a small speciality chemical manufacturer with a technical staff of eight to one of several corporate laboratories of a large multinational group, with a staff of over 1,500. Of these roughly 25 per cent had matrix structures of some kind. Our findings, not surprisingly, were difficult to interpret in organizational terms, mainly because there were so many types of structure, or perhaps we should say that the matrix organization, which is so often heard of as being appropriate to R&D, is really so flexible that it can take on an almost infinite variety of forms. Even within a single establishment there are many different forms of organization around at one and the same time.

We concluded therefore that we would gain more knowledge of the management process if we focused attention on individual projects. This led us to making a distinction between what we subsequently called the 'leadership' matrix and the 'coordination' matrix.

The leadership matrix

(a) assumes that people tend, if left to themselves, to pursue their own ends, which are likely to be related to their professional, specialist goals, and need galvanizing into working on the organization's goals;

(b) needs drive, motivation, and leadership towards tackling the task goals;

(c) the leader of the project or lateral group therefore has to have influence and status so that he is not dominated by the heads of the specialist or vertical groups; and

(d) the lateral groups need to be cohesive and strongly motivated to solve the problems necessary to complete the task.

The coordination matrix

(a) assumes that people are rational and objective, work to achieve the organization's goals given adequate information, and balance priorities in a way acceptable to all concerned given the facts of the situation;

(b) needs everyone to be kept informed about what is happening to the task and when they will be required to do what;

(c) the leader of the lateral groups is therefore seen as a coordinator, with the most complete knowledge about what is happening to the task and what it will involve in due course, and influences events by signalling to the vertical authorities when the project deviates from its plan; and

(d) the lateral groups only need to be a set of nominated individuals concerned with the completion of the task, each knowing who else is involved. The nominated individuals are primarily members of the functional groups, and project work is secondary to their functional work.

Like all models, these caricature reality, and elements of each type can be found within single organizations. Our experience is that one reason for the difficulty which R&D organizations have with matrix organizations is that the underlying differences between the coordination and leadership matrices often have not been recognized. People think they are operating in one while the dominant ideology of the organization reflects the assumptions of the other. In one laboratory, for instance, project leaders are encouraged to see themselves as operating in a leadership matrix—and the more ambitious take to this naturally. The organization is, however, very hierarchical, and unless the project leaders are old, experienced individuals they stand little chance of influencing the heads of the vertical groups. The rules and operating procedures in fact are those of the coordination matrix, and the frustration that results arises from this confusion. These points, with some added comments, are summarized in Table 1. The comments suggest that the differences have significant implications for the style of leadership and operating characteristics of the group.

Table 1   Two models of matrix organization

	Leadership matrix	Coordination matrix
The model assumes people	—tend to pursue their own goals: —professional —specialist —need galvanizing into working to project goals	—are rational, objective —act predictably on adequate information
Role of Project Leader is to	—motivate team to work to project goals	—keep everyone informed about —project status —when their contributions will be needed
Consequences for Project Leader	—need status, authority —gets action by personal authority, influence, negotiating skills	—is coordinator, with most complete information on status and future needs of project —gets action by signalling deviations from plan
Consequences for Functional Manager	—scope of authority, responsibility limited by project needs	—must consider project needs in conjunction with needs of functional activities
Consequences for Project Team:	—must be cohesive group —functional activities interfere with project work	—meetings of nominated individuals —project work interferes with functional activities

The leadership–coordination distinction also helps us to draw together some of the points made earlier, for example the effect of external (i.e. outside the project) pressures on the type of leadership required. Basically the coordination matrix will work best when there are adequate facilities available to ensure that conflicts for resources are not continually arising. If this is not the case then more of the leadership characteristics are required, but such characteristics will tend to be of a management nature rather than an integrative technical nature. This agrees with the findings of many researchers about the influence of external factors on internal management structures and, as stated earlier, the way in which the performance of projects is affected by the leaders' ability to get resources. Linked to this is, of course, the priority given to the project. The coordination matrix style will also be supported in organizations in which formal planning systems are operated in such a way as to provide forward resource loading information which can be used to anticipate and eliminate potential bottleneck situations which lead to conflict (Gunz and Pearson, 1977b).

Still under the heading of organizational structure it is now possible to include a further set of dimensions which are very important determinants of the management task facing a temporary group. At the same time these further dimensions actually allow us to identify more specifically the different types of groups with which we are concerned. The dimensions relate to the time allocation of the project leader and of the team members to the project, and a simple analysis gives the breakdown shown in Figure 6.

Examples of temporary groups which fit into each of these categories are recognizable in most organizational settings.

The full-time leader, full-time team members (box 1) shows itself frequently in the form of a task force. The project is likely to have a high priority and this is often clearly shown by bringing together all the people to a common location for the duration of the project.

Full-time leaders with part-time team members (box 2) fits neatly many of the projects in a matrix organization. Box 4 describes an even more common situation, namely where the leader has other duties as well.

Part-time project leaders and full-time team members (box 3) are probably

| | | Team members | |
		Full time	Part time
Project leader	Full time	1	2
	Part time	3	4

Figure 6

encountered less frequently, but the situation does arise, for example in discipline-organized structures where heads of departments may act as project leaders on a number of projects simultaneously.

An additional category which we do not propose to go into here is an essentially ad hoc one in which a number of people are brought together at a particular point in time in the life of a project to assist the team with ideas for possible new directions and/or to help in identifying areas of concern for which contingency plans may need to be drawn up well in advance. Such approaches have been used in a wide variety of situations (see, for example, Woods and Davies, 1973; Knowlton, 1976; Davies, 1979) and the evidence is that a great deal of commitment can be generated even though the imported members of the group do not necessarily have any organizational commitment to the project.

Team Development

In setting out some of the characteristics of temporary groups it might be argued that the variety is so high as to preclude any attempt at drawing conclusions about appropriate management styles. We do not think this is necessarily true because there are some fundamental characteristics which can be identified in all project groups. These are basically the project itself and what is to be achieved, the team members and the contribution they can make towards the desired ends, and the structure or the way in which they choose to interact with each other and with any external influences. To put it more simply, the common threads to project management are the goals, the roles, and the procedures. It is not argued that these are always set down in a very formal way or that they necessarily need to be but that they do have to be considered and a project leader ignores them at his peril—more so in temporary groups because of the many distractions which arise due to overlapping group membership and priority conflicts because of overload positions.

These points then lead us to ask two questions about the potential for team development (see Plovnick, Fry, and Rubin, 1975). If, as is commonly the case, a project leader is not given the authority to choose the team members what can he do to encourage the best possible team performance? If he can choose the composition of the team, on what basis should he make the choice? The implication of our analysis of the dimensionality of project problems is that the questioning must start with the very basic: do we need a team at all (in the sense used in this chapter of people who have to work closely together towards a common and agreed goal which they are motivated to achieve)?

Team Goals

Even in modular or multidisciplinary-type projects commitment to an agreed goal is likely to be necessary in most situations—the only exception being where there are adequate resources both in quantity and quality to progress all the separate activities in the required time-scales, which will probably be fairly flexible and certainly not short term. Agreement on goals and primary tasks must therefore be given due attention. We would argue that this is more important for the temporary group because the ability to keep team members motivated is mainly influenced by their interest in and perceived progression towards a defined and agreed goal. In the research and development field such a goal will almost certainly have a strong technical focus, but from our earlier analysis we would argue that an agreement about other issues—for example, the degree of urgency—is most important. We can point to many examples of projects which were less successful than they might have been because of a lack of agreement about the degree of urgency of the work sometimes arising simply because it was never discussed openly and hence different viewpoints were held. This can have serious implications, most particularly when people are members of more than one temporary group at the same time, as is often the case.

In addition, problems arise frequently owing to a lack of agreement and acceptance of the level of urgency by other people in the organization who may not be members of the group, e.g. those responsible for supplying service facilities. However, an important point to note is the influence that people completely outside the project group can have through, for example, their competing claims on scarce resources and their changing view of external circumstances. This is the source of our earlier argument for looking carefully at the different types and levels of decision which must be made during the course of a project and for reviewing these with appropriate parties, both inside and outside the team, at regular intervals.

Despite the constant references in the literature to the overriding importance to successful team performance of everyone understanding clearly the project goal, we think it is essential to emphasize again the point made earlier about the pluralistic nature of goals in practice. The needs and aspirations of individual team members vary, and each individual will naturally be concerned with the way in which a particular project will meet their own. Failure to recognize this is likely to lead to a failure to meet either personal or project goals at a sufficiently high level. However, it must be accepted that some incompatibility will occur in a number of situations but that this can be made acceptable by bringing goal definition into open debate at the earliest possible point in time. As mentioned earlier, a failure to recognize this potential divergence between the goals of the individual and of the project has often led to delays and a lowering of performance.

In this context it is interesting to note that experiences of researchers in a number of different countries is that the output from a university-based interdisciplinary project is often *not* papers of an interdisciplinary nature but rather a series of individual papers which report on that aspect of the work which is most closely related to an individual's specialism and which can be submitted for publication in the journals most likely to be seen as relevant to his or her career development. A recognition that this may be the situation is important and may be turned to advantage, for example by allowing people time after completion of the project to develop some of the material for their own purposes.

Team Roles

The possibility of achieving research goals within any given project will depend upon the contribution which an individual is required to make which will in turn be influenced by the role he is required to adopt in relation to other team members. There have been many attempts made to identify the roles which are required within a balanced team.

It has been argued that the following four are necessary: generators, integrators, developers, and perfectors (see Clutterbuck, 1979). Belbin (1976) has gone further than this, and identified seven which he has labelled as chairman/shaper, plant, monitor/evaluator, company worker, team worker, resource investigator, and completer.

It is important to recognize the existence of these roles within any group, whether permanent or temporary, but it is also important to recognize that the relative importance of each role will depend upon the type of project and also the stage which it is in. Again the categories of urgency and predictability are useful dimensions for analysis. For example, projects which are low urgency and high predictability may well benefit from having people who place an emphasis on finishing rather than on idea generation, whereas the reverse may be the case in situations of low urgency but low predictability. Turning to the modular–integrated dimensions it can be argued that the former will benefit from an emphasis on the chairman/shaper role because of the value which is placed on the coordination as distinct from the leadership characteristics.

We would therefore argue that it is very important to look carefully at the choice of team members in temporary groups in an attempt to ensure that the required roles are filled by people whose contributions will be in line with the needs of the organization, but who will also obtain personal satisfaction and development from the project. This is particularly important in temporary groups because the individual rewards from participating in such an activity are not always so clearly seen to have arisen from the success of the project as they are in permanent groups.

Obviously there will be times when it is not possible to achieve an ideal match between the overall needs of the project and the choice of individuals who are most likely to see the roles required as fitting their own needs. We would argue that any major differences between the two will tend to lead to a reduction in performance unless the differences are seen as unavoidable, relatively short-term, and unlikely to have significant adverse effects on future career prospects. If this is the case then it should be possible for many people to agree to cooperate in a role which is different from what they would choose if other opportunities were available. However, for optimum performance such changes must be negotiated and agreed before the project is set up and re-negotiated during the course of the project if changes occur, or are anticipated, in key variables such as predictability and structure.

A factor often overlooked in the selection of project group members is the career stage they have reached. Here the business of performance evaluation, both of the project and individual, plays an important role. This is often assessed externally to the group, and the legitimacy of the person or people carrying out this appraisal needs to be established and agreed. The implication of this is that people outside the team must be seen as performing an essential role. This is likely to be particularly important for the younger, less experienced team member, and even more so for the new recruit into the organization. Such people are likely to have fewer distractions because of their newness and will be very much involved in the organizational socialization process on which the contribution they are asked to make to a project will have a large influence (Schein, 1978). They will therefore have a high commitment to the project and to its success which will be reinforced by any indication that their performance is noted by people who are in a position to influence their career development. In contrast, it can be argued that older people will face many distractions, including, for example, administration. If they feel that a particular project will make little or no impact on their future in either a positive or negative way, they may choose to put in the minimum of effort. The reduction in motivation of the older person is a subject of considerable interest at the present time and ways and means of overcoming this are of prime concern to the project leader and to the organization.

The temporary nature of the working relationship clearly raises questions about the criteria for judging performance. A great deal of attention has been paid to this, particularly in the innovation and research and development area. Some studies have focused on the technical output from the group, others on the success or otherwise of the exploitation, i.e. in the commercial output. Many of the groups studied were of a temporary nature although some had a fairly long life-span. Rothwell (1977) analysed and summarized the findings from nine studies covering a variety of groups in a number of different countries. In his analysis he identifies a number of key factors associated with the more successful groups. For example, good communication is seen as very important, as is support of the group from senior management. Communication covers not only internal, that is within the group, but also external, so that ideas and information from outside sources are incorporated into the group thinking. If attention is not paid to them there is a great danger that the N.I.H. (not invented here) syndrome appears—with a potentially adverse effect on performance.

Other researchers, for example Pelz and Andrews (1966), have found that the performance of a group increases with the average length of time the members have been together up to a certain point, after which it can fall off. A reasonable explanation for this is that group members need to get to know each other, to understand each other's way of working, etc. but that the benefit from this can go off if the group becomes too introspective and cosy. More recently, in a study of a number of academic groups involved essentially in fundamental research, Stankiewicz (1979) found that group size had an influence on performance. Of particular interest was the finding that the scientific recognition accorded to a group fell off after a certain size when individual members did not identify closely with the group. Cheng (1979) found that integration between members was affected by, amongst other things, interpersonal compatibility, suggesting that it may be useful, even necessary, to have compatibility as a selection criteria for deciding group composition. This is important to consider because our experience suggests that in many cases the project leader does not have a very large say in the choice of team members, particularly in matrix organizations. This would be particularly true in the case of younger, inexperienced project leaders who also may well be put in charge of low-priority projects. The potential for failure is obvious and the longer-term implications for the individual and the organization are likely to be serious. In this case it is important to consider how such potential incompatibilities might be reduced, if not completely eliminated, by team building.

In looking at performance, however, we must remember that the criteria for judgement will very rarely be unidimensional, and that failure on one dimension may well be compensated by a higher than expected success in another. For example, in research and development a project may not achieve the desired outcome by providing a company with an immediate commercially viable product but the results of the work may open up new avenues for exploration which in the longer term could have much more significant effects. Finally, as remarked earlier, an individual team member may well achieve success or personal kudos from a project which is not seen as a group success. (For a discussion of some of these issues see, for example, Barth and Steck, 1979.)

Team Procedures

Attention must then be paid to the procedures and social mechanisms which will be required to ensure that the project is progressed satisfactorily. In considering the form such procedures might take we are very conscious of the vast amount of research which focuses on this subject. Our own work on organizations clearly demonstrates the ways in which various forms of functional, matrix, and project structures can influence the progress of individual projects. However, as mentioned earlier, factors which can have a significant impact on the performance of temporary groups in all these structures include the degree to which resources are made available at crucial points in a project life-cycle and the way in which priority clashes are resolved. In many areas, of which research and development is one, the influence of changes in the external environment, technical and commercial, can have a considerable influence on progress.

The importance of communications cannot therefore be over-stressed, and this is emphasized in the research literature (see, for example, Allen, 1977). This literature makes it clear that a continuing interest in information-seeking is a fundamental part of a scientist's training, and it is important that this should be encouraged with opportunities being provided for formal and informal interchange. However, the more recent literatures does note some significant differences between the needs of different types of projects and makes a distinction between the influence of, for example, scientific, administrative, and external information inputs. The conclusions one can draw from a careful study of this area is that communication can be managed and that the good project leader and team is aware of this.

The value of communication is also emphasized in most of the more useful planning and monitoring procedures which have been developed over recent years as aids to project management. For example, networks, planning diagrams, and milestone or phase breakdown charts are all basically devices for encouraging communication at the earliest possible stage of planning and then further encouraging this at subsequent review dates. Detailed consideration of such approaches is beyond the scope of this chapter, but an examination of their use in practice indicates that they can be of considerable help in clarifying some of the key areas for attention which we have been discussing, i.e. goals, roles, and procedures.

A final point to make, however, is that there will always be an element of uncertainty in the management of projects, and that some of the important characteristics of leadership include the ability to recognize changes which were not planned for and to take action, or to draw other people's attention to the need to take action when things look to be changing. Obviously, the frequency with which such on-line, almost ad hoc actions will be necessary will depend upon the type of project, but we contend that this frequency can be reduced in almost all cases by the adoption of a more structured approach to management, involving a combination of formal planning methods and team-building methods focusing on goals, roles, and procedures. Above all, emphasis on the latter will help to identify the important characteristics of a project including the environment within which it will be carried out and the people who will be involved. This will lead to an improvement in performance not least because of the recognition it gives to the personal development needs of individual team members which are not often adequately recognized in temporary project groups.

References

Allen, T. J. (1977) *Managing the Flow of Technology*, Boston, Mass.: M.I.T. Press.
Bärmark, J. and Wallen, G. (1979) 'Interaction of cognitive and social factors in steering a large interdisciplinary project', in Barth, R. T. and Steck, R.

162   GROUPS AT WORK

Barth, R. T. and Steck, R. (1979) *Interdisciplinary Research Groups: Their Management and Organization*, International Research Group on Interdisciplinary Programs.

Belbin, R. M. (1976) 'A practitioner's guide to team-skills management', Industrial Training Research Unit, 32 Trumpington Street, Cambridge.

Bower, J. L. (1970) 'Managing the resource allocation process: a study of corporate planning and investment', Boston, Mass.: Harvard University, Graduate School of Business Administration, Division of Research.

Cheng, J. L. C. (1979) A study of coordination in three research settings, *R & D Management Special Issue* **9**.

Clutterbuck, D. (1979) 'R & D under Management's Microscope', *International Management*, February, **1979**.

Davies, G. B. (1979) 'Small group creativity in food product development', Proceedings of Creativity Week 11, Centre for Creative Leadership, Greensboro, North Carolina, September.

Farris, G. F. (1978) 'Informal Organizations in research and development', Joint National Meeting of the Institute of Management Sciences and Operations Research Society of America, New York, May 1978.

Galbraith, J. R. (1973) *Designing Complex Organizations*, Reading, Mass.: Addison-Wesley.

Gordon, G. (1966): 'Preconceptions and reconceptions in the administration of science', in M. C. Yovits *et al.*, eds., *Research Program Effectiveness*, New York: Gordon & Breach. (Article was reprinted in *R & D Management* **2**, 1, October 1971).

Gunz, H. P. and Pearson, A. W. (1977a) 'Matrix organization in R & D', in K. W. Knight, ed, *Matrix Management*, London: Saxon House.

Gunz, H. P. and Pearson, A. W. (1977b) 'Introduction of a matrix structure into an R & D establishment', *R & D Management* **7**, 3, 173–81.

Gunz, H. P. and Pearson, A. W. (1979) 'How to manage control conflicts in project based organizations', *Research Management* March, **1979**.

Handy, C. (1976) *Understanding Organisations*, Harmondworth: Penguin.

Katz, D. and Kahn, R. L. (1966) *The Social Psychology of Organisations*, New York: Wiley.

Keller, R. T., Szilagyi, A. D. Jr, and Holland, W. E. (1977) 'Boundary-spanning activity and employee reactions: an empirical study', *Human Relations* **29**, 7, 699–710.

Knowlton, R. E. (1976) 'Hazard and Operability studies and their initial applications in R & D', *R & D Management* **7**, 1, October.

Likert, R. (1961) *New Patterns of Management*, New York, McGlaw-Hill.

Organ, D. W. and Greene, C. N. (1972) 'The boundary relevance of the project manager's job: findings and implications for R & D management', *R & D Management* **3**, 1, October, 7–12.

Pearson, A. W. (1978) 'Review of selected information transfer studies', Advisory Group for Aerospace R & D Conference, Paris, October 1978, AGARD Proceedings.

Pelz, D. C. and Andrews, F. M. (1966) *Scientists in Organisations: productive climates for R & D*. Ann Arbor, Michigan: Institute for Social Research.

Perrow, C. (1972) *Complex Organisations*, Glenview, Ill.: Scott, Forseman.

Plovnick, M., Fry, R., and Rubin, I. (1975) 'New developments in O. D. Technology: Programmed Team Development,' *Training and Development Journal*, April, **1975**.

Rothwell, R. (1977) 'The characteristics of successful innovators and technically progressive firms (with some comments on innovation research)', *R & D Management* **7**, no. 3, 191–206.

Schein, E. (1978) *Career Dynamics—Matching Individual and Organizational Needs*, Reading, Mass.: Addison Wesley.

Stankiewicz, R. (1979) 'The effects of leadership—the relationship between the size of research groups the their scientific'performance', *R & D Management Special Issue* **9**.

Woods, M. F. and Davies, G. B. (1973) 'Potential problem analysis: a systematic approach to problem prediction and contingency planning—an aid to the smooth exploitation of research', *R & D Management* **4**, 1, October.

Woodward, J. (1965) *Industrial Organisation: Theory and Practice*, London: Oxford University Press.

Groups at Work
Edited by R. Payne and C. Cooper
© 1981 John Wiley & Sons Ltd.

Chapter 7

Negotiating Groups

John Carlisle and Malcolm Leary

Introduction

The title of this chapter, Negotiating Groups, is a very deliberate one. Too often negotiating has been discussed as a process in which the participants are, at the most, psychological singularities, and at the least, incidental to the process. A great deal of emphasis has been placed on strategies, issues, conflicts, and targets arising during the process, while the role of the group as both determinant and vehicle of the process has been ignored. Part of our aim is to redress that balance; the other part is to share insights arising from our research and experience of negotiating.

Two-factor Model

This chapter is about two areas:
1. Negotiating and
2. Groups.

We shall examine these separately and jointly as part of an interacting, symbiotic (or mutually destructive) development process over time. The groups will be examined at two levels: intra-negotiating groups—I groups, which comprise the other party's negotiating team; and the inter-negotiating groups—N groups, which form the actual negotiation (Figure 1).

Negotiation as a Necessity

Why do we negotiate? Why does everyone at some time or another become entangled in a process in which any final decision is arrived at after what seems to be endless hassle and even, at times, open dispute.

The answer is threefold. First there just is not enough of everything to go around sufficiently to satisfy everyone's wants. Secondly, most people and organizations simply do not have sufficient power to seize what they want. Or, power is not appropriate. Thirdly, the desired objective is very often impossible to achieve without another party's cooperation. You either get together or you get nothing. This can be considered a corollary to the second point.

However, this is not to assume that because a negotiation situation arises people automatically negotiate. If only people would! There are three choices when a negotiation is imminent: flight, fight, or negotiate. The first two are the easy options, requiring less skill but often leading to long-term disasters. In

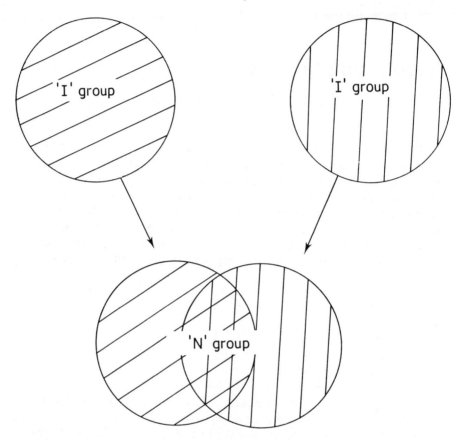

Figure 1. The relationship between the intra-negotiation groups (I) and
inter-negotiation group (N)

Britain, for example, many managements have a history of flight and the unions a
history of fight, so that when, as today, they are forced to negotiate they are at a
loss, not having the skill or experience, and tend to fall into pretty damaging
conflict.

In the end negotiation is the hardest, but most effective option, or as Churchill
said, 'Jaw-jaw is better than war-war', and running away does not always mean
you will live to fight another day.

Negotiation—a Power Paradox

People often confuse a negotiation with a conflict process, because they feel
uncomfortable with the awkward, unsociable bargaining behaviours. In fact, an

oil company executive once commented to one of the authors that negotiating was 'uncivilized'. (War is civilized?)

In fact what people see is not destructive conflict, but a potentially creative tension arising from the necessity for cooperation between two parties who want different things from the same situation, which are not completely achievable because of the other party's demand, but which would not be at all achievable without the other party's presence. So the parties undertake the 'process of agreeing the distribution of scarce resources'—which is a good working definition of a negotiation.

This interdependence in conjunction with differing objectives is the *power paradox* arising from the fact that each party has the power both to prevent the other party from achieving his objectives, or to assist the other party so to do. This directly is central to the whole theme of negotiating and is worth examining in some depth. Opposition in itself is therefore not necessarily destructive. It is how it is handled that is important. If these differences turn into a negative conflict rather than a creative confrontation, then we have problems. Negotiation provides a potential process for handling differences more positively.

Interdependence

The very fact that negotiators meet is an acknowledgement of their need for each other, and again we get this equal and opposite effect; interdependence paradoxically gives each party the ability to damage the other. This reward/punishment theme is insistent in the negotiating process and is a tacit admission of the power parity condition necessary for successful negotiation. If A feels B is too strong, then A will do his best to demonstrate his power to damage B. While B, if he is experienced, will not use his extra power as a club; very often he will emphasize the better deal for both parties. (Even the Godfather 'made an offer'.) Unfortunately there are quite a few unskilled negotiators who behave like Billy the Kid and draw their guns at the first opportunity.

What emerges from this forced interdependence is a battle between the rational and non-rational. These are complementary conditions of a negotiation and much of the structure is given to maintaining the right balance, not necessarily a perfect equilibrium but often a shift in either direction at the appropriate time to strengthen or weaken a case. Consider the careful positioning of even the physical proximities of opposing parties in the Paris negotiations over Vietnam, or the Zimbabwe-Rhodesia conference. It is usually at the beginning and end of a negotiation that the most attention has to be paid to the emotional aspect; when there is a good deal of uncertainty or anxiety. The rational, or issue aspect is prominent before and in the middle of a negotiation. Ultimately, however, both rational and emotional needs have to be satisfied before agreement is reached.

Group Formation

In summary, negotiators get together generally for two reason.

1. Because the parties need each other, and only each other, in order to achieve their objectives.

2. Because one or both parties feel that, of all the available options, meeting the other party seems to be the best.

Thus, they carry out a process which Walton and McKersie (1965) call Distributive Bargaining, and they do this within the constraints set by their own organization or reference group. The targets, therefore, are not only their targets, but also reflect some sort of imperative from their group. (This has additional emotional connotations, increasing as it does the personal risk element—especially when making concessions.)

If the negotiation has been well-planned, then negotiators do not have *a* target; rather they have a target area, ranging from maximum to minimum, within which they can bargain. This reduces the 'loss-of-face' risk factor, but also, more importantly, increases the likelihood of agreement because it allows flexibility. Herein lies the *real* bargaining skill of the negotiators, in using movement to gain movement, and is here that they earn their keep.

We therefore have to consider the characteristics and performance of two kinds of negotiation groups.

The Intra-negotiation Group—I Group

Separate teams of negotiators formed by each represented party.

1. These groups come together to reflect the various sub-interests which are deemed to need a voice during the negotiations. For example, there needs to be someone there (a) to make sure the needs of key individuals or groups are satisfied (to some extent); (b) to ensure that the power and influence of each interest is fully exerted when decisions are made; and (c) to add important skills, understanding, or technical information to the collective pot.

2. The assumption is generally that the person with most authority or influence in the group will take the lead at the negotiation. This is often a miscalculation since they do not necessarily have the right skill. There should be some sorting out of roles and duties, both for the I group stage and later for the N group processes. The front man, seen perhaps as a controller, the old fashioned 'chairman' will be identified. Back-up roles will be allocated, someone to coordinate, a person to keep notes. The role of the expert, the one with specialist knowledge, requires considerable clarification here.

3. The I group members represent a wider reference group—management policies and objectives, shopfloor aspirations, and the interests of a particular function or department. To some extent the targets and boundaries of the I group are set by the outside reference group. These may be at variance and in themselves need reconciling.

4. The form, structure, and practices of the I group, have to be worked out between group members. Very rarely is any framework set and the group themselves are left to 'sort things out'. Often this is done much more informally than in an N group.

The Inter-negotiation Group—N Group

The separate teams of negotiators jointly work together to reach an agreement.

1. The individual I group's aims and aspirations, translated into actual targets or ranges are reconciled and compromised to reach a jointly acceptable agreement (in a successful negotiation).

2. The pressures and limits of each I group will impinge on the freedom and judgement of the members of the re-constituted N group.

3. The agreement reached by the N group will arise from the process and interaction of the N group. The effectiveness of this process will depend on the skills and awareness of N group members, appropriate to what is needed at a particular stage in the negotiations.

4. There needs to be a shared responsibility for the effectiveness of the total negotiation process.

5. Because of these increased pressures, the influence of history and ritual, etc. the N group process is likely to be much more formalized. The I groups and the N groups have a separate identity and existence. They also have a linked purpose and a shared process to go through (Figure 2).

It is increasingly a feature of today's organizations that negotiating *teams* are the prevalent mode of successful negotiating, and the genesis of the I group can already be seen in the planning group which is often taken into the negotiation itself. It is worth looking more closely at this group's development.

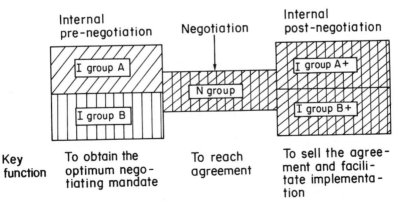

Figure 2. Roles of the I and N groups

The Development of the Intra-negotiation Group (I Group)

In our complex, organization-oriented society groups are taken for granted; we rarely question their utility. It can be said, however, that most experts such as Karrass (1970) and Rackham and Carlisle (1978) recommend negotiating in a group or team for business or industrial relations negotiations. Why?

First, negotiations in both fields are around highly complex issues with important legal, financial, and technological implications. It is impossible to expect one person to plan effectively on the basis of all these requirements. So the experts are invited in and if they work well together (which is not always the case) they arrive at an effective plan which the negotiator can use with more confidence than one derived from this own limited knowledge and understanding of the issues.

Secondly, this team can be invaluable during the actual negotiation. As the negotiation proceeds various esoteric points are raised and debated, and it is very useful for the prime negotiator to check out with specialists the implications of these issues as and when they arise. This is the obvious case for the expertise of the multifunctional team.

However, there is also another less obvious, but perhaps more important, case for a negotiating team and that is simply to help handle the information and arguments which flow back and forth across the table. In addition to being able to marshal their own facts and present their own case, the negotiators must also be able to consider the points of the other party, listen for flaws, build on common ground, and ensure they understand the implications of each. It is an extremely difficult task for one person to handle. Having someone else there can help control the process and provide additional thinking time. In fact some organizations, such as Rank Xerox (Mitcheldean) in England, have actually organized their purchasing department into commodity teams whose members provide both the expertise and process aid in negotiations with suppliers. This procedure (a recent innovation) has had most impressive results over the past two years; not least of all because each member of the team knows his role and acts in concert with the buyer who orchestrates the process (see Carlisle, 1980).

There is also the phenomenon whereby a group is liable to take and reinforce a higher level of risk than would an individual negotiator and sometimes it is just such a risk which injects life and hope into flagging negotiation.

A final telling argument in favour of negotiating teams is that they can review the interaction jointly and provide very useful feedback to each other about the success or failure of various manoeuvres and exchanges. The group thus becomes a learning group, consciously improving its performance from negotiation to negotiation. The ability of lone negotiators to provide themselves with reliable and significant feedback is very limited, clouded as it is by rationalization and recency effects. It is here that management negotiators often fall down.

Over the life of a negotiation the function, purpose, and constitution of the I

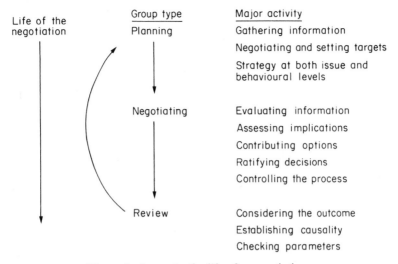

Figure 3. Stages in the life of a negotiation

groupings may alter to meet differing requirements arising from the needs of the negotiation as whole. Figure 3 indicates the various stages of a negotiation. Thus each group, although it may comprise the same members, takes on a different identify at each phase. The skill of the I group members at accommodating interactively to each phase is of key importance.

The Development of the Inter-negotiation Group (N Group)

So far the need to look at negotiations as a set of interdependent relationships which develop in different ways over the life of the negotiation has been emphasized. As well as the dynamics of what happens *within* the negotiating teams, the relationship *between* the various groupings involved also needs to be considered. The inter-negotiation group (the N group) comprising the negotiating parties brings us into another dimension of interrelationships which will be examined further in this paper.

Much has been written of the detail, the nitty-gritty of negotiating techniques and ploys. We have resisted the temptation to become too involved in this rich and seductive field. Rather, we have concentrated on what we consider to be so far a neglected view of negotiations. We are primarily interested here in what happens to the negotiation as a whole over its life. Our focus on the negotiating group therefore includes both parties sharing responsibility for the effectiveness of the total negotiation as a development process. In examining the time sequence of the negotiation we will be looking at a living, organic, and human process. Issues of birth and formating, living and death will be raised and scrutinized (see Figure 4).

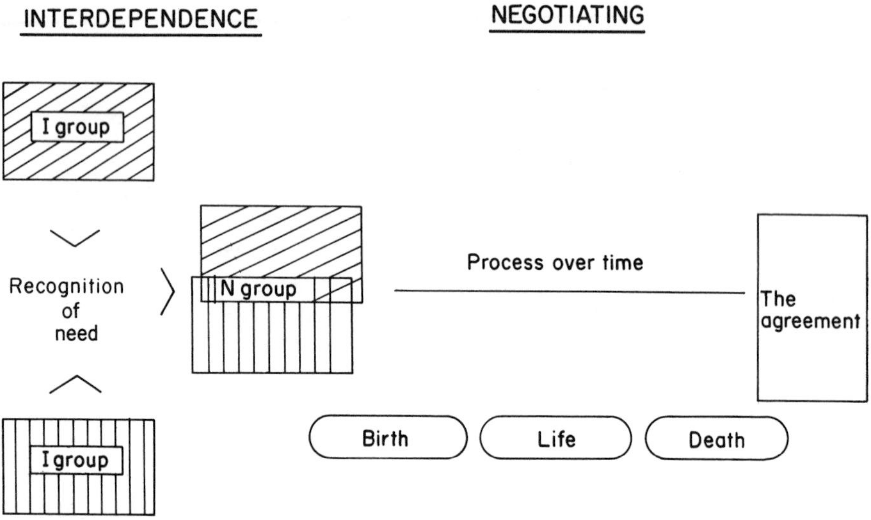

INTERDEPENDENCE   NEGOTIATING

Figure 4. Life processes of a negotiation

Groups over Time

A real understanding and feel for what negotiations are all about cannot be achieved unless the process is examined over a completed time-cycle. We are not therefore dealing with a series of events which has a neat, precise, ordered inevitability about it. Characteristically a negotiation, as with any social interaction, will have its own phases and trends, peaks and troughs, ebbs and flows. A negotiation tends to trace out its own individual pattern compared with other groups and we will try to identify what this is. First, however, a few words about the importance of bringing time and movement into the study of negotiations.

A New Perspective—The Importance of the Time Dimension

Existing studies of negotiating groups give little emphasis to developments over time. Morley and Stephenson (1977), for instance, devotes some space to looking at the typical phases of a negotiation as sequential events without time movement, as does Douglas (1957). There is a need therefore to look at the following elements over time—see Figure 5.

A time dimension provides particularly valuable insights when the behaviour of a good negotiator is examined. They have a relationship to the process of a negotiation as a whole, 'in the round' which is most important for achieving the responses required at particular stages to move things forward. 'Appropriateness' of actions and behaviour is a key element in negotiations. To have an idea of what is needed at a particular time, and to do the right thing at

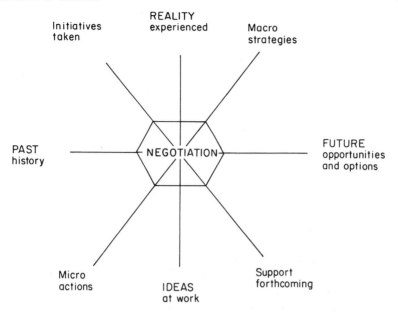

Figure 5. Elements of a negotiation

that time, requires a combination of acute perception and skilled behaviour. To be aware of the total process as it lies ahead is invaluable in finding the right relationship to the negotiating process as a whole. This is not to say that all negotiations will go the same way of course. They will all have a peculiar life of their own, made up from the unique mix of circumstances and characters involved; but all will flow through an identifiably common course.

Events are likely to move in certain predictable broad directions over the life of the negotiation. How those involved relate to these patterns will determine how effective the negotiation might be. How do the actors involved respond for example to any crisis point which may be met along the way? When particular skills, insight, or initiative are needed at a precise moment, will the group be found wanting? Who will ask the key question, provide the right commentary to maintain momentum?

In order to see what is required at various phases of the negotiating process, the patterns need to be identified. These patterns will follow some of the features of all development processes, particularly as seen in the social field, and will include, for example:

(1) a step-by-step, incremental movement from one stage of the negotiation to the next (Figure 6);

(2) each successive 'layer' will be characterized by new qualities needed from the group;

(3) a movement from one layer to the next will undoubtedly involve some

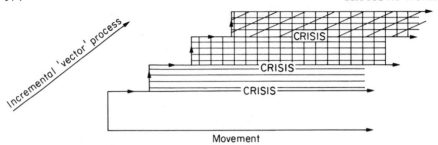

Figure 6. The 'layered' movement of a negotiation

tension and problems which need to be overcome, as well as extra energy.

The features most likely to appear in order of precedence in a negotiating group have been explored before. Douglas (1957) for example itemises:

(a) establishing the negotiating range;
(b) reconnoitring the negotiating range;
(c) precipitating the decision making crisis; and
(d) conducting the agreement.

Morley and Stephenson (1977) go a little further by looking at changes in behaviour roles and major features as the negotiation passes through phases at distributive bargaining, problem solving, and decision making. These regrettably, are insufficient to connect observation and causal explanation.

The Life Process

Unless the group process is brought to life the agreement cannot reach maturity. There is a shared responsibility for providing the energy at appropriate points. As the negotiating process proceeds along its way, it needs to be understood, respected, and guided by those taking part. The negotiation must be handled through its crises, and assisted to maturity until the optimal distribution for the parties involved is achieved. To do this effectively needs first of all an acceptance of shared responsibility for the process *as well* as the outcome and the awareness and skill to be able to work with rather than against the natural flow of the negotiation.

If our starting point is an appreciation and acceptance of the natural pattern of development of a negotiation, then something more than just a few static signposts is needed. The following journey/map of a negotiation (see Figure 7) is offered as a more detailed guide. Along the way some of the key roles which need to be played within the total negotiating group are highlighted, as are some of the major features or landmarks.

It can be clearly seen that the negotiation demands different approaches and responses at various times during the life-cycle of the process. A variety of skills and qualities will be needed by those who take part. There is therefore the

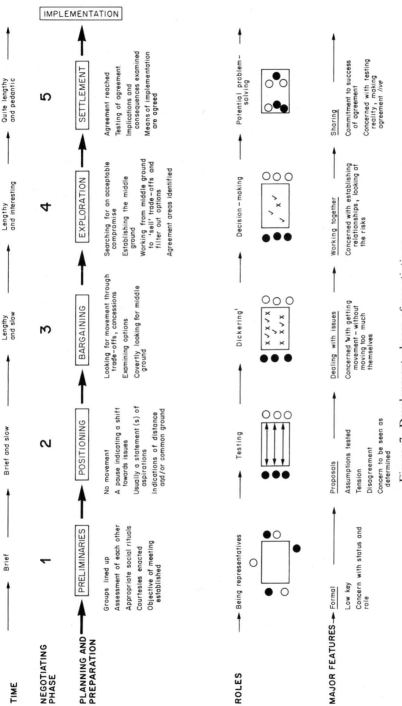

Figure 7. Development phases of negotiations

possibility of a wide range of different options making a vital contribution at some stage or other during the proceedings. This perhaps points towards the need to have such a range of skills and qualities available during the negotiation. This seems to be another very effective argument for having a negotiating team—a range of people, perhaps on both sides, to be able to call on the variety of approaches and stances required as the negotiation takes its course. Not to have these around often leads to jerky, interrupted progress, if progress is achieved at all.

Too often, too great a reliance is placed on one strong figure to lead the negotiation and provide a focus for all substantial contributions. Even if the negotiator were the type of genius who could cover all the areas needed, might it not be a little imprudent to rely too much on one figure? Where do you pick up after their defeat or departure? Genius and champion are impossible to duplicate!

All this points *not* to the superstar status British Standard Negotiator, but to the development of a flexible, sensitive, but tough capability in negotiators so they understand the negotiation as a process and can do what is necessary, however difficult, as and when it is needed. The practical requirements for achieving this are examined next.

Possible Directions to a Negotiation

Much of the effort of effective negotiators needs to be directed towards channelling the proceedings in the most appropriate directions according to the kind of development path outlined below. This might involve the following.

1. Identifying that the process is 'stuck' and needs some specific action to bring it to life again. This would then lead to the next point.

2. Bringing in a new quality which is needed to reach up to the next level, e.g. an openness in order to move the group from Bargaining to the Exploration phase; a summary of the agreement as they move to the Settlement phase.

3. Overcoming tensions and conflicts as the crisis between each phase is met.

4. Ensuring that the next stage is not entered into before the last one has been effectively consolidated—not moving too quickly. Recognizing that the process has a life and rhythm of its own.

There is not therefore an inevitability about a successful negotiation. Things can and do go wrong; progress through the various stages is certainly not a foregone conclusion. The possible directions the negotiation can take are summarized in Figure 8.

Anomie, deadlock, and agreement are all possible outcomes to the negotiation. All are possible ways of effectively keeping the ubiquitous thread of conflict under control. To be conscious of the possible directions the process can take and to be able to identify the likely turning points might make navigating the troubled waters of a negotiation that much less problematic.

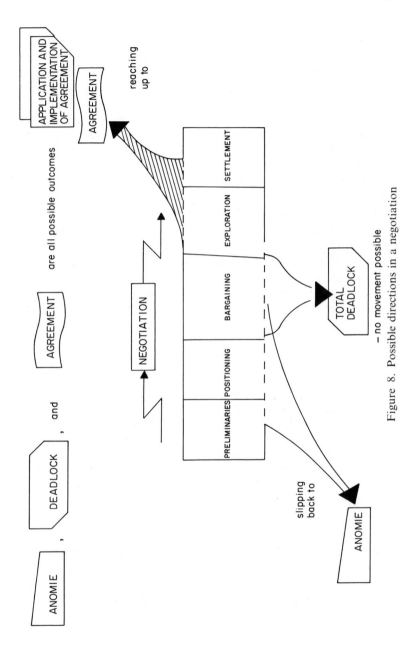

Figure 8. Possible directions in a negotiation

Directions

Anomie

Here we distinguish a damaging conflict from the less serious misunderstandings, tensions, and minor crises which characterize many social interactions. Here the negotiation degenerates into a pattern of relationships between the parties where they are no longer conscious of, or in full control of, their negative images of each other, and the violent behaviour which has taken the place of normally acceptable standards. The tendency for this degeneration to take place is always present and needs to be consciously guarded against in the process. If tensions are seen to be increasing, then specific action needs to be taken to prevent this degeneration. Once such a conflict has started it is very difficult to stop. As the negative mechanisms take hold, the parties themselves become increasingly unable to get themselves and the negotiation off the slippery slope.

Raising the temperature is a risky business in negotiations since it may be difficult to control thereafter. A minor neurotic response at an early stage of a negotiation can turn out to be pathological later on if it is allowed to fester. Some situations will obviously have a greater propensity to degenerate into conflict than others. Small-scale tensions which often appear at the 'pre-liminaries' stage of a negotiation should carefully be kept in check. To do this negotiators should look for advance signs of negative *trends* that negative patterns are being set up, not just isolated incidents. Most likely initial tensions will be felt within the parties themselves and this inside pressure then translates itself to the outside. The most likely focus for this tension is normally found in the following areas.

1. *Issues*—the subject matter of the negotiation may give rise to high tension. It could be, for example, over status, grievances, or fair treatment as well as widely differing objectives.

2. *Environmental Pressures*—the pressures applied to representatives by the broader group are well known. The reference group can act as a powerful unseen influence on the negotiator, particularly when concerned with questions of whether the agreement reached will be acceptable to the wider audience.

3. *Emotional responses*—the personality and temperamental mix of the negotiating group can have a strong influence on the likelihood of conflict being contained or not. A volatile mixture may be formed through natural inclinations or clumsy, unskilled group interaction.

Even if conflict tendencies can be contained, however, the route towards an eventual agreement may still be partially blocked through the following possible outcome.

Deadlock

Without evidence of any real conflict this is the point where the negotiations seem to be stuck, at an impasse. Naturally the barrier to overcome always appears to be enormous, insurmountable, at that particular moment. If it is carefully handled it can be reduced to its true proportion, as the skilled negotiator realizes that it is part of the total process, a natural stage along the way to an agreement. Sometimes environmental pressures prevent this effective approach, for example pressures from the outside for a 'quick' agreement are likely to be crowding out a more relaxed approach which might well be needed to resolve the impasse. The tendency to panic, give up, or do something dramatic increases as the deadlock continues.

To break a deadlock an appreciation of the flow of the whole process is essential. It must be understood that a natural pause in the proceedings has been reached. It is an opportunity to take stock and to gather strength before the next stage is entered. Often specific tactics are used to foster this kind of response. Negotiators adjourn for a while, separate to reduce the pressure, with the emphasis always being placed on 'coming back later'. Often stamina and the determination to eventually reach an agreement is the most important element at this stage. Eventually when the momentum is regained the negotiation moves towards an agreement.

Agreement

Here a contract is needed which is acceptable to all parties, and which will last. This indicates some formality in the expression of the agreement. It has to have the feel of a firm undertaking. Perhaps a little solemnity sets in as the importance of what has been agreed is made fully apparent to all parties. There is always a Go/No-go element about an agreement. Have we got one or not? Often it needs a definite risk to be taken to clearly confirm that commitment to the agreement has actually been reached. Often agreements are close at hand but go by default for the want of someone to confirm the fact. Nods and winks should give way to definite statements, e.g. 'I say yes to that!' 'I'll back that to the hilt.'

Determination and stamina are again important here, as agreements can prove too elusive, particularly as the final decision nears. So near and yet so far is often the case as feelings of personal risk and anxieties have to be assuaged. 'We are not leaving here until we have an agreement!' is often just the kind of statement of intent by a negotiator which can clinch the deal.

Expectations and the Negotiation

The direction which the negotiation will actually take, and how long it takes to move, will be determined to an extent by the dynamics of the negotiating process. What is said or done, how things are presented will have an influence on whether it descends to irresolvable conflict, gets stuck in a deadlock or reaches up to an agreement. This is not the full story, however, for the expectations which the parties bring to the negotiation proper also play a very important part in the process. They are well worth examining.

There is a tendency that negotiators will veer towards the most violent option open to them, given a discrepancy in expectations. So if one party expects a conflict to break out immediately whilst the other anticipates only a deadlock, then the likelihood is that they will end up with real friction—there will be always a pull towards the more extreme pole. A mismatch between expectations causes a raising of tension and negative images. For example, if party A has a less extreme expectation of conflict than B, then A is regarded as an unrealistic dreamer. A, on the other hand, probably regards B as something of a warmonger.

Even slight discrepancies create serious breaches and interruptions in the process. It may well be worthwhile attempting to classify the expectations and hopes which all parties carry with them into the negotiations and make these as explicit as possible in the beginning. At least then they can be worked on openly, and perhaps even adjusted to allow normal development. The matrix on Figure 9 indicates the range of expectations which have to be dealt with by negotiating groups.

The Slippery Slope

It is worth repeating that whenever expectations are out of line there is a strong tendency towards the more violent prophesy being fulfilled. This creates ample opportunity for 'I told you so', since our expectations are mostly about the other side, not ourselves. They are projections of the negotiator's own fears and doubts onto the other party. In them they see their more unstable, violent selves. So, although they may vehemently deny that they were predisposed to conflict ('No! *We* want agreement! It is they who want deadlock/conflict') the end result tends to be the same dysfunctional conflict. Negotiators interviewed during breaks in 'set piece' bargaining always claim that is the other side who are the aggressive ones. There is an element of playing to the gallery invariably in this stance but often there is also a strong element of self-justification.

The likelihood of conflict breaking out will be increased even further if the potential areas of agreement are hard to justify. Unless some common ground is located, however vague, then disillusionment can quickly set in and slipbacks occur. If the overall, transcendental objectives of the parties involved in the negotiation do not overlap to a minimum degree, then we are hardly in the negotiating business anyway. This is when the parties' expectations may be congruent with each other, but not with reality!

If the paths of both parties cannot be made to merge at any point, then agreement is impossible and deadlock and conflict likely as the negotiators search for the non-existent common ground. It would be better not to continue the negotiation beyond the preliminaries stage.

To summarize, the negotiation will retreat from agreement if:

PARTY A: 'I think that in the negotiations
             we are likely to get...'

Outcomes	Conflict	Deadlock	Agreement
Conflict	Conflict of an extreme volatile nature almost inevitable **SYMMETRICAL EXPECTATIONS**	Initial deadlock likely to slip back to conflict after a period unless positive action is taken to prevent it. Party A will feel disappointment, but may get over this in the long term. **ASYMMETRICAL EXPECTATIONS**	Conflict – highly probable. The party expecting agreement is likely to feel the gap acutely. There could be the danger of a breakdown of any long-term relationship. **ANTITHETICAL EXPECTATIONS**
Deadlock		Deadlock probably slipping back to conflict if agreement is not seen as a long-term possibility **SYMMETRICAL EXPECTATIONS**	Probable deadlock – how long the possibility of an agreement remains visible may depend on how strong Party A's convictions are. There is the danger that Party B will make too many concessions to meet A's desire for an agreement **ASYMMETRICAL EXPECTATIONS**
Agreement			Likelihood of agreement high – many of the rituals and preliminaries of negotiation could be dispensed with **SYMMETRICAL EXPECTATIONS**

PARTY B: 'I think that in the negotiations we are likely to get...'

Figure 9. Expectations matrix

(a) the expectations the parties have of each other are not symmetrical or

(b) the expectations the parties have about the likelihood of agreement are not met by reality.

Meeting Expectations—Acceptable Levels

Within this framework of expectations of possible outcomes will be also built up a sensitivity regarding the likelihood of movements and shifts in direction. Some of these potential movements will be looked on in alarm, others keenly anticipated. Danger signals or signs of optimism will be picked up and translated as indicators that things are going well, or not. The correct interpretation of these signals and trends will provide an invaluable platform on which to develop the skills needed to steer and guide the negotiations in the most positive direction. Within each phase of the negotiation certain characteristics will be anxiously looked for, others studiously avoided (Figure 10).

PERCEPTION BY THE NEGOTIATOR	Preliminaries phase	Positioning phase	Bargaining phase	Exploration phase	Settlement phase
HEALTHY	An element of personal 'meeting' tension Concern about seriousness of issues	A certain element of issue dis-tancing and objec-tivity Transition-ary dead-lock	Temporary deadlock -tension Personal and issue differen-ces clearly stated	Agreement on issues Commitment and feas-ability explored	Agreement – looking at full implica-tions, risks, and payoffs
UNHEALTHY	Deadlock Agreement anticipated too early and easily	'Fudging' of real differences between parties Inter-personal antagon-ism	Stasis Agreement in too much sacrifice by one side	Personal-izing of issues	Conflict Deadlock

Figure 10. Healthy and unhealthy 'signs' at different phases of a negotiation

Movement and Growth

Expectations are built up by the parties concerned not only about the probable outcome of the negotiation as a whole but are also focused on what the process is likely to involve as movement comes about in one direction or the other. The more this expectation about what could happen and what is likely to happen is translated into a real awareness of possibilities and responsibilities for giving life to those possibilities, the more skilled the negotiations have to be. This will reflect ultimately on the maturity of the negotiating group as a whole.

An understanding of the internal dynamics of the negotiating process is a key quality to be developed by the negotiating group. This covers:

(a) what causes changes in direction and

(b) which factors need emphasis and which require playing down.

This sensitivity to the subtleties and nuances of the process as a whole will really separate the professionals from the amateur. To be able to identify, then channel and divert the internal energy of the negotiating process demands real presence and skill. This sensitivity and skill is carefully nurtured by those who recognize its importance, and build it into an art with a surrounding mystique. This phenomenon of a mysterious 'feel' for negotiations which negotiators either have or do not have accounts to an extent for the awe and uncertainty with which many negotiations are approached. The universally recognized and respected 'good negotiator'—such as Kissinger a few years ago—is seen with this kind of aura. We cannot envisage what exactly he does but, by gum, it must be clever! Not so, he was merely good at recognizing what works and then doing it.

We have hopefully already shown that this 'feel' can be brought down to fairly precise descriptions of the flow of negotiations and the way in which the parties understand and relate to this. More particularly, however, it also involves carrying out fairly specific duties and responsibilities to maintain and nurture the life of the negotiating process. The way in which these are realized forms the final part of this discussion.

Maintaining the Group and the Negotiation

Every negotiator should have an awareness of the life and developmental processes of the group. This is the medium within which any agreement is to be reached and it must be sustained through the birth pains, nurtured to maturity, and eased into its death—whence emerges the agreement.

The negotiator is simultaneously required to protect the N group and to preserve his I group's objective, and this causes a remarkable tension which inexperienced negotiators are often incapable of handling. They either concentrate on sustaining the relationship and suddenly find they have sacrificed their own goals, or preserve their target intransigently only to find themselves stranded without a medium for achieving it.

It is impossible consciously and purposively to pay attention to both dynamics simultaneously. What usually happens is that the skilled negotiators intuitively handle the interactive, relational elements of the exchange for most of the time, while carefully, consciously evaluating the pragmatic issues. It is only when they feel a crisis looming in the relational area that they transfer all their attention to handling that aspect of the negotiation, putting issues to one side for a time. But usually they have such a 'feel' for the process that they can often consciously predict and pre-empt crises which occur at certain stages in the life of negotiating groups. Once again it is obvious how much the team approach can facilitate this process.

Maintaining the Group

In 1977 Roger Harrison published a paper called, significantly, 'The development of long-term working relationships', and because negotiations normally involve long-term relationships Harrison's paper is particularly relevant. The paper, which deals 'with the processes which occur when people work together', divides behaviour into two categories, namely Behaviour Categories for *Work*, and Behaviour Categories for *Relationships*. This parallels our thinking in this area, except that we address negotiating from a slightly different perspective:

(a) understanding the macro-process by looking at the negotiating group (N group) as a living, developing entity with a purposeful and limited existence, and

(b) by looking at the qualities and actions which sustain this existence for as long as it is useful.

Looking at the second case first it is clear that 'faith without good works is nothing'. Good intentions never kept a relationship healthy nor drew up a concordat. Actions did, and when we examine the skilled negotiator's behaviour we can see just how significantly these affect outcomes.

A Huthwaite Research Group study carried out between 1968 and 1976 indicates specific behaviours avoided and used by skilled negotiators in achieving successful agreements. We will examine some of these.

The skilled negotiator, when compared with the average negotiator, *avoids*:

Counter proposals—a proposal which directly follows the other party's proposal. It is very often seen as a statement of disagreement, and can also lead to too many issues being presented at once.

Defend–attack spirals—a series of subjective and sometimes emotional attacks, becoming progressively more intensive.

Irritators—these are not attacks, rather the opposite; but having the same effect, i.e. putting the emotional climate up. Characteristically these comprise gratuitous self-congratulatory statements such as: '*Our* reasonable proposition',

'A generous offer we made'.

The skilled negotiator will *use*:

Questioning behaviour—over twice as often as the average negotiator. These are issue *and* relation-centred, and for the latter are particularly useful at the crises characterizing the beginning and the agreement stage. A primary use of questions for the skilled negotiator is to establish common ground and avoid misunderstandings.

Giving feelings commentary—here the skilled negotiator drops the occasional comment about his internal state, i.e. 'I find what you've just said particularly helpful', etc. In the end people make agreements with people they feel they can trust to carry these out. Feelings commentaries facilitate these.

These two behaviours correspond directly with Harrison's category of 'Moving towards others', which in fact keeps the Negotiating Group moving forward, going with the flow.

Comment

A particularly interesting facet of the conscious application of negotiation activities is that the skilled negotiator is seldom aware of their behaviour in the relational area, but very clear about strategies and tactics. In other words, these interactive skills have become internalized, and unless there is an obvious breakdown they are applied subconsciously. The hypothesis is that perhaps the unskilled negotiator has to divert too much attention to face-to-face stimuli and this gives him less energy and time to devote to practical issues. (It would be worth considering the even greater importance of the team effort for the inexperienced negotiator.)

The 'feel' for the negotiating process works its way through into the actions and will of the negotiator at a largely secondary level of consciousness. Basic social and interactive skills are brought to the negotiating situation, link with a deeper understanding of the organic process of negotiating, and result in an ability to do what is necessary according to

(a) the role the individual negotiator has to play;

(b) the objectives of his/her side; and

(c) a concern for the overall effectiveness of the negotiation and the negotiating group in total.

In this way the negotiator and the negotiating process come together.

Final Summary

The Negotiator and the Process of Negotiating

Effective negotiations are more likely to take place within the right atmosphere and conditions. Part of the skill of conducting effective negotiations may depend just as much on creating this facilitative climate as skill at the eyeball-to-eyeball confrontation itself. This will be done through making certain aspects of negotiation open and clear before entering the negotiations proper. It will involve discussions about the process—how the negotiations are to be conducted and not the end product. This joint concern for preparation and how things are to be done will not come easily. For many involved with traditional forms of negotiation the whole idea of openness and discussions before a negotiation begins will be an anathema. More likely, an all-pervading atmosphere of dark suspicion and mistrust is promoted, cards are played closest to chest, and as little as possible about anything is revealed. Under such circumstances a great deal of effort must go into creating conditions conducive to negotiating. The task may be impossible but an attempt needs to be made to work on the following points.

1. Bringing expectations into line—at least discussing differences in expected outcomes.

2. Ascertaining whether there is any real overlap of aims, objectives, direction—at a fundamental level as well as superficially.

3. The real willingness to compromise—defining to an extent what is meant by a compromise. What do I expect of myself/others when compromise is called for?

4. Developing more skilled behaviour—in the whole range of social skills but more specifically in certain key negotiating areas (see Leary, 1980).

Perhaps a start could be made by asking better questions. Given that some of these *conditions* have been established, at least to a limited degree, what do we expect from the skilled negotiator? What separates them out from the rest? To see what is really important we will attempt to look behind the immediate phenomena to see what qualities are perhaps working at a deeper level. Above all the effective negotiator needs some, if not all, of the following qualities.

1. *Process sensitivity*—a sensitivity, a relationship to the negotiating process as a whole; a familiarity with the ebbs and flows of a negotiation, being in touch with those elements of negotiation which make it distinguishable from other methods of decision making and interacting.

Along with this 'feel' for the total, there is the key ability of being able to see onself as part of the process. Whilst being involved in what is going on deeply, nevertheless finding another way of looking at the totality with a helicopter vision, thus seeing more clearly what is needed at any given moment.

2. *A sense of time and movement*—a deep understanding of the time process and how this affects negotiations. This overall sense of time and movement can more specifically be brought down to an understanding of how the process of negotiations moves over time. The development phase of a negotiation provides a background for this understanding, but again is not enough if used as blueprint without being allied to a qualitative sense of what is following through this process.

3. *Judgement*—being in touch with the movements and trends of the negotiating process. This translates itself into an ability which correctly

anticipates future moves and changes in direction and reacts to them in a meaningful way. This means to bring personally, or call for in others, those qualities which are needed at a particular time in the negotiations. In this way the various tensions, sources of energy and movement within the negotiation can be used for positive ends.

4. *Behavioural skills*—even within this broader framework there will be the need for certain highly specific actions and behaviours at certain stages of the negotiation.

5. *Negotiating maturity*—above all, the one extra quality and dimension that may be required. Although we have talked of the conditions which ideally would be present as a lead into an effective negotiation, in the real world it is highly unlikely that all these conditions will be met. There will be barriers and constraints which need to be acknowledged and overcome. The ability to live with the pressures these obstacles present, whilst at the same time getting on with the task in hand will be a real test of the maturity of the negotiator.

Over time this maturity should build up. Social skill will meet a response on the other side. Shared responsibility for the health of the process as a whole is fostered and each side brings out the best in each other in a negotiating sense.

If any of these elements is neglected, then the effectiveness of the negotiation is seriously threatened.

Future Developments

For a long time a broad understanding of the negotiating process has been available. The development of negotiating skills and techniques has certainly not been neglected. The problem is that both are involved in successful negotiation and little work exists which examines the interaction of these two parts of the process.

Negotiating skills are largely concentrated on individuals. Little consideration is given to the overall skill capacity of the negotiating group. At best only one side is considered at any one time and even then not within the context of the group. Normally one individual is relied up on to come up with the goods.

Overall, little attention is paid to the additional elements identified here which are vital to the negotiation. Particularly:

(a) *Concern for the midwifery of agreements.*
   Bringing movement towards an agreement.
   Sensing and providing for the right pacing.
   Having the courage to look at the full consequences for the future of agreements considered.

Then

(b) *Concern for the life of the negotiation.*
   Handling the total process skilfully—including the death and finish as well as the birth and life of the N group.

Appreciating the need for an autumn and winter as well as the spring and summer and coping with these changes.

These concerns have to be the shared responsibility of the negotiating group as a whole, all sides and parties. Any efforts directed at increasing awareness of these factors, and developing the capacities of those involved to guide and direct the process, might best be done using the negotiating group as a whole as the training focus. If movement along this path is accepted, then joint training in the above areas for negotiating groups might not be far away and a better future for negotiations even closer.

References

Carlisle, J. (Huthwaite Research Group) (1980) 'Training negotiators', *Journal of European Industrial Training, MCB* **1**, 4.

Douglas, A. (1957) 'The peaceful settlement of industrial and intergroup disputes', *Journal of Conflict Resolution*, **1957**.

Harrison, R. (1977) 'The development of long-term working relationships', Unpublished paper.

Karrass, C. L. (1970) *The Negotiating Game*, New York and Cleveland, Ohio: World Publishing.

Leary, M. (1980) *Poles Apart—Conflict and Conflict Handling*, Gower Publications (in press).

Morley, I. and Stephenson, G. (1977) *The Social Psychology of Bargaining*, London: George Allen & Unwin.

Rackham, N. and Carlisle, J. (Huthwaite Research Group) (1978) 'The effective negotiator', *Journal of European Industrial Training, MCB* **2**, 6.

Walton, B. B. and McKersie, R. B. (1965) *A Behaviour Theory of Labor Negotiations: An Analysis of a Social Interaction System*, New York: McGraw-Hill.

PART III

Common Problems Facing Groups in Organizations

Groups at Work
Edited by R. Payne and C. Cooper
© 1981 John Wiley & Sons Ltd.

Chapter 8

The Use of Task Groups and Task Forces in Organizational Change*

Frank Friedlander and Barbara Schott

Introduction

There is an increasing use of groups in organizations which operate outside of and as a supplement to the formal hierarchy. These may be temporary or ongoing, ad hoc to a specific task assignment or free to develop their own agenda, representative of all major segments of the organization or of only specific parts, span several hierarchical levels or be drawn only from a single level. Frequently, the work group is appointed by top management or possibly by the organization to explore a specific question or issue affecting the total organization. It then reports back its recommendations and may or may not be responsible for implementation. In this latter sense the work group functions within the role of change agent inside the organization. How far it proceeds in the cycle of problem diagnosis, implementation, and evaluation is a function of both its organizational mandate and its own inclination.

We will refer to such a work group as a Task Group. Task groups are similar to and a type of collateral organization (Zand, 1974). They are similar to parallel organizations (Stein and Kanter, 1980) although they do not necessarily become part of the formal permanent structure of the organization. They are to be differentiated from hierarchical groups (in which formal authority still exists), employee problem-solving groups (formed to solve a specific production problem), and worker councils (formed to politically represent workers).

The reason for forming a Task Group rather than using the regular organization structure is that the latter is geared primarily for productivity and efficiency. The mobilization of people and equipment to optimize output calls for a hierarchical structure which lends itself to top-down authority and routinization of task efforts (Burns and Stalker, 1961). Plans and objectives are generally defined at the top, sub-divided by function, and directed downward. Such a structure serves to effectively allocate work, control, costs, and delegate responsibilities. An inevitable cost of this directive structure is a lack of sensitivity to emergent problems and to utilizing the human resources at lower levels in the organization (Schein and Greiner, 1977). These call for a more organic structure which is geared for knowledge generation and problem solving

* We appreciate the many helpful suggestions that Dr William Pasmore of Case Western Reserve University provided in reviewing an earlier draft of this chapter.

191

rather than productivity, control, and efficiency (Burns and Stalker, 1961). An organic structure promotes a climate of informality, creativity, and sensitivity and minimizes hierarchical levels and control in the service of problem exploration, knowledge gathering, and change.

The use of groups (rather than a single internal change agent) as a mode of organization development would seem to make sense. Work groups are better able to manage complex production systems (Pasmore and Sherwood, 1978), generate norms which influence the behaviour of their members (Roethlisburger and Dickson, 1950), provide learning for and linkages to their organization, and are used as counter-weights to formal organizational leadership (Zand, 1974). In terms of orienting a Task Group toward organization development values and methods, Lewin has commented that it is easier to affect the personality of ten people if they can be melted into a group than to affect the personality of any one individual separately (Zander, 1979).

Zand (1974) describes the purpose of collateral organizations as one of identifying and solving problems not solved by the formal organization. It creatively complements the formal organization, operates parallel to it, and draws its members from it. The outputs from the collateral organization are inputs to the formal organization.

Despite the proliferation and wide use of Task Groups (and collateral organizations), surprisingly little is known about how and when such groups are selected and formed, the processes they utilize both internally and with the remainder of the organization, problems they encounter, and what factors contribute toward the effectiveness and implementation of their recommendations. The purpose of this chapter is to explore these issues.

Three case studies are first presented. In each a Task Group was formed for the purpose of problem identification and problem solving. In each case the mission of the Task Group eventually went beyond these functions to one which included organization development functions. In the first case, the Task Group was formed by its own members, in the second case by the consultant, and in the third by the organization. These three cases were selected on the following bases: all represented the use of a Task Group; all became organization development projects; and finally, at least one of the authors was a consultant in each project.

After a description of each of the cases, an analysis is presented which focuses on three major areas which influence the group's effectiveness: its internal processes and identity, its interface with the rest of the organization (particularly top management), and how the implementation leads to outputs such as performance change, structural change, and organizational learning. Within these three major areas, we have derived inductively (Glaser and Strauss, 1967) sixteen concepts which are important to understanding the use of Task Groups in organizations. These concepts are linked together toward the construction of a theory of Task Group process within an organization. Finally, in the concluding section two major issues are discussed. One of these concerns the trade-off between the autonomy of the Task Group (which leads to innovative recommendations) and the degree to which it collaborates with the organization and top management (which leads to more traditional recommendations). The second issue concerns the negative consequences of disempowerment efforts that may occur between the Task Group and top management.

Chemtire Corporation—Administrative Group

The Administrative Group is composed of fifteen top managers at a major research and development facility. This case is an example of a task group that is structurally a permanent part of the organization rather than temporary in nature. Its purpose is general and ongoing, rather than specific and limited. Membership in the group is by virtue of one's position in the organization rather than by selection or appointment. These factors have specific consequences on the task group's development, its interface with other parts of the organization, and finally on its ability to implement change.

The group is responsible for managing a facility that is the centre for all research and development for a major international corporation which we will refer to as Chemtire. The company has a diverse product line. The Research and Development Centre, as it is called, employs about 400 scientific, technical, service, and support people. The managers in the Administration Group represent both divisional product lines and staff support.

Presenting Issues

At the request of the Administrative Group, an attitude survey process had been developed and conducted by the corporate organization development staff. The Administrative Group was facing a complex and demanding task—how would it respond to employee recommendations for change resulting from this process?

The attitude survey process had two phases. The first phase involved giving the attitude survey to all employees and feeding back the general results to the entire population. In the second phase, small cross-level groups were formed and facilitated by a consultant where specific data from the survey was fed back in order to check the validity of the survey results and develop recommendations for change based on employees' opinions and knowledge. What the Administrative Group was facing was: 'How do we respond to the recommendations we receive? Who will be responsible for turning the recommendations into action plans? Will we involve employees in the process? How will we keep the employees informed as to the action being taken?'

The author, who was an external consultant involved in the attitude survey process, was asked to present preliminary findings of the recommendation sessions to the Administrative Group. By that time it was clear that (1) the employees were sceptical about management's commitment to change and (2) management was uneasy about their own ability to handle the recommendations constructively.

Neither the Administrative Group's cohesion nor their problem-solving skills were developed well enough to tackle the job ahead. This was evidenced by managers severely limiting the amount of information they were willing to share, unwillingness to put aside individual concerns for the good of the Centre, lack of building on one another's ideas, and sporadic follow through on the rare occasions when decisions were made. This resulted in the author being asked to work with the Administrative Group to help improve their task team effectiveness.

Internal Dynamics

The next step was a 'needs assessment' questionnaire aimed at helping the Group understand how it viewed itself, where it might go, and some barriers it might encounter. There was consensus within the Administrative Group regarding its purpose which was to share information. This information-sharing was seen as the primary means of improving the Centre. Problem-solving skills were considered inadequate.

Some of the following concerns came to light: additional time would be needed for working together on the recommendations; fear that employee participation might mean loss of power and control; concern over what kind of leadership the group wanted/needed; difficulty of being effective with a group of fifteen; and large differences in the level of trust members felt in dealing with sensitive issues within the group.

Influence. Although all members occupied similar positions in the organizational hierarchy, the amount of influence each exerted within the Administrative Group varied. This variance can be explained by two factors: personal style and divisional representation.

Personal style of influence refers to one who is talkative, extroverted, and willing to take risks and thus is allowed more influence. Within the group there were three common ways in which personal style was used to exert influence. The first was by setting the agenda. This method was used most frequently by the Employee Relations Manager, who would have the agenda typed and given to the moderator prior to meetings with the suggestion that other items could be added. The second method, used by about half the members, was to introduce areas of special interest during the meeting. These presentations often lacked specificity, thereby inhibiting the group's engagement with these issues. In this way the presenter was able to inform others and appear collaborative while avoiding the influence of others. The third way members influenced the group was through blocking or diverting; this was a means of stopping someone else rather than advancing one's own cause. For example, when something was being discussed that a member was not in agreement with, the member would switch topics, precluding closure on the original issues.

The second factor, divisional representation, refers to the size or number of people employed in one's division and the amount of profit one's division accounts for in the total organization. The manager of the Chemical Division, for example, could easily resist unwanted change by virtue of the fact that his division was the corporation's biggest money maker.

Structure. The group structure was flexible in the sense that nothing about its policies and procedures was in writing. Formal leadership was restricted to a moderator, who was chosen by consensus for an undetermined length of time. The person who was serving as moderator when the consultant worked with the group was one of the least influential members. His job was to see that there was an agenda for the meeting and to 'keep things moving'.

In conclusion, the feedback of this information sparked considerable energy in the group. Two things were occurring. First, the group was beginning to build a joint perception of itself including its strengths and weaknesses. Secondly, as a group they were becoming actively involved in the survey feedback process, as evidenced by their feelings of responsibility for whatever outcomes would result.

Interface

As the Administrative Group gained a further sense of itself, it now faced the task of managing its interfaces with its relevant environments. The two most significant interfaces were with employees and the organizational development group at corporate headquarters.

Employees. The boundary between the Administrative Group and the R & D Centre employees in the beginning was handled quite differently by each manager. Some managers regularly reported to their employees the activities of the Administrative Group, while other managers did not. Some employees regarded the Administrative Group as 'a light-weight group that does not really accomplish much' because communication between the two groups was negligible.

There was no formal way for employees to have input into the Administrative Group. Informally a manager could bring the Administrative Group's issues or decisions to his employees, but this was not common. At the same time, because members of the Administrative Group also represented their own functional area (employee relations, chemicals, etc.), some managers were accused of promoting their individual 'kingdoms' to the detriment of the total Centre.

As the recommendation sessions progressed and the Administrative Group began to contemplate their new role of helping to implement some change based on the recommendations, the managers began, as a group rather than individually, to respond to the R&D employees. Bulletins were posted on a regular basis and the in-house newsletter carried articles keeping the total Centre informed of the progress and actions of the Administrative Group related to the survey process. Employees began to express some mild hopes and expectations that the Administrative Group would respond to their recommendations.

Corporate OD. The second interface, Corporate OD, became critical as the Administrative Group began to assume responsibility for the outcomes of the attitude survey process. Up to that point the interactions across the boundary had been polite and politically respectful. Corporate OD had considerable power to assess and restructure departments and divisions to the extent of creating or eliminating positions up to the Vice Presidential level. The Administrative Group's attitude toward Corporate OD was initially one of caution that grew out of both a fear of OD's motives and doubts about their expertise. As time passed and the Administrative Group gained momentum, they sent suggestions to Corporate OD regarding the nature of the information they wanted from the final analysis of the recommendation sessions. After considerable debate, the Administrative Group decided to hold a three-day off-site workshop that would include group development for the Administrative Group and action planning around the attitude survey recommendations. They further planned to have consultants who were not a regular part of the organization conduct the workshop. They reasoned that this would provide them with greater freedom to explore their own shortcomings than if OD people with a direct line to corporate headquarters were present.

This decision had serious repercussions for the Administrative Group. First, Corporate OD insisted on running the workshop since it had come about as a result of the attitude survey they had conducted. This brought the managers together as a group around the perceived external threat. The Administrative Group considered resisting Corporate OD by refusing to have their staff conduct the workshop. However, with some help from the consultant, the Administrative Group developed a clearer sense of how they were a part of a complex and interactive network of groups within the larger system. They came to understand that their resistance would lead to alienation from Corporate OD which might, in turn, have negative consequences for either the Centre or some managers. Finally, by developing a strategy which included the use of both internal and external consultants, the manager met some of their needs to retain control over the workshop.

In conclusion, both the interface with employees and Corporate OD presented some problems, but the Administrative Group was developing to the point where it could recognize and cope with its needs, limitations, and power in relation to other relevant parts of their environment.

Outcomes

The Administrative Group has been in existence for about seven years. It continues to meet on a regular basis. Some of the changes that have occurred are the following.

Spin-off groups, made up of employees and managers, have been created. An example of this is a scientist/manager group that has visited other R&D labs around the country to see how the career ladders of technical people and managers could be made more equitable. The results of the study led to policy changes related to career development.

The use of subgroups within the Administrative Group occurs on a temporary task basis where, for example, Maintenance and Employee Relations might tackle a problem jointly and report back to the total group.

Both the size and composition of the group has been altered slightly. The numbers of people who are included have been reduced, thus eliminating a few managers who were not directly involved in the overall operation of the Centre and had little to contribute. An informal change in composition has resulted from managers being more willing to send assistants or other employees who have something to contribute. So, while the size has decreased, the variety of input has increased. Although information sharing remains its primary function, the Administrative Group has somewhat higher expectations for itself concerning accountability and follow-through.

St James Plant—Study and Communications Group (SAC)

The St James Lamp Plant is part of the Lamp Manufacturing Division of Woodmere Electric, a large, diverse, multi-national electronics corporation. St James is a non-union plant located in a relatively rural area. It has a workforce of about 400; 90 per cent of the non-supervisory employees are female and 100 per cent of the supervisors are male.

Presenting Issues

The plant had experienced ongoing, unexplained complaints from employees of physical soreness, mostly on the hands and arms. Over a period of three years prior to the consultants' entry, 30 per cent of the workforce had experienced some soreness. This had led to absenteeism, loss of productivity, increasing numbers of workmen's compensation claims, and nineteen cases of surgery.

The plant had been opened in 1971 and for the next two years had gained a reputation among corporate management as a 'country club'. In 1973 new management took over the plant with the clear mission of increasing productivity by clamping down on employees. The supervisor of Shop Operations became known as the 'drill sergeant', providing harsh, impersonal pressure upon factory workers for increased productivity, punishing absentee and tardy employees, and generally being intolerant of laxity. This pressure was sustained by foremen, who had little opportunity to practise anything but a high task-oriented, autocratic leadership style. The foremen were given production figures to be met and orders to be carried out. Their input was rarely elicited. The foremen, in turn, passed on their pressures and frustration to employees, without much consideration for workers' problems. The result of this autocratic management style was impotency of the foreman level and passive resistances at the worker level.

The consultants were first contacted by Division Management (two levels above the Plant Manager). After two meetings, Division Management recommended to Plant Management that it consider the use of consultants in exploring the soreness problem. Although Plant Management had some mixed feelings, they welcomed the consultants eagerly, quite willing to hand over to the consultants the entire soreness problem and what should be done about it.

Internal Dynamics

Early on, the consultants made the recommendation that a 'core group' be formed of plant employees. The core group, which became known as the Study and Communication Group (SAC), would work collaboratively with the consultants in (a) gaining a better understanding of the plant climate and the causes of the soreness problem; (b) gathering and conveying information to the workforce; and (c) making suggestions to management for organizational changes. The rationale for the proposal was based on the following: (a) the soreness problems were experienced by the factory employees; *they* would, therefore, be in a good position to diagnose the causes of soreness, including undue psychological stress, machine-determined methods and psychological climate factors, which might be causing soreness; (b) employees were feeling oppressed, powerless, and under-utilized; consultants working with them collaboratively and sharing responsibility with them would afford them the opportunity of using their ideas, feeling greater responsibility, and empowering them; (c) the core group would create a model within the plant of management, foremen, workers, and consultants working collaboratively to share this responsibility and power; and (d) that whatever changes were eventually recommended would be more fully implemented by the workforce if these changes were derived from the workforce. Over the longer term, it was hoped that a capacity for identifying and analysing issues, for suggesting solutions, and for implementing these could be built into the workforce.

Formation. The idea of a core group was accepted by management. It was formed by the consultants who asked management to propose a list of twenty names of which six hourly workers were chosen by the consultants based on the following criteria. Two workers were chosen from each of the three major departments, one worker from the first and second shift, half the group was pro-management and half anti-management (as viewed by management), and half experienced soreness as a result of work. Two foremen known and respected by factory workers were also to be in the group. The Employee Relations Manager was to be in the group and to serve as a link with management. After the six names were selected, management notified workers to come for interviews. Most were genuinely interested, but some who accepted felt they did not have a choice. One person declined.

Development. Concurrent with the formation of the SAC group, several other groups were formed. A Steering Committee composed of the Plant Manager, the Supervisor of Employee Relations, Supervisor of Shop Operations, and the Supervising Engineer were members of this group. The purpose of the Steering Committee was to review all SAC recommendations and make all implementation decisions. This committee also worked with the consultants to understand and improve its management style. A Review Committee (of counterparts of each of those positions, but at the division level) was formed as an umbrella group to support plant management in making needed changes.

Initial meetings of the SAC were focused on creating the identity of the group in terms of its purpose, method of operation, and in building an aggregate of people into an operative group. Because this represented a new role for employees, it took some time before the group fully understood its charge. One of the challenges to the group in its early and middle stages was its own pessimism and sense of powerlessness. Members had learned to be reactive and passive and to not assume responsibility for anything other than the specific job functions that they were to perform. They had also learned that management was reluctant to accept suggestions and was unresponsive to most upward messages.

The first concrete task for SAC was to work jointly with the consultants in designing a questionnaire for all hourly employees. A three-hour SAC meeting was spent in members suggesting questions, possible causes of soreness, and other relevant plant issues. The final questionnaire was a result of that session. This was an initial step in developing group identity as SAC now saw itself as able to influence the consultants and produce something concrete.

Interface

Questionnaires and interviews were analysed by the consultants and this data were reported back to SAC through various charts, tabulations, and graphs. SAC and the consultants put a good deal of work into understanding, analysing, and interpreting these results. The next task was to interface with the Steering Committee and employees regarding the findings.

Steering committee. Copies of these charts and tabulations were then sent to members of the Steering Committee on the day before a joint meeting of SAC and the Steering Committee. It is worth noting at this point that there was little formal interaction between SAC and the Steering Committee prior to this meeting. The intent of the joint meeting was for the consultants and SAC to feed back the results of the questionnaire and interview data, to discuss these findings jointly, and to collaborate on possible action steps that might be taken at that point.

The meeting was marked with explosiveness, conflict, and defensiveness. Management felt the data were overly critical. They claimed the questions themselves were biased, that employees did not know the 'facts', and SAC with the help of the consultants had interpreted their responses in order to make a point. The gap between management and workers widened. The credibility of the consultants was endangered. On one hand, SAC members were angry and questioned whether management ever meant to make any changes. Underlying the anger was a good deal of anxiety and hopelessness. On the other hand, they experienced more loyalty to one another and greater dedication to their task.

The consultants worked with the Steering Committee from this point on to strengthen their understanding of themselves and their abilities to manage change. Defensiveness began to fade, some constructive energy was developed, ill feelings towards SAC lessened, and slowly the credibility of the consultants was reinstated. Several joint SAC–Steering Committee meetings followed. Each one was increasingly constructive.

Employees. The next step for SAC was to help design the feedback process to the workforce. The consultants suggested that a report be written and circulated to all employees, but SAC members preferred a face-to-face feedback to workers in groups of twenty to thirty. SAC exerted its influence over the consultants in establishing their method. A consultant and one SAC member fed back data to each group.

SAC entered the next phase of developing recommendations for changes based on the data with renewed energy. The one overriding suggestion by SAC was 'a group such as ours should be a permanent part of this organization'. In addition, recommendations were made to the Steering Committee: (1) to provide job rotation experiments and (2) to begin a foreman's training program. These recommendations were approved by the Steering Committee at joint meetings of the two committees.

Outcomes

The Steering Committee, meanwhile, was making some recommendations of its own. These included revision of work methods in three different locations during the following six months. In each of these cases the Steering Committee called upon SAC to help initiate these experiments and work jointly with management. In each case the SAC representative from the relevant department played an instrumental role in helping set up and legitimize experimental job redesign groups composed of workers who held the jobs in question, method experts, and a mechanical specialist. In all three cases the SAC member helped workers in that department join in a highly participative exploration of methods that would be both efficient and yet prevent the re-occurrence of 'sore arm'. All three projects were successful in increasing the production rate and in preventing soreness symptoms.

A follow up some two years after the above changes indicated that SAC was still very much in existence, although it is now called the Sounding Board. It has become somewhat formalized. Members are nominated by workers from their respective departments. They receive an orientation either by the group or by a member of the Industrial Relations Department who has group facilitator skills. Members serve a six-month term on Sounding Board and seem to have high energy for taking on a variety of task functions. Management sees one of the main functions of the group as a communication link with employees. In addition, thirty workers have now served on the Sounding Board and have thereby become exposed to and participated in its activities. Management reports that the Sounding Board has broken down some barriers between labour and management.

The Steering Committee and the Sounding Board have joint meetings once a month. Most of their work is in response to ideas initiated by the Steering Committee. Management asks Sounding Board members for their views on ideas for new or revised programs and methods. Thus, most of the Sounding Board activity is in response to ideas initiated by the Steering Committee. Examples include a scrap reduction programme, absenteeism procedures, a break schedule change, and several production methods changes. Examples of programmes initiated by the Sounding Board include new procedures for job bidding and job rotations. In general, the Sounding Board acts more as its name suggests—as a sounding mechanism rather than as a group responsible for tracking, following up, or evaluating changes.

The joint meetings between the Sounding Board and the Steering Committee are going quite well. In general, there is a fairly balanced initiation on the part of each group. The Sounding Board feels supported and the Steering Committee feels receptive.

The substantive outcomes from the total project are more clear than the process outcomes. The former include increased productivity and lowered absenteeism, scrap rate, and soreness. Whether the organization has learned how to use the full resources of its workforce in studying and making recommendations is not as clear. It would seem as though management has re-directed the mission of the original SAC concept from a pro-active group which takes responsibility for identifying problems, diagnosing them, recommending action steps, and evaluating the repercussions, to a more reactive group which primarily responds to management initiatives and serves as a conduit for management programs. Yet, perhaps a SAC concept needed to occur as it did before a Sounding Board activity would be acceptable and effective.

ABC Law Firm—Retreat Committee

The ABC Law Firm is a large firm of approximately seventy-five partners and about seventy associates. Its primary offices are in a major midwestern city with about one-quarter of its staff located in the Washington, D.C. area.

ABC, like most law partnerships, has relatively few formal hierarchical levels. The highest level is an elected seven-person group called Managing Partners. The second level is Partners—those who have been elected to Partnership, and finally a third level, those not elected to Partnership, referred to as Associates.

Presenting Issues

At a recent Partners meeting, ABC had decided upon having a three-day retreat for members at a remote location. The reasons for having a retreat were somewhat nebulous at this point, but seemed to concern improving the relationship between the headquarters and Washington offices and with a vague stated need for members to engage in more social contact. A 'Retreat Committee' of seven Partners had been appointed at the Partners meeting, and this was to become the liaison group or client group. It was responsible for the retreat and, as such, its initial step was the actual selection of the consultant.

Internal Dynamics

Two facts are noteworthy at this point: first, that the Retreat Committee was formed by the organization (not by the consultants) for the clear and express purpose of managing the retreat, and secondly, that the selection of consultants and agreements with them were made by this group (rather than top management—the managing Partners).

Formation. The Retreat Committee was appointed at a meeting of all partners on the basis of a heterogeneity of interests and perspectives. Similarly, its chairman was appointed at that meeting. Its members varied in age, tenure with the firm, and legal specialization. No Managing Partners were members of the committee. It thus represented homogeneity in terms of status levels. This had the effect of allowing members to express their opinions freely; yet it presented a disadvantage in not allowing overlapping membership (and therefore ready access) with the Managing Partner group.

At the initial meeting, the consultants discussed with the Retreat Committee the possibility of using the retreat to do problem solving and action planning on issues which were affecting the law firm as a whole. The consultants suggested that interviews be conducted with a sample of Partners in order to find what major issues the firm was facing, as perceived by Partners. Questionnaires were also to be given to all Partners in order to deduce their opinions on a variety of issues that emerged from the interviews. Thus, the Retreat Committee expanded its initial missions and revised its identity. Its mission had been expanded from responsibility for the retreat to responsibility for diagnostic data gathering and the retreat, with both of these activities seen as potential steps in a context of longer-term organizational change.

Development. The group and consultants met on about ten occasions during the succeeding two months. The task for these meetings followed those of an action research cycle. Early meetings focused on reaffirming the contract and process to be used by the consultants, designing interview questions, selecting which Partners (between twenty and twenty-five) would be interviewed, designing and wording letters sent by the Retreat Committee which introduced and explained the interviews, and arranging for interviews. During these meetings, expectations, courage, power, and energy increased significantly as the committee saw the importance of its mission and purpose: organizational change. The group became more invested in this mission, in its own cohesion, and in the consultants. In turn, the consultants became more energized and more credible to the group. In addition, a significant amount of 'inside' information was shared by the committee members on their perceptions of the organization and its problems. This became an invaluable input to the consultants as they designed and conducted the interviews. Finally, the committee and the consultants jointly developed a careful strategy intended to optimize the opportunity for organizational change. This was evidenced, for example, in the committee's suggestions of those to be interviewed, and the questions to be asked in those interviews.

The next set of meetings with the Retreat Committee focused on feedback of interview data, building a framework of the firm from this data, and designing questionnaires based, in part, on the data. During these sessions, members of the Retreat Committee freely offered interpretations of the interview data, added data of their own, and found the framework constructed by the consultants an enlightening and useful method for conceptualizing their organization. This framework incorporated, and thus legitimized, the diversity of perspectives represented in the Retreat Committee, and thus allowed each committee member not only to feel his perspective was included and accepted, but that other perspectives need not be excluded or rejected. These sessions were enhanced by members freely sharing their individual views and perceptions, building upon views of each other, and gathering momentum and power as a high energy and diagnostic team.

Interface

Thus far the Retreat Committee had been in continual contact with the remainder of the organization through occasional memos and through informal verbal conversations. The latter were generally achieved by each individual Retreat Committee member discussing issues with other Partners in their representative departments. The memos were concerned with the process the Retreat Committee was planning to use and its subsequent process. The Retreat Committee, in turn, received suggestions and feedback on its progress from Partners concerning both the Retreat Committee process and the retreat design. The questionnaire to be constructed and sent out next took into account a number of these suggestions. Its purpose became not only to collect more representative, more objective data (compared to the interviews) but also to respond to many of the Partners' feelings of being excluded from the interview process. The Retreat Committee provided many ideas for the questionnaire which the consultants used in its construction. A draft of the questionnaire was reviewed and finalized by the Retreat Committee, which then sent it with an appropriate cover letter and a return envelope addressed to the consultants. Results were then tabulated and fed back to the Retreat Committee.

At this point the Retreat Committee and the consultants worked collaboratively toward a design for the three-day retreat which would be stimulating and engaging for partners, provide full feedback of the collected data and framework, encourage Partners to add further data, and focus on using these data toward problem-solving and action implementation steps. Its self-perceived power, insight, and energy aided the Retreat Committee's process of designing and strategizing the three-day process which would accomplish this. It built into the design key roles for its own members in both plenary sessions for all seventy-five Partners and in smaller discussion groups in which Retreat Committee members became discussion leaders. One week before the retreat the consultants spent a half-day training the Retreat Committee members in group leadership skills.

From discussions with the Retreat Committee, concerns arose about the implementation of action steps during and after the retreat. As a result, contact was made with the Managing Partners' group early in the project in reviewing the retreat design. Suggestions and concerns by the Managing Committee were fed back to the Retreat Committee and incorporated into designs. Plans were also made for a joint meeting of the Managing Partner and Retreat Committee during the retreat.

The retreat itself was organized around the major themes which emerged from the interviews: provision of opportunities to renew interpersonal and professional relations, an exploration of the causes and effects of disunity and differentiation within the firm; an examination of the changing environment for the field of law and how this affected the fields in which ABC practises or should practise; how the firm organizes itself to cope with expansion and change; and an exploration and discussion of the conflicting styles and disagreements between the midwestern and Washington offices. In each of these areas feedback was given to the total Partnership, small groups explored possible remedies and solutions, and each group presented its suggestions (which were recorded on tape) to the total Partnership. A more pervasive issue, which cut across all themes, was how ABC might change its process, structures, and climate in order to enhance planning, coordination, control, a sense of involvement, utilization of Partners' ideas and views, and monitoring ABC's changing environments.

During the retreat the Retreat Committee played an active and visible role both in leading discussions and in linking up with other partners who were particularly relevant to the process and to its future implementation of action recommendations. A joint meeting between the Retreat Committee and the Managing Partners was held which resulted in the latter conducting the last one-hour session reviewing the retreat and looking toward future action steps.

Yet it was clear at this meeting and in the final one-hour session that the Managing Partners were not totally supportive of either the data or the solutions which emerged at the retreat. The Managing Partner committee felt responsible for the shortcomings and weaknesses discussed at the retreat about ABC, and became somewhat defensive. They claimed that the firm was highly successful as it was, and saw little need for any major changes. Their response was more diplomatically stated as: 'There is no need to rush into action steps. We will need to go over the final report thoroughly and then see what action is called for.'

Outcomes

One outcome of the retreat was the report compiled by the Retreat Committee of the interview and questionnaire results and the reports on each major theme by sub-groups. This report was sent to all ABC members. During the following weeks a few (but by no means a majority) of the recommendations made during the retreat were implemented. These concerned changes in staffing and eva-luation procedures, and the initiation of efforts to review law specialization needs and resources within the firm. But many of the more underlying change recommendations were not implemented, and the membership lost much of the excitement and energy that developed during the retreat.

Perhaps a longer range outcome was the introduction to the organization of a process and structure for exploring and surfacing issues, for collaborative problem solving, and for creating the energy and commitment for change. This 'learning capacity' on the part of the organization was enhanced by the creation and development of a high energy, enlightened group (the Retreat Committee). Although the existence of the Retreat Committee ended when it distributed its report, it learned not only substantively about its organization, but more importantly learned through its own experience a process for achieving organizational change.

Analysis

The method used to understand Task Group development and effectiveness in the organization is based on Glaser and Strauss's concept of grounded theory. Starting from the point of actual experience (i.e. the three cases just described), the method proceeds to a content analysis of the cases and moves toward building a theory of Task Group process.

A summary of some of the salient characteristics of the three Task Groups is presented in Table 1. This table provides the reader with a convenient way to

Table 1 Summary of characteristics of the three Task Groups

	Chemtire Corporation Administrative Group	St James Lamp Plant Study and Communications Group	ABC Law Firm Retreat Committee
Internal dynamics			
Formed by	Self	Management	Total organization
Espoused purpose	Exchange information and improve organization	Diagnose and recommend change	Arrange retreat
Actual purpose	Information exchange (not problem solving)	To help diagnose and influence plant problems; to help management influence plant	To help diagnose, analyse, feedback data toward potential organizational change
Membership	Open—any manager	Restricted to appointed or elected representatives	Closed—appointed by organization
Number in group	Fifteen	Ten	Seven
Initial intervention	Feedback of preliminary recommendations; needs assessment questionnaire	Discussions of group identity and purpose; team building	Discussion of group's mission; design and manage retreat and/or organization development
Group leadership	Moderator only	Formal by members; informal by consultants	Committee chairperson

Interface			
Seen by rest of the organization	Not too powerful as a group	Not powerful, but provided hope	Power to organize retreat; not powerful to implement change
Input methods	Written analysis of attitude survey; written analysis of recommended sessions	Workers, steering Committee, attitude survey, interviewer	Informal discussion, interview questionnaire, retreat discussion groups
Primary interface	R & D employees; Corporate OD	Steering Committee; workers in respective departments	Managing Partners Group
Boundary interaction	Initially restricted intake; sporadic output	Initially withholding, then formal presentation of all information at once	Restricted, then formal
Tone	Frustration with lack of decision making and follow-through; commitment to improve the organization	Balance of scepticism and hope	High energy, vital but scared
Outcomes			
Structural and substantive changes	Spin-off groups; some restructuring in Administrative Group; policy change in career development; job posting	Created an ongoing employee group to test out ideas and improve communication between management and employees; job redesign; job rotation; increase productivity; decreased 'sore arm', scrap and absenteeism	Changes in staffing and evaluation procedures; mechanism for identifying issues, gathering information, analysing and feeding back
Organizational learning	Improved problem-solving skills; greater employee participation; uses and limitations of confrontation and collaboration	Improved use of workers' resources through participation; greater responsibility assumed by employees	Improved use of partners in identifying problems and generating alternatives

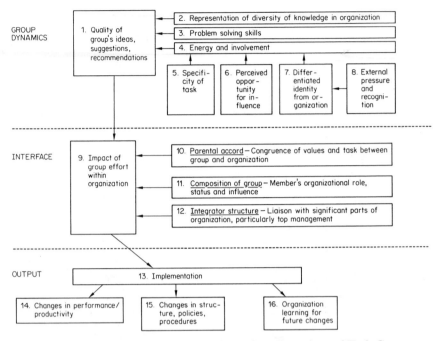

Figure 1. Development of internal and interface dimensions of Task Groups

recall, compare, and contrast the three cases. These characteristics, in turn, fell into three main categories: *internal dynamics* within each of the Task Groups; *interface* between the Task Group and all other relevant parts of the organization; and *outputs* resulting directly or indirectly from the Task Group's efforts.

These three categories later serve as the conceptual ground upon which the Task Group process is conceptualized. Further analysis indicates several dimensions were particularly crucial to the development and effectiveness of the Task Groups. These are depicted as crucial concepts in Figure 1 together with hypothesized cause–effect connections between concepts. A discussion of these crucial concepts and connections is presented below. Numbers in parentheses refer to the numbered concepts in Figure 1.

Internal Dynamics

In order for a Task Group to offer (1) high quality ideas, suggestions, and recommendations (2) based on a sound data collection and analysis, it must have within its boundaries adequate and diverse substantive knowledge and (3) adequate group skills to tap this knowledge. These group skills include such things as the group's ability to make decisions, solve problems, build on one another's ideas and confront one another in a constructive manner. In the three cases presented, we found that (2) a diversity of knowledge was needed in the Task Group which matched the diversity in the organization. We include here not only the technical knowledge, but also political knowledge which represents and parallels the various departments or specializations in the larger organization. By political knowledge we mean an understanding of what is important to who, how to interpret information according to who said it, and who in the organization needs to be included in the Task Group knowledge base. Without this, either the mission of the group suffers, the Task Group works with insufficient knowledge, or the Task Group is unable to sense the political issues in these departments and specializations. For example, SAC tended to lack the diversity of a production/engineering perspective and was hampered by this. Diversity of skills offers the group greater flexibility in its task (Hackman, 1976). And finally, ideas and recommendations by the Task Group which represent diverse technical and political knowledge are more likely to be accepted by the diversity in the organization and, therefore, implemented. Diversity also may lead to either conflict among various parties or withdrawal of one party. For example, in the Administrative Group (the most diverse of the three groups) differences and conflict tended to be submerged until group skills were provided to the group. Thus, Group Skills (3) are needed for tapping the representative knowledge and for making productive use of the differences, conflict, and competition among diverse interests.

A third major ingredient which contributed to Task Group effectiveness was (4) high energy and involvement in the specific task at hand. Thus, a group may have the appropriate breadth of knowledge and group skills for using that knowledge, but unless there is a sense of excitement about the task, energy and motivation will dissipate. We found that in groups where (5) the task was specific and concrete (i.e. Retreat Committee) or where a concrete task emerged from a more vague one (i.e. Administrative Group), energy and involvement noticeably increased. These results parallel findings in socio-technical experiments that autonomous work groups which are effective have a well-defined, identifiable, clearly differentiated, whole and significant task (Hackman, 1976; Cummings, 1978).

Similarly, as all three groups perceived themselves as potent in terms of (6) possibly influencing and changing the organization, they became increasingly energized and involved. This sense of potency was enhanced as the group saw opportunities for and the viability of influence and change in the organization. In a sense, the identity of the group took on as one of its purposes change and influence. For example, as its task became one of using the data from the attitude survey for possible organizational changes (as compared to its initial purpose of information exchange) the Administrative Group members became increasingly involved and motivated.

Another variable leading to increased energy and involvement was the group's self-perceived identity as (7) differentiated from the remainder of the organization. As clearer boundaries developed, the group took on a more distinct meaning and distinct responsibilities which made it separate from, yet part of, the organization. It felt acknowledged, responsible, a force to be dealt with. The formation of this differentiated identity was often fostered by (8) some pressure or confrontation from the organization or from a more powerful group. For example, SAC's identity in its own eyes became clearer after its confrontation with the Steering Committee. It felt an increased sense of its own boundaries and cohesion and clearer about its responsibility to the Steering Committee. Through this confrontation the Steering Committee acknowledged SAC as a force to be dealt with.

Interface with the Organization

Obviously, a Task Group can develop and recommend high quality ideas for planned change based on a thorough data collection and diagnosis, yet fail in getting any of these ideas and changes accepted or implemented by the organization. Thus, a second major cluster of concepts derived from our studies was concerned with the relations between the Task Group and other relevant groups in the organization. The concepts in this cluster all related to (9) the impact of the Task Group's effort in relation to the remainder of the organization. But specifically, the crucial element was the power the Task Group had and the strategy it used relative to the top management group in that organization. Insufficient power or poor strategy led to subtle or more blatant action by top management in disconfirming the group, questioning its credibility, changing or co-opting its mission, disagreeing with its diagnosis, or procrastinating on action decisions (ABC Law Firm). All of these top management reactions obviously inhibited or prevented implementation of action steps recommended by the Task Groups. What was needed was a sharing or even mutual enhancement of power between the Task Group and the top management group.

The concepts in the interface cluster each contribute to the impact of the Task Group in different but related ways. *Parental Accord* (10) represents the degree to which the group membership, values, and perceived task are congruent with those of the organization. Congruence of values seems to be the underlying variable in this cluster. If the values of the Task Group are consistent with those of the organization, its findings and recommendations are likely to be more acceptable to top management and the organization. We are implying that organizational diagnosis is a process not simply based on factual data gathering and analysis, but that the very questions asked in a diagnosis and the way they are interpreted are governed by the value stance of the Task Group. Perhaps the most relevant way that the degree of value congruence is acted out by the Task Group is the boundary within which its task is defined. Again, a congruent definition of the task between the Task Group and the organization contributes to parental accord. Congruence of both values and task boundaries would seem to be a more likely occurrence if the Task Group is appointed by the organization or by top management rather than if it is self-appointed. Yet in two of our three cases, this did not occur.

Several examples from the cases demonstrate these findings. In ABC, although the retreat committee was appointed by the total partnership, its task boundaries expanded to organizational diagnosis and change from its assigned mission of simply planning a retreat. Furthermore, the group was dominated by members with a more progressive change-oriented viewpoint than held by the more conservative Managing Partners of the organization. Most of the members of the SAC group in the St James Plant were factory workers, half of whom had experienced soreness. The values they expressed in the questions asked and the results of the questionnaire were obviously quite different from those of the Steering Committee. In a similar manner, to include management practices, as these affected 'sore arm', might have been seen by management as going beyond their assigned task boundary. In an even deeper sense, management philosophy over the preceding three years had been closer to Theory X than Theory Y (McGregor, 1967). The entire idea of dealing with recommendations made by a factory worker's group toward greater worker participation was foreign to them. The Plant Manager expressed this candidly when he admitted, 'I'm not sure at all that I have the skills to run this plant participatively.'

The more general issue of congruence between Task Group and the structure and climate of the organization of which it is a part is an issue discussed in the literature on autonomous work groups in socio-technical experiments. Cummings (1978), for example, notes that the larger organization has a major impact on whether autonomous work groups can be implemented effectively. Specifically, if the work group is operating more organically while the organization has a more mechanistic structure (Burns and Stalker, 1961), this affects both the internal dynamics of the group and its relationship with other organizational units. In both ABC and the St James Plant the organic Task Groups saw their mission as somewhat more flexible than did management. But not only was their process more organic, their recommendations were even more so in what were basically mechanistically structured organizations.

The second concept in the Interface cluster concerns (11) the composition of the group as it relates to its impact in the organization. We found that the higher the position and status of its individual members, the more influence and power the group had with the remainder of the organization, particularly top management. Similarly, and correlated with status, is the power of individuals and the degree to which their informal role in the organization was an influential one. It is clear that members of Task Groups carry with them to varying degrees the status, power, and role of their regular work lives. Thus, Task Groups are a part of and draw upon the system of interlocking roles within the organization (Katz and Kahn, 1966). For example, the Administrative Group in Chemtire was composed of fifteen top managers; it thus had high power in influencing the remainder of the group. Members of SAC had low status and power; thus they were not in a position to exert power over the organization, particularly the Steering Committee.

The third major concept in the Interface cluster concerns the degree to which the Task Groups developed (12) structures which integrated their activities and ideas with the organization, and in particular with the top management group. It is hypothesized that the greater the prevalence of integrator structures, the more were the group's efforts enhanced.

In all three Task Groups the degree to which the Task Group achieved liaison with its top management group empowered its ideas and activities. Both inputs from top management and outputs to it are important in this respect. And of particular significance is that this flow of ideas be continual rather than delayed until all data is collected and analysed or until a more formal presentation is made to the top management group or the organization. The SAC at the St James Plant agreed early in its life not to share any of the data it collected through questionnaires or interviews until a formal presentation to management had been made. Thus, management was kept in the dark for prolonged period of time in spite of its expressed interest and curiosity about the findings. When SAC finally revealed its findings in a formal presentation, the management Steering Committee was highly uncomfortable with both the findings and the data-collection method. Very little contact occurred between SAC and the Steering Committee during that two-month period in terms of getting management inputs to the SAC process or progress. Similarly, but to a lesser extent, the Retreat Committee in the ABC Law Firm restricted its output to the Managing Partners group. One meeting was held between the Managing Partners and the consultants, with two members of the Retreat Committee present. The consultants, in this case, served as a liaison structure between the two groups. By the time formal presentations of the data and analysis were made at the retreat and a meeting was held between the two groups, it was too late to build the necessary rapport and to exchange relevant inputs that would affect the Retreat Committee's process.

There is clear evidence in the literature that integrative structures are valuable in increasing the flow of information and rapport between differentiated or autonomous groups (Lawrence and Lorsch, 1969; Stumpf, 1977). Integrative structures in the cases in this study would have provided inputs to the Task Group which would have made their effort more relevant and acceptable to top management, and outputs to top management would have given management more opportunity to consider and respond to the Task Group in terms of *its own* suggestions. Integrative structures would have facilitated mutual feedback as well as management's sense of participation. Together these would have empowered the Task Group's recommendations within the organization.

These three factors—parental accord, the composition of the group, and integrator structures—directly affect the impact of the Task Group's Effort (13) to implement (13) whatever suggestions or recommendations it makes to the organization. We also noted earlier that a second factor which empowers the Task Group is its own effectiveness—the quality of its ideas, suggestions, and recommendations. These, in turn, are affected by a number of internal dynamics, such as its problem-solving skill, the degree to which it represents the diversity in the organization, and its energy and involvement. But it should also be noted that the quality of the group's ideas and recommendations are also affected by its strategy and power in the organization. For example, the quality of its suggestions are partially a result of favourable parental accord, composition of the group, and integrator structures. In this sense, the quality of the group's ideas are equated to the acceptability and relevance of these ideas. Similarly, the interface between the group and the organization (parental accord, composition of group, and integration structures) affects the group's energy and involvement, its perceived opportunity for influence, external pressures, and differentiated identity.

In a sense, the concept of the impact of group effort is a culmination of all of these factors and, in turn, this power provides the energy and strategy for implementation of the group recommendation. Implementation need not take the exact same focus of that recommended by the Task Group. At a minimum it implies the organization takes *some* action steps toward a revision in its work processes, its structures, policies, or norms.

Outputs

The three case studies provide an array of qualitatively different outcomes. These range from (14) performance/productivity changes, to (15) organization changes, to (16) changes in organizational ability to cope with future change through organizational learning (16) (Argyris and Schön, 1978). In discussing the outcomes of these case studies, we are not implying that these will necessarily follow in future cases from the series of events which preceded them. Outcomes are discussed to provide some guidelines as to the kind of repercussions that occur in Task Groups. At the St James Plant, Task Group recommendations resulted indirectly in increased rates of production, lowered turnover and scrap rates, and lowered soreness incidence. In the remaining two cases such concrete performance changes were difficult to ascertain, since the Task Groups focused upon revisions in organization policy, structure, procedures, and norms.

These latter four kinds of revisions are a second-level outcome—that is, their direct effect upon performance cannot be measured, yet they represent change at a more pervasive level with the clear intent of increasing performance. At the St James Plant these included the development of mechanisms for sounding out management and employees' ideas for policy and production changes and for the education of employees on management's perspectives. At Chemtire, this included the Administrative Group restructuring itself to focus on organization-wide issues and the creation of spin-off groups to explore and make recom-mendations on specific issues. It also included policy changes in the career development of technical personnel, job posting, and improvement of com-munication within the Maintenance Department. At ABC it included changes in staffing and evaluation procedures and a review mechanism for specialization needs and resources.

At a still more pervasive level are changes in the ability of the organization to learn from its own experience, to improve its problem identification and problem-solving processes. In all three cases the organizations improved their ability to use the resources of middle and lower level employees through participative methods and improved teamwork. The resource development included employees and groups learning that their own identification of problems and recommendation of solutions were useful and important inputs into the organization. Similarly, upper management learned that such processes did provide important and useful inputs and that merely because employees participate in such activities does not imply that management will lose control. In short, the organizations learned that they can invent and develop new processes in order to cope with the changing problems and conditions of the firm.

Consultant Role

Although the role of the consultant will vary with the unique needs of each group, just as it did in the three cases cited, we believe there are five functions the consultant should facilitate in the development of any Task Group. First, s/he will help the group define the nature of the task and its own role in relation to the task. Questions such as Why was I chosen? What are we going to do? How are we going to do it? need to be addressed by the group and the consultant working together.

A second clear function for the consultant is to aid the group in data collection where further information is necessary. The consultant can offer expertise in suggesting the modes of data collection (interview, questionnaire, etc.). The consultant is regarded as the best person to collect the data since s/he is not a direct member of the system and therefore can more easily be trusted not to represent any particular point of view. The consultant is limited in his or her knowledge of the problems and the questions which should be asked. Here s/he needs to rely heavily on the Task Group.

The third function which we referred to earlier in the chapter involves developing skills in the group so that it can operate effectively as a team. These include listening, being able to build on other's ideas and confront one another constructively as well as the group's ability to come to decisions and put those decisions into action.

A fourth and we believe very important function of the consultant is helping the group to understand the larger system or organization in which it is embedded and how it needs to relate to that larger system: What are the Task Group's capabilities and limitations in the organization? What other parts of the organization must it be attentive to? How should the group interact with those other relevant parts of the organization?

The fifth function will not be evident until after the Task Group has completed its work, but it must be attended to in the very early life of the group. Necessary bridges must be built and continually developed with people who are in positions within the organization to lend support to implementing Task Group findings. This can be done both through informing them of the situation under study and the Task Group's activities and by involving them actively where appropriate.

Conclusions

The strategy of developing Task Groups for the purpose of improving organizations has a great deal of merit, yet is also marked with potential pitfalls. In this section some of the advantages and precautions on the use of Task Groups are discussed.

There are clear advantages of the Task Group rather than an individual as an agent of change within an organization. Task Groups provide an opportunity for members to share all phases of the organization development process. This is particularly so for the diagnosis, implementation, and evaluation phases. Thus, diagnosis of a pervasive organizational issue by a group which is representative of the wider organization is based on more valid data since the group has improved access to a variety of parts of the organization. Similarly, implementation of change activities and evaluation of the impact of these can be gauged more adequately.

The Task Group also has the potential advantage of increased mutual learning, and generating mutual energy and motivation through member interaction. Finally, a group is frequently more powerful than a single person in influencing the organization and in recovering from temporary setbacks. It is easier for the organization to disaffirm an individual than a cohesive, high energy group.

The degree to which the Task Group is superior to a single agent of change is quite obviously contingent upon the extent to which the group possesses or develops problem-solving skills and teamwork. Team building and a focus on the group process is essential (Schein, 1969).

Equally important in determining the Task Group's advantage over a single change agent is the strategic selection of its members. The general principle here is that group composition is contingent upon its purpose. For example, it would seem wise to have representation of those people and organizational units which are most acutely sensing the organizational problem and are part of it. Similarly, it is well to have organizational units represented in the Task Group which are most affected by problems and by any proposed solutions. More respected and powerful units should also be represented if Task Group recommendations are to receive a better chance of implementation. The organization status, age, tenure, and sex of members are additional characteristics to consider strategically. For example, older, higher status members generally have more respect and influence in the organization, but may contribute toward less innovative remedies to organizational issues. Thus, the strategic choice of Task Group members has much to do with the effectiveness of the implementation of the Task Group's ideas.

Task Groups have the potential of not only learning about many parts of the organization and educating these parts, but also learning change agentry skills as well. These include building structural rapport with the organization, initiating diagnostic action and evaluation processes with it, and helping to build into the organization a capacity to learn from its experience. These are concurrent processes. Thus, in the diagnostic, action, and evaluation phases, the Task Group is gaining knowledge of the organization, analysing these data, feeding back its findings, reconsidering action steps, and evaluating these steps. But as it learns about the organization, it shares its discoveries and educates the organization. And, as these occur, it shares with the organization the process it has utilized. These processes should be contagious to the organization. It acquires a similar capacity through the formation of other Task Groups or through spin-offs from the initial Task Group.

One of the crucial issues which underlies the effectiveness of Task Groups is the structure of the interface between the Task Group and the remainder of the organization. The Task Group can have high overlap, participation, and involvement with the organization and highly permeable boundaries, particularly in regard to top management. This structure is likely to allow the Task Group to produce ideas and recommendations which are more congruent with and more acceptable to the organization. Ideas are likely to be largely a reflection of not only the *status quo* of the organization but also of the malfunctional processes which fostered the current condition and problems facing the organization.

On the other hand, the Task Group may be autonomous and have relatively impermeable boundaries which allow only limited and delayed interaction with top management. These structural conditions are likely to create ideas and recommendations which are more innovative and less traditional. Since these ideas are less affected by the current norms, policies, and malfunctions of the organization they are likely to be more incongruent with and less acceptable to top management and the organization. The crucial issue, then, is autonomy versus participation since these affect the degree to which the Task Group's ideas and recommendations reflect the organization's traditions versus its creativity. Autonomy is necessary for innovation; collaboration is necessary for implementation. Maintaining autonomy, yet creating and developing personal, procedural, and structural linkages with top management and the organization, seem essential to effective Task Groups.

The issue of autonomy versus collaboration between the Task Group and top management has much to do with the power struggles that occur between these two groups. Little collaboration will occur if either the Task Group or top management feel attempts toward disempowerment by the other. Rather, an active stance toward empowerment by each of the other seems essential. Top management must provide active support, essential information, and adequate protection for the Task Group. The Task Group, in turn, should provide continual updating of its progress and a genuine recognition of top management's involvement and ideas.

Thus, mutual empowerment becomes the basis for collaboration. And respect and acceptance for the integrity of each other's knowledge becomes the basis for granting autonomy.

References

Argyris, Chris and Schön, Donald A. (1978) *Organizational Learning: A Theory of Action Perspective*, Reading, Massachusetts: Addison-Wesley.

Burns, Tom and Stalker, George M. (1961) *The Management of Innovation*, London: Tavistock Publications.

Cummings, Thomas G. (1978) 'Self-regulating work groups: a sociotechnical synthesis', *The Academy of Management Review*, **3**, 3, 625–634.

Glaser, Barney G. and Strauss, Anslem L. (1967) *The Discovery of Grounded Theory*, Chicago: Aldine.

Hackman, J. Richard (1978) 'The design of self-managing work groups', in B. King, S. Steufert, and F. E. Fiedler, eds, *Managerial Control and Organizational Democracy*, Washington, D. C.: Winston and Sons.

Katz, Daniel and Kahn, Robert L. (1966) *The Social Psychology of Organizations*, New York: John Wiley.

Lawrence, Paul and Lorsch, Jay W. (1969) *Organization and Environment*, Homewood, Illinois: Irwin.

McGregor, Douglas (1967) *The Prefessional Manager*, New York: McGraw-Hill.

Pasmore, William A. and Sherwood, John J. (1978) *Sociotechnical Systems*, LaJolla, California: University Associates.

Roethlisberger, Fritz J. and Dickson, William J. (1950) *Management and the Worker*, Cambridge, Massachusetts: Harvard University Press.

Schein, Edgar (1969) *Process Consultation*, Reading, Massachusetts: Addison-Wesley.

Schein, Virginia E. and Greiner, Larry E. (1977) 'Can organization development be fine tuned to bureaucracies?', *Organizational Dynamics*, Winter, **1977**.

Stein, Barry A., and Kanter, Rosabeth Moss. (1980) 'Building the Parallel Organization: Creating Mechanisms for Permanent Quality of Work Life'. *The Journal of Applied Behavioural Science*, **13**(14), 507–517.

Stumpf, Stephan A. (1977) 'Using integrators to manage conflict in a research organization', *Journal of Applied Behavioral Science*, **13**, 14, 507–517.

Zand, Dale E. (1974) 'Collateral organization: a new change strategy', *The Journal of Applied Behavioral Science*, **10**, 1, 63–89.

Zander, Alvin (1979) 'The psychology of group processes', *Annual Review of Psychology*, **1979**, 417–451.

Groups at Work
Edited by R. Payne and C. Cooper
© 1981 John Wiley & Sons Ltd.

Chapter 9

Interface Issues

Alan Dale

Our choicest plans
  have fallen through.
Our airiest castles tumbled over,
  because of lines we neatly drew
and later neatly
  stumbled over.

(Hein, 1969)

Every occupant of the castles, which are our modern organizations, knows these lines to be true: knows that Kafka's and Parkinson's visions of their compartmentalization have been realized to such an extent that 'getting it together' is now a major preoccupation. Many of us, indeed, make our livings attempting to help the hapless occupants achieve this modest aim. But how has this state of affairs come about?

The Origins and Significance of Interface Issues

Natural Variety and Social Groupings

Human beings have a great variety of needs, interests, wants, goals, and so on. Furthermore, these are constantly changing as each matures, grows older or has new life experiences. Thus, in the jargon of organization theory the world is naturally *differentiated*.

Individuals have a number of common and collective interests. A common interest is one in which they share an external objective, such as making money. A collective interest is one in which the interest is mutual, such as a friendship or memberships of a community, where their own relationships *are* the interest. Sherif (1967, p. 88) makes a similar distinction between common goals and superordinate goals, the latter being: 'those goals which are *unattainable by one group, singly*' (my emphasis).

In pursuing their interests, individuals associate with others in developing a great variety of social groupings and other structures. Some of these serve *task* functions and others *sentient* ones (Miller and Rice, 1967). Now add a further distinction, that between *crescive* and *enacted* structures (Sumner, 1906).

The research on which this paper is based has been supported at various times by the Social Science Research Council (Project HR 3480/1), by 'Environmenta Ltd.', and by other organizational sponsors who were good enough to pay me to do my thing in their organizations.

Crescive structures are those which grow up naturally, not deliberately: perhaps even unconsciously. Enacted structures are those which are deliberately and consciously created. Thus, four possible origins are revealed:

(a) crescive sentient groupings (e.g. friendships);
(b) enacted sentient groupings (e.g. marriages or social clubs);
(c) crescive task groupings (e.g. information networks); and
(d) enacted task groupings (e.g. bureaucracies).

No individual is a member of only one grouping, but simultaneously a member of several, which serve different task and sentient interests and which may arise in (at least) any of these four ways.

Neither is a single-function group a possibility for long. For example, it is well established that proximity or frequency of interaction tends to lead to friendships: therefore, an enacted task group also tends to create conditions in which other sentient groupings can arise crescively.

Every individual is also the setting for intergroup conflicts, problems, and issues. This is so because s/he is simultaneously a member of several groupings which may have different values or preferences. Which role to activate, which values to give priority and similar questions are normal and ubiquitous for every individual. Thus, every individual carries interests and outlooks from each group of which s/he is a member into every other one. (See Lewin, 1973, p. 147 for a very clear account.) As a result, there are always intergroup issues *within* any particular group. Sherif (1967, ch. 4) and Merton (1968, ch. 11) offer full discussions and examples of such processes.

We may note in passing that the existence of intergroup conflicts within the person and the group leads to very powerful arguments in favour of the strengthening of individual identity and capacities, for if everybody is a pawn in the game, then there are few means available for resolving issues or otherwise *changing* the game. Conversely, and paradoxically, the discovery of new collective interests is more easily possible when individuals can transcend their 'worlds-taken-for-granted' and the norms which go with them.

Nevertheless, certain sentient relations, at least, develop within all face-to-face groupings, regardless of their origins. Most obviously, groups develop 'we/they' feelings and distinctions between 'us' and 'them'. Therefore, there are always at least some perceived issues *between* groups. Sherif (1967) has demonstrated that such phenomena are extremely regular and predictable, a finding since confirmed by many other investigators. (This is, of course, quite apart from any *actual* issues due to competing action preferences.)

So, to summarize so far, the human world is naturally differentiated, but quickly becomes formed into various groupings pursuing common or mutual (collective) interests: *simultaneously*, this very process establishes new differentiations.

Effects of Complexity, Interdependence, and Change

This is not, however, the end of the story. Three other factors, namely complexity, interdependence, and change, complicate it.

In general, the greater the complexity faced by any social unit, the more likely it is that she or it will further differentiate (specialize). For the individual, this means a proliferation of mental frameworks or 'bits' of knowledge. For the group, the result is similar, except that the differences may be distributed between individuals. In either case, the problem is how 'to get it together' in any one instance, either within or between groups.

The latter point is crucial, of course. It may well be that we do not always *need* to get it together. Even the individual may be perfectly well able to hold mutually contradictory views or frameworks, each of which works well for him/her in a different setting. It is only when the contradictions matter in a particular case that their integration becomes a problem. The cases in which it does matter are where there is real interdependence between the different positions in relation to possible *actions*. So, the greater the interdependence, the more is differentiation likely to produce interface issues.

The third factor, change, is relevant at all levels. We have already noted that an individual's interests, etc. change as s/he matures, grows older, or has new life experiences. Groups also go through such changes (Tuckman, 1965) so that the individual is thus exposed to different social realities in the same group as it develops. Perhaps more importantly, the wider environment faced by the individual or the group constantly throws up challenges or problems to be solved. Whatever the source of change, it tends to lead to new differentiations (specialisms, roles, outlooks, frameworks and so on) and to new sentient experiences together in new groups. If interdependent action is then relevant to these differences, more interface issues result. Furthermore, the faster the *pace* of change, the more is this process emphasized. (This logic of continually differentiating when faced by changes is ultimately self-defeating. I shall later discuss what may be done to transcend it. Meanwhile, it is important to pursue it, because it is the logic of most organization theory and, if we want to improve upon that theory, we must first see what is wrong with it. For the moment, let us just note that, in unstable conditions, interface issues tend to be rather prominent!)

The Significance of Interface Issues

I now come to the central argument of this essay: that *interface issues are signs of the two fundamental problems in organizing: how to get it together, and for whom*. In one sense, this is a re-statement of the question, 'How organize', but in a way which emphasizes the possibility of integration and conflict existing simultaneously in the same situation. (See Giner and Silverstone, 1978, for a similar argument at the level of culture.) By comparison, conventional approaches to organization theory and practice are *bureaucentric*, that is to say, they use (apparently unconsciously) the logic, the cognitive frameworks, the values, and the structures of bureaucracy to study bureaucracies (Dale, 1980). From this perspective, interface issues tend to be regarded, *per se*, as *bad*. For the anthropologist to understand how the natives make their reality is one thing: to go native is quite another! A non-bureaucentric style of enquiry leads to different conclusions, as follows.

The existence of issues is not itself necessarily either a good or bad thing, although it is true that it is all too easy to create more than are appropriate, by dividing organizational work too much. In enacting organizational task groupings, there is of course a conscious recognition of the value of dividing the task, because of the impossibility of one person, or an undifferentiated group, doing it all. It is not so common to find such a strong belief in the utility of actually *creating* certain kinds of issues by particular task groupings. In reality, no organization—short of a total monopoly—can survive *unless* there are such issues and they are resolved successfully. Imagine a manufacturing company in which there was no difference of views between Finance and Production functions, no recognition of their interdependence and no acceptance of constraints on resources. It is partly *because* there are such issues that such organizations are able to produce at a price that customers will pay.

There are even fewer organizations, however, which recognize the positive values of the non-enacted task groupings (private information networks, for example). Probably even fewer recognize that the pursuit of specifically group interests can also be in the interests of overall task accomplishment, as well as against them on occasions. The dangers of pursuing group interests and 'sub-optimizing' have been so often stated that it seems unnecessary to do so again here. There are dangers, certainly, but as Moscovici (1976) points out in his original and provocative study of social influence and change, thought and practice on this question in organizations are dominated by a 'conformity bias' which is both profound and largely non-conscious. He argues instead that divergent interests and sub-group memberships are essential as sources of innovation, originality, and a clear statement of preferences which assists in the modernization or renewal of organizational norms. The Law of Requisite Variety (Ashby, 1962) is another way of stating similar points. George Bernard Shaw, as usual, makes the point more pungently: 'The reasonable man adapts himself to suit the world, while the unreasonable man seeks to adjust the world to suit him. Therefore, all progress depends upon the unreasonable man' (Shaw, 1971).

I must, however, go one step further in advancing the interest of the various groupings against those of 'the organization'. There are two reasons for this: 'the organization' is merely a euphemism for a particular grouping, the owners or controllers. Why then should the interests of one grouping take precedence over that of any other? (This is not to deny that there are many actions in which the various groupings can and should fruitfully collaborate.) The formally enacted task organization is a Johnny-come-lately, superimposed on the more fundamental social interactions and groupings, which are determined by sentiment as well as task, arise crescively, and are primary in the sense that they can and do exist regardless of whether an enacted organization does so. Why then should criteria of organizational success necessarily take precedence over the criteria of success for such a grouping? (This implies, of course, that there may be perfectly valid reasons for supporting the survival of organizations which are 'failures' by conventional criteria. They may meet so many sub-group needs that their true value to society is very great.)

Looked at in this light, the organizing problem is: 'How to get sufficient variety *and* integration'—variety both in terms of the interests of individuals or groupings and also in terms of the organizational forms needed to serve them. This is not to say that the insights and prescriptions of other organization theories are without value, but that they need to be set within such a framework. Modern contingency theory is a case in point: it is superficially 'neutral' but actually ignores competing interests.

Returning to the question of interface issues, then, the questions to pursue are:

(1) *in what ways may their outcomes be good or bad for the various social units involved; and*

(2) *in what ways may they be handled?*

Environmenta U.K. Ltd: a Case History

Environmenta U.K. Ltd (that is not its real name) is a pretty typical example of a contemporary organization with 'interface problems'. A famous and prosperous company, it designs, manufactures, sells, and installs systems for dividing and furnishing large open-plan office areas. Its products are expensive, of high quality, are specified by many architects, and widely regarded as setting the standards which others follow. The Company was founded in the U.S. and grew rapidly during the 1960s before setting up in Europe, where there are common manufacturing and distribution facilities serving separate sales organizations in several countries.

In 1978 the U.K. Sales and Marketing Company, Environmenta U.K. Ltd, comprised about sixty people: sales people, managers, designers (specialists in designing office layouts from the modules and components of Environmenta's catalogue), sales administrators, secretaries, a telephonist, and a house-keeper. Its manifest organization structure at that time is shown in Figure 1.

The management of the company thought it successful but were acutely aware of a number of issues and problems. I had long discussions with Alex Hildreth, the Managing Director, Sales and Marketing, and his boss, the Managing Director of the European company, Martin M. Jones, who was the only

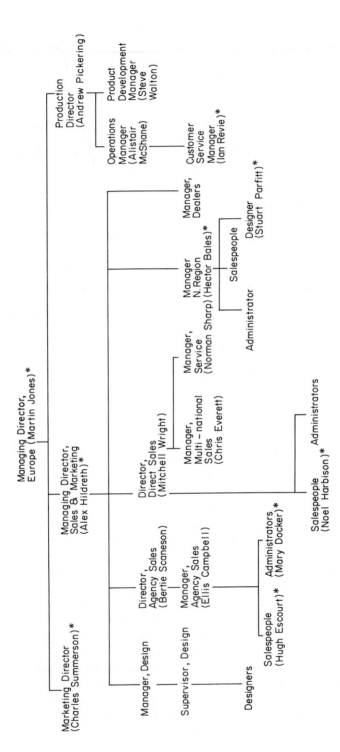

Figure 1. Partial organization structure as manifested before the start of the project in Environmenta, showing characters identified in the text. (O.P.G. members marked with an asterisk)

American national in the organization at the time. They described to me a number of issues which they faced, including the following.

1. Should sales people specialize in particular products or market sectors? Was the present division of the sales force into two groups appropriate?

2. How many levels should there be in the organization?

3. What could they do to ensure management succession, i.e. that people were prepared for a promotion and that individual careers were advanced as much as possible?

4. What could they do to prepare the organization for its continued projected growth?

5. Jones wished to move one of Hildreth's two sales managers, Mitchell Wright, out of his organization to set up a European-wide specialist group selling directly to multi-national companies. How should the U.K. company cope with this situation?

The two managers went on to describe a number of aspects of the existing situation and their concerns about it. The main points were as follows.

1. Environmenta U.K. was organized into two main sales groups, the Direct Sales division (selling directly to the ultimate customer) and the Agency Sales division (selling through architects and other specialists). They felt that this split had been an important innovation in giving them credibility in their market, but were aware of serious conflicts between members of the two divisions. Indeed, Hildreth complained of having to spend a lot of his time sorting out disputes, particularly commission payments, between them.

2. There were other specialist sales activities in the U.K. organization, one concentrating on multi-national companies based there, and another concentrating on providing service to established customers. A further division was concerned with selling through dealers, most of which activity was then concentrated in two small overseas markets where there were no local sales organizations.

3. There was a central group of designers who always seemed to be having great difficulties in coping with the workload and in producing the required quality.

4. Within the Agency Sales Division there were tensions and interpersonal difficulties between the sales people and the two levels of management between them and the Managing Director.

5. Although Hildreth carried the title 'Managing Director, Sales and Marketing', there was also a separate Marketing Director for Europe, Charles Summerson, located in Hildreth's offices but responsible to Jones. He had recently been brought in from a multi-national company in quite a different field and was regarded as far more cosmopolitan and specialized than most of the company's management, who were mainly people with a background exclusively in their own industry. Previously, there had been two other Marketing Directors, neither of whom had lasted more than a few months, and had been regarded as incompetent.

6. There were a number of tensions also with the Manufacturing and Distribution operations, both of which were controlled by the Production Director, Andrew Pickering, in a different location. There was some attempt to integrate these various activities through a Customer Services Department, also located within the factory and managed by Ian Revie. There were, however, very frequent complaints by both the Sales and Production companies about the unreasonableness of each other's behaviour.

7. Both managers were very concerned that the company should present a clear point of contact with its customers. They were worried that the customer tended to see a long succession of different people from Environmenta and become confused or get inferior service on occasions. Indeed, there was an unacceptably high level of customer complaints and work which needed to be re-done.

8. The Company had a very explicit management philosophy, developed in the U.S. and exported as a series of written statements to the U.K. company. In essence, this 'Mandate' was a fairly detailed account of 'the business we are in' and 'our style of managing and behaving'. Jones and Hildreth both expressed their strong belief in the Mandate but were doubtful whether it was universally followed or accepted.

In addition to these discussions with the two top managers, I spent some time observing operations, both in the Sales organization and in the factory which served it. My main impressions at that time were:

1. There was a long chain of highly interdependent stages from the time when the first contact was made with the customer through to the point when an order was finally delivered and installed. The elapsed time could be anything up to two years and was rarely less than two months even after the order was finally confirmed. Since every order was made to specification, the factory carried virtually no stock and there was a very heavy premium on efficient integration of supply, manufacture, delivery, and installation. At the same time, it was necessary both to keep the customer informed and to educate at least some of his/her staff in the proper use of the product.

2. There was a good deal of confusion about exactly who was responsible for managing this process, both within the sales force and the factory. Hildreth and Jones said categorically that responsibility lay with the sales people to manage each project, but this was frequently not done, or not well done, and Customer Services and the factory staff complained that often the sales person would lose interest as soon as s/he had secured an order and been paid his/her commission.

3. People at lower levels in the organization regarded both top managers, particularly Jones, as rather distant and out of touch with the problems which they faced. Many people were extremely concerned about the lack of clarity of their own situation and their possible future in the company, although almost all were confident of its economic success. There was a good deal of anxiety associated with this ambiguity.

The Organization Study Project

Environmenta Ltd contracted with a University Institute, of which I was a member, for myself and a colleague to work with them over a period of a few months. Our task was to help them study their issues and problems, decide what action might be necessary, and to implement any necessary changes indicated. They specified that this should be done 'in a participative manner', which they said was part of the style of the Company. However, they hoped and expected to be able to make major decisions about the organization within three months. We told them we believed it would not be possible in such a short time to use a fully participative approach, but that we thought that it would be feasible to work through a specially-constituted and powerful representative group. This was agreed and the process commenced with a one-day workshop attended by every member of the organization, plus Martin Jones and two managers from the factory, Ian Revie and his boss, Alistair McShane, the Operations Manager. These latter were invited because of their interest in the interface issues between Production and Sales. In effect, the organization was closed down for a day, leaving only a switchboard operator on duty, while the study was inaugurated. The consultants (my colleague, Ken Knight, and myself) provided a structure for the workshop.

1. The sixty people were divided into seven groups by level and function, with the top managers, including McShane, in a separate group. Every group was asked to spend an hour and a half listing on a chart their major concerns about the organization, with any related issues of which they were aware. The charts were then pinned around the walls of a large conference room and a rule of 'no talking' enforced for 30 minutes. Everybody was asked to walk around, read what all the other groups had written, and to formulate any questions they wished to ask them, in order to clarify these data. That clarification process took a further hour.

2. The workshop members were asked to re-group heterogeneously in order to produce a list of criteria for membership of an Organizational Project Group to be set up as the major vehicle for the pursuit of the study. The functions of this group were listed as being (i) to *sense* the issues in the organisation, (ii) to *steer* the study, (iii) to *sanction* the work to be done, (iv) to *test* the findings at all stages, (v) to *design* any possible changes, and (iv) to take action to *develop* the understandings and capabilities of the rest of the organization. The group was to be chaired by Martin Jones, with Alex Hildreth also in attendence at every meeting so that it would have the managerial authority present within it to decide any issue raised within the boundaries of the Sales organization.

At this stage there was a good deal of anxious discussion within the groups. However, each produced a list of criteria fairly quickly and a common list was settled upon, including such considerations that the representatives between them should be able to represent all power blocs in the organization; male and female staff; all parts of the work flow; and all functions. Additionally, it was considered that representatives should, at least in some cases, be able to bargain hard!

3. The election which followed this step was the occasion of a good deal of anxious lobbying and politicking. There was clearly suspicion as to the intentions both of the top managers and the consultants: not to mention a good deal of cynicism in some quarters. Nevertheless, the election was swiftly conducted and six representatives appointed, who between them satisfied all the criteria previously indicated.

4. The workshop then concluded with a discussion between the newly elected representatives and the rest of the organization as to how the former should conduct the study process.

A summary of the Organization Study Project structures is given in Figure 2. Members of the O.P.G. are asterisked on the organization chart given in Figure 1.

The consultants undertook to summarize the contents of the charts produced by the groups at the beginning of the workshop and to present this summary to the first meeting of the Organization Project Group, to be held a few days later. This was duly done and the Group, chaired by Martin Jones and assisted by one or both consultants, met for between a half and one full day every two weeks over a period of about four months. During this period they organized the data from the workshop into seven themes and developed success criteria for working on each theme. In between meetings a Study Group, consisting of two members of the O.P.G. and the consultants, interviewed virtually everybody in the organization and undertook various observations and other data-gathering activities. The results of their labours were fed back to the O.P.G. meetings until the Group members gradually were able to clarify and focus on the issues which they faced. This process involved a considerable number of surprises, both at the rational and emotional level, for all of the Group, especially Jones and Hildreth. There was a good deal of frank criticism: both of them and of the organizational arrangements which they had created. However, both proved able to listen to what was said and to respond constructively.

In addition to the manifest work of the O.P.G. and the Study Group, a number of other kinds of behaviour were apparent. Of the six elected members of the Group, two were salesmen. One of these, Hugh Escourt, was also a member of a clique of somewhat disaffected sales people together with the Marketing Director and others who regarded themselves as competent but unrecognized. At times, this clique behaved as though opting out of the organization and retreating to a position of criticism of it: at other times it functioned more as a cabal of power-seeking—aspirants to top positions. Much of this activity was centred around after-hours or lunch-time social activity, and a certain amount of it to character assassination of particular individuals in the organization. Both salesmen appeared to use the O.P.G. meetings as a place to be noticed, although their styles

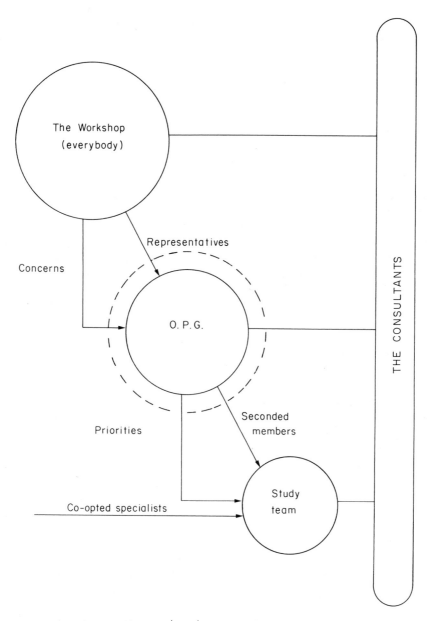

− − − − − − signifies an 'open' group: anybody could
observe and take part at certain points.

Figure 2. The organization study project

in this respect were radically different: the second one, Noel Harbison, adopting a cool, reasoned manner in contrast to the passionate arguments of his colleague.

A major concern in the early meetings of the O.P.G. was the high level of conflict between the two sales divisions and also between the two managers and the sales people within the Agency Sales Division. Escourt was a member of the latter division and, together with the majority of his immediate colleagues, made no secret of his low regard for its Director, Bertie Scaneson. Between the sales people and their Director was a Manager, Ellis Campbell, a popular and highly successful salesman, who had been given his position some time before when it was feared that he would leave.

Great efforts were made by the consultants to help the O.P.G. understand the roots of these conflicts and to avoid personalizing them. This was never fully possible, but the O.P.G. gradually came to realize that they were at least partly structural in origin.

Hector Bales, the Sales Manager on the O.P.G., was in charge of a separate regional group based in the North of England. The Designer member on the O.P.G., Stuart Parfitt, worked for him. Throughout the meetings their contributions, whilst always supportive and reasoned, were often selected to emphasize and support the practices of their own operation which (as was acknowledged by the others) was working much better in many ways. Like the sales people on the O.P.G., they were at times clearly protecting and advancing their own sectional interests, although all members of the Group were supposed to represent the entire organization and not to carry a mandate from one part.

The fifth member of the Group was Ian Revie, the Manager of the Customer Services function in the factory, whose work brought him into continuous and close touch with the Sales company. Of the six elected members, it was he and the Sales Administrator member, Mary Docker, who were most consistent in taking an overall view of the company organization.

The data-gathering programme between O.P.G. meetings revealed a number of other groupings and interfaces within the organization at large. The specialist sales manager in charge of sales to multi-national organizations in the U.K., Chris Everett, was partly involved in the cliques and cabals already referred to, but was also involved with a further cabal with his former boss, Mitchell Wright. Wright had been in charge of the Direct Sales Division, but was moved out just before the start of the project to develop sales to multi-national companies in Europe, leaving a vacancy filled by Alex Hildreth while the study was conducted. Other sub-groupings cut right across the organization and included the following:

(a) 'the keepers of the conscience'—a group of people who were critical of the company's present practices, which they regarded as undermining its special traditions and the excellence of its products;

(b) 'the old-timers'—a group of people who had been involved in setting up the U.K. company;

(c) 'the President's Club'—a group of highly successful sales people who had been admitted to membership of an exclusive club patronized by the President of the parent company in the U.S., involving a number of extra benefits and privileges (Ellis Compbell was a member of this Club); and

(d) 'the cosmopolitans'—a group of people with experience of other industries and companies, who were generally critical of the management practices within Environmenta U.K. Ltd.

In addition of these groupings, there were less sharply delineated ones which provided emotional support for each other; various social sets; and a significant number who took a deeply British view in opposition to what they saw as the encroachment of American culture. More evident than any of these 'overlays' (Pfiffner and Sherwood, 1960) were the project teams and task forces which were frequently formed in order to push through a sale or new product and/or progress it through the various stages of planning, manufacture, delivery, and installation.

When the O.P.G. had become clear about the issues, a one-day seminar was organized by the consultants with the aims of equipping the O.P.G. members with the tools to analyse their organization more systematically and to assist them in considering design options.

The seminar was followed by a two-day working conference at which all of the data and discussions of the O.P.G. were considered and systematically analysed, using the frameworks provided by the consultants. As with all O.P.G. meetings, this was open to others in the organization to attend. On this occasion, seventeen people did so at various times. (At other meetings, attendance varied from none to about six.)

The conference considered some radical re-design options and decided on a re-organization based on regional groupings, each one including designers, administrators, and sales people, with the aim of greatly reducing the inter-functional conflicts. Perhaps more importantly in the long term, the conference recognized that the task of the Sales organization was in fact a much broader one than 'selling' (including the 'tailoring' of the Company's standard components to fit the needs of a customer, so that the real product was 'solutions to customer problems').

The implications of this conception of the task of the Sales organization included that the Customer Services function was logically located within the Sales organization and not the factory. (There was a Production Planning function in the factory as well, which could carry out all the necessary progressing work.) It was considered that, if the Customer Services function could be moved into the Sales company then, as a corollary, the factory should be insulated as far as possible from direct contact with sales people. This would allow it to routinize its production and run as efficiently as possible, with the uncertainties mainly absorbed by the Customer Services function. Furthermore, a Customer Services function would be decentralized within the regional groupings, so that each administrator would be able to see the project for a particular group of customers through from beginning to end. The existing two Sales divisions were to be dissolved, leaving a small central group of specialist sales people with a knowledge of the Agency market to be assigned to regional groupings as required, on a project basis. The design group was to be similarly decentralized, leaving a manager and one or two designers in a central group. These and other aspects of the proposals resulted in a matrix form of structure.

The conference proposals were summarised in a 'White Paper', circulated and widely discussed within the organization in a series of meetings and finally modified and endorsed by another meeting of the O.P.G. During this period, members of the various groupings described above, both official and unofficial, were very evidently jockeying for position and staking out their claims for positions in the new organization. This process was neither more nor less rational and emotional than one would expect to find in any other organization in a time of change of structure. All of the managerial posts in the new organization were advertised only within the organization, together with full job descriptions developed with the aid of the consultants. The selection process was made as public as possible and involved a much more thorough approach than had previously been used within the organization. There were widespread assumptions that the appointments had been decided long ago and that the whole process was merely a 'white-washing job'. However, the appointments made were a combination of the expected and unexpected (in one case of a candidate believed to have been permanently written off within the organization). Nevertheless, both of the salesmen members of the O.P.G. were appointed to be managers and there was some comment within the organization of the 'unfair advantage' they had had in being able to get so close to the two top managers. On the whole, the selection process was favourably received throughout the organization and almost all the appointments made have been successful.

Not all of the 'decisions' made at the O.P.G.'s conference have been implemented, however, First, there has been a back-tracking of the decision to decentralize the Agency Sales Division people to the regions. This seems to have been achieved by a process of 'foot-dragging' as much as anything else. Perhaps more significantly, there has been a virtual duplication of the Customer Services function, because the original group remains within the factory, while new Customer Services Coordinators have been added to the regional groups in the Sales organization. It is widely believed within the organization that this situation has arisen because Alex Hildreth is unwilling or unable to really confront the Production Director, Andrew Pickering, on this issue and that Martin Jones is unwilling to arbitrate in favour of one or the other. It seems likely that a possible reason for this is that Jones, as the only American in the European organization, is highly dependent on the long experience of Hildreth and Pickering. Both were involved in setting up the U.K. and European operations and have an encyclopaedic knowledge of their organization, unequalled by anyone. Such is the *realpolitik* of organizational life!

Interactions and Memberships in Groups: the Process of Grouping

The conventional wisdom about groups and their interfaces in organizations is that things are, or at least should be, much simpler than was the case in Environmenta. The majority of textbooks, management journals, and consultants espouse a model in which membership of a single task-based group is the norm. In such groups, all individual needs, goals, and interests are, ideally, to be integrated with those of 'the organization'. Any deviation from this norm is regarded as regrettable at best, and pathological at worst.

Quite apart from the blatant ideological bias of such a position, its *naiveté* (or self-deception?) is astonishing to anybody experienced in studying organizational life at close quarters. To the latter, the multiple interactions and memberships; the confusions and conflicts; and the self-interested territorial behaviour evident in Environmenta are surely usual.

The reality of social life is that almost all of us have a wide variety of overlapping interactions through networks or webs of contacts and affiliations. Such interactions may be patterned, regular, and bounded to the point where a 'group' may be said to exist, or less regular and/or bounded, so that we might experience them as a 'flocking' or 'cluster' (Spink, 1975), a 'serial' (Sartre, 1977), a crowd or some other type of social collectivity. Whatever their form, such collectivities have to support a wide variety of task and sentient functions.

To the extent that any one collectivity is unable to support all these functions, either for the individual or for the organization, the number of memberships of a particular individual will tend to increase. Correspondingly, the individual has to handle an increased number of interfaces between the groups of which she is a member.

Sentient Groupings in Environmenta

In Environmenta, the sentient functions of the various groups included the following.

1. Providing friendships or other affective bonds for their members. Examples were 'the old-timers' and a sub-group among the Agency Salesmen. (According to Simmel, 1950, this is *the* fundamental basis of social groups.)

2. Providing a 'home base' for emotional security, support, and for the confirmation and development of individual identity. An example in Environmenta was the group of 'keepers of the conscience' of the company who were using this identity as a secure base, often in the face of great uncertainties about their own roles. On the whole, however, home bases were poorly provided for by the official task grouping and, instead, a high level of anxiety prevailed. (For a more detailed account of the effects of the lack of a psychological home base, see Hjelholt, 1976, pp. 232–243). Perhaps the most obvious home base group was the female employees, although even that was under a good deal of tension since one or two of their number were under other pressures to behave like men—particularly one saleswoman.

3. Providing a reality-testing mechanism: a way of checking out one's own interpretations of events. Such groupings were numerous and fluid in Environmenta. People spent a good deal of time comparing their views of the latest happenings or rumours on the personal front: who was in favour or on the way down; which way was opinion forming; what were the latest 'buzz words' and their significance for the individual, etc. This was done both face-to-face and through networks of contacts which even involved people in the American parent company. Such interactions often took place on the occasion of other official task meetings, such as Hildreth's regular Sales Progress Meetings with his managers. In the breaks, sub-groups of the latter would confer with each other or with other valued contacts in the building, often in apparently casual meetings (yet it was noticeable how certain people always managed to bump into each other). Other key figures in the reality-testing networks were people in Product Development (not obviously much to do with their concerns, but well informed about some trends in the company) and the sales administrators, whose position in the workflows also gave them much valued sentient information.

4. Providing a source of values and standards of behaviour. Again, there were many such groupings in Environmenta. They included a group of design-orientated people (including some in the factory and Product Development); the members of the 'President's Club' and their followers; and the 'cosmopolitans'. Such groups were, respectively, orientated mainly towards design standards, sales performance, and modern management. Each also had its symbols or heroes, notably one Edward J. Brown who, in a brief stay in the Company, had become regarded as the model of design flair and creativity.

5. Providing a means for advancing or protecting individual interests, most obviously through overt association and bargaining, but less so through cliques, cabals and other coalitions (see Burns, 1955, for a detailed account of such processes). Examples were the disaffected group of 'British' people; the Northern Sales Group (particularly in using its two members on the O.P.G. to consistently advance its position and defend it from changes); and the power-seeking cabal centred around the Marketing Director, Charles Summerson.

This is by no means as exhaustive list of types of sentient groupings, nor of their examples in Environmenta. It is sufficient, however, to show that such groups served at least five functions for their members: *psychological, social, economic, political,* and *moral.* It seems likely that such groupings would be found in all organizations of any size.

Task Groupings in Environmenta

Almost all individuals in the Company were also members simultaneously of several groupings serving a variety of task functions. At the very least, they were involved in different groupings for different sales projects. Other task functions served by the various groupings included the following.

1. Acting as the organization's 'memory' when required. The 'old-timers' had an obvious function here, as well as their sentient functions. Sales Administrators and Customer Services people were also important in this respect (although not always recognized to be so), especially since the sales management did not keep uniform or consistent records.

2. Handling change. For example, there was a frequent use of task forces or project teams to innovate, and larger sales conferences were regularly used to announce or discuss changes. The O.P.G. and its associated groupings was a major example of an ad hoc structure created to consider and decide upon change in the organization.

3. Information-gathering and performance monitoring. In Environmenta this was usually done in meetings, rather than through formal information systems, which were under-developed. Examples were Hildreth's Sales Progress Meetings; innumerable ad hoc groupings to progress a particular project (often involving even Martin Jones, the Managing Director, Europe, in quite low-level decisions and problems); and the departments such as Customer Services which had a specific monitoring function.

4. Coordination and integration of the work of other groupings. Sales Administrators were important here and, again, Customer Services. However, as has been described in the case, there was much confusion and disagreement about such responsibilities, particularly as to who was managing a project. This was further complicated by the 'matrix' structure, with people like the Multi-National Accounts Manager, Chris Everett, attempting to coordinate different aspects of the work of other groups.

5. Noticing business opportunities and finding new directions. Examples here were almost all centred around Martin Jones. Some were official groups, such as the company committees dealing with new products, but others were unofficial groupings to whom Jones paid particular attention or set out to influence strongly. Hildreth and Wright were prominent in both, while the Product Development Manager, Steve Walton, figured mainly in the latter.

6. Routinizing the work. It was widely recognized in Environmenta that this was not given sufficient attention. One example, however, involved the manager in charge of follow-up service to customers, Norman Sharp, with other managers and administrators in trying to draw up more systematic procedures for servicing existing customers and capitalizing on further sales opportunities.

As with the sentient groupings, this is by no means an exhaustive list of task groupings in Environmenta. However, it does support Katz and Kahn's (1966) conclusions that all organizations need task groups to encourage *technical, support, maintaining, adaptive*, and *integrative* functions.

In Environmenta no individual worked always with the same people on the same tasks and, indeed, this is only conceivably possible in a totally routinized situation. (That is, one in which there is no variability in the task demands and where all activity is programmed.) Conversely, the greater the variation and complexity in task demands, the greater will be the need for more interactions, groupings, and memberships: hence, the greater the number of interface issues. In Environmenta the task demands were complex and highly variable: activity in response to them was very difficult to programme. Its task structure, however, in spite of rhetoric to the contrary, was fairly strictly divided at the start of the study by function and type of customer. The result was a plethora of interface issues.

Interface Issues and their Manifestations

Definitions

The definition of 'issue' used is the one given by Dale and Spencer (1977, p. 14): 'A choice of actions which involves competing preferences or sentiments within or between social units, and which is constrained by resources, power structures, time or other contingencies.'

Such a definition allows for conflicts or problems which do not produce issues. For example, there may be a conflict of values but no action implication involving both parties; or there may be a problem with a neutral constraint, such as time, but no conflict of preferences between the parties. An issue, then, has three components: *conflicts, constraints,* and *actions* involving the interests of both social units simultaneously. This is not to say that conflicts and problems are unimportant: merely that they are less inclusive.

An 'interface issue', then, is an issue between social units. Perhaps 'inter-unit' issue would be a less ambiguous term although, as will be seen later, the interfaces can also be between conceptual units or categories which are simultaneously social (for example, 'Leader' and 'Follower'). So I will stay with the term 'interface issue'.

As issue *within* a social unit exists when the whole unit (whether individual or social collectivity) holds conflicting values or preferences which have constraints and action implications in a particular instance. However, issues which are apparently 'intra-face' are frequently in reality merely reflections of interface issues. An indecisive individual, say, may be trapped between the competing demands of being 'a good Christian' and 'a good businessman'. Similarly, a group attempting to pursue incompatible goals in a particular case (say, selling goods which violate its own ethical standards) may be simply reflecting the issues between its own external referents. For more thorough discussion of such phenomena, see Sherif (1967, chs. 1 and 2). Wholly intra-unit issues are uncommon, it seems.

Issues, Latent Issues, and Pseudo-Issues

As we have seen, issues arise because of conflict between various social groupings under conditions of constraint and interdependent action. However, not all such issues are recognized, and therefore remain 'off the agenda'. For example, the rights of women as a class in employment went unrecognized for a very long time before the emergence of issues connected with them. Before that, so did the rights of children at work, etc. There are still many other issues which are not anywhere near being 'on the agenda', such as the rights of male parents as a sub-group of employees. In some organizations the absence of functional task issues is conspicuous, such as cash-flows in Rolls Royce Ltd before it collapsed.

The reasons for the non-emergence of issues may be reduced to two broad categories: *non-consciousness* of interests (or *false consciousness*) and *domination* by one party to an issue, whether through open coercion or more subtle forms of suppression or repression, such as consultation about or participation in trivia. See Clegg (1979) or Billig (1976) for more thorough discussions from a sociological and psychological viewpoint, respectively.

Pseudo-issues arise when there is a simple misperception of the situation or the pseudo-issue is a 'cover' (consciously or not) for the real one. For example, studies of decision making in organizations have shown that there are many 'decisions' which are never implemented. The reason may be that there never was a decision to be made or that the 'decision-making process' actually served other functions, such as reducing anxiety, socialization, or distributing glory and blame. March and Olsen (1976) present many examples and offer further discussion of such phenomena.

Manifestations of Issues

How shall we know when issues exist and are recognized? In Environmenta at the start of the project there were plenty of manifestations. For task issues they included:

—work 'falling between the cracks' or being duplicated;
—squabbles over the right to a particular customer or piece of work;
—disputes about work standards;
—accusations of irresponsibility and lack of cooperation between the two sales divisions and between them and the factory;
—customers confused as to who was dealing with them;
—blaming others for problems and failures; and
—stereotyping other groups.

For sentient issues, the manifestations included:

—verbal aggression towards other groups;
—anxieties about personal and group futures;
—frequent forming of cabals and cliques;
—defensive behaviour and cynicism;

—a great concern for territory and status, particularly in the over-use of titles to
the point of confusion; and
—gossip of a malicious kind and character assassination of those in other groups.

Some of these issues were handled in an 'adult' mode (Berne, 1964) but a great
number in 'parent' or 'child' modes, so that the senior managers were very
concerned about the conflicts existing at the start of the project.

The organization study project attempted, with some success, to help the
recognition and handling of such issues, from initial clarification through an
'adult' mode of discussion and negotiation to decisions and actions. It must be
emphasized, however, that the success was partial, especially since the new
groupings created by the project could be and were used for other purposes.
Thus, the O.P.G., in addition to its official functions, also served at times as:

—a place to be noticed and advance personal or group claims for promotion:
whether by flattery, reasoned argument or other means;
—as a place to defend territory and independence (particularly by Hector Bales
and Stuart Parfitt, the two from the Northern Regional Sales Group); and
—as a place to block changes (probably not always consciously) by 'talking
things out' or by never getting round to them. This happened particularly with
one of the seven themes considered by the O.P.G.: that to do with career
development and related topics.

Environmenta manifested signs of most kinds of issues, but a few which are often
found in organizations did *not* appear so often there. The included:

—cold, apathetic, and impotent relations (things were generally lively!);
—individual withdrawal and subsequent fragmentation of groups (a huge
amount of effort, particularly by the top managers, was devoted to driving
work along and getting groups together for frequent meetings); and
—purely instrumental involvement in the firm (many people identified closely
with it).

Manifestations of Latent Issues (Unrecognized Issues)

It may well be wondered how a 'non-issue' can have manifestations! There seem
to be two relatively easy ways of recognizing them, however. Probably the more
reliable indicator is *taboos*; the subjects which obviously cause embarrassment or
provoke sanctions, emotional denials, or similar signs of serious concern when
they are raised. A less reliable test is simply to note what is not recognized as an
issue in one organization while it is recognized in a similar one elsewhere.

Two possible ways of identifying the latent issues via a more detailed analysis
are (i) by tracing the interdependencies between social groupings to find who
actually needs, gets, and gives what resources, information, and values; and (ii)
examining the extant functions of particular groupings, especially those which
are *supposed* to be dealing with issues.

In Environmenta, certain taboos were very clear. First, any discussion of owner/manager/employee interfaces was avoided, or provoked dogmatic and vague assertions of 'the realities of business', taken more or less verbatim from popular business magazines. Slogans such as 'managers must manage' tended to inhibit any serious discussion of management functions (although this did change as the project proceeded). Secondly, there was no public discussion of the Company's use of transfer pricing mechanisms (and thus its true profitability world-wide and in the U.K.). Indeed, it was publicly a 'non-subject', and although all managers had some idea of its importance, such decisions were reserved to Martin Jones and discussed only with a handful of people, such as the Finance Director, who had to know.

In other organizations we have seen many examples of quite different ways of keeping issues off the agenda, and we were at some pains to prevent these happening in Environmenta. Among those we sought to avoid were allowing particular groups (such as the O.P.G.):

(a) to be used for public 'trials' or 'assassinations';

(b) to be used as a displacement mechanism to direct attention away for more deeply felt issues;

(c) to be used to coopt or neutralize dissent; or

(d) to become 'containers' for the 'too difficult' issues or, worse, a repressive, 'Church-on-Sundays' setting having no influence on issues day-to-day.

The processes for the Organizational Workshop and the subsequent structures of the project, already described, were of course designed to achieve those ends. They appeared reasonably successful in this respect. However, in one other important respect they *created* a further difficult interface issue, since a 'hierarchy of information' developed, with the Study Group at the top, then the O.P.G., and finally the rest of the organization. The two groups become interest groups themselves, so that interface issues developed between them and the organization much as in any 'social democracy' based on representative systems (Molin, 1979).

Manifestations of Pseudo-Issues

The 'other' functions of the O.P.G., described earlier, give clues as to the pseudo-issues in Environmenta. For example, there was an enormous amount of time and effort devoted to analysing the primary task of the Sales organization and 'deciding' that it necessarily included the Customer Services and Installation functions. Thus, the work of the O.P.G. 'demonstrated' the company's serious concern with doing an excellent job to solve its customers' problems and organize itself rationally and efficiently. Nevertheless, in spite of the involvement of the chief executive, Martin Jones, there was never any serious attempt to carry out the 'decision'. Instead, a duplication of effort was arrived at in which both Sales and Production companies maintained a Customer Services function. Efficiency was clearly a pseudo-issue and I dare say that the concern expressed for the customer ranked lower than for the territories of Production and Sales Directors. I do not suggest that this was necessarily deliberate, or even conscious, particularly in view of the serious commitment and subsequent action of Jones and Hildreth in almost all other respects. However, this view of the situation in very widely held in both the Sales and Production organizations.

Pseudo-issues are, by their very nature, elusive, and likely to be understood only on close acquaintance with an organization. Similarly, they are likely to vary greatly from one organization to another. Nevertheless, once one is sensitized to their possible existence, they are naturally easier to spot and cope with: often by doing nothing, one imagines! March and Olsen's book (1976) is probably the best current source on such matters.

The Outcomes of Interface Issues

When two social units, A and B, are involved in interface issues (conflicting action preferences under constrained conditions) there is a logically limited set of possible outcomes:

  (a) they realize their individual interests unequally;
  (b) they realize some of their individual interests, to an equal extent (but never *all* of their interests, since there would then be no issues);
  (c) any mutual (collective) interests are realized to some extent; or
  (d) any mutual (collective) interests are not realized.

Way of Describing and Evaluating Outcomes of Interface Issues

Note that 'preferences' are not necessarily equivalent to 'interest', since the one may be realized without the other. The question of what constitutes 'true' interests is, of course, a matter of fierce controversy: are they what people think they are, or is there some external criterion, such as acquisition of resources or control? A relatively straightforward way out of this dilemma is first to describe outcomes, in terms of 'who gets what', 'who controls what', or other criteria, and then to ask the interested parties to evaluate them. This process will not appeal to whose who wish to dominate, however, since it tends to sharpen awareness of interests. (For example, when black people in America began closely to examine and compare outcomes for themselves and white people in the political and employment fields, they rapidly developed stronger and clearer ideas of their true interests.) A possible framework for describing outcomes has already been presented, considering functional outcomes in terms of technical, supportive, maintaining or stabilizing, adaptive and integrative criteria (for the *task functions*) and in terms of psychological, social, economic, political and moral ones (for the *sentient functions*). Relatively few organization specialists have recognized the possibilities in such a procedure. Pondy (1967) makes a clear statement of them but pursues only certain task criteria. Some of the studies conducted by the Tavistock Institute probably come closest, although they usually omit any consideration of really divergent group interests. See, for example, Trist *et al.* (1963) or Miller and Gwynne (1972).

Types of Outcomes

The combination of the four possible general outcomes gives rise to a range of possibilities from Domination to Negotiation, Synthesis or Deadlocks. These are outcomes where the interests of first one party, then both, and finally neither, are met. A final possibility, of course, is to split up. Considered in terms of both individual and mutual interests simultaneously, some possibilities are outlined and slightly expanded in Figure 3.

Working from this diagram, a few common practical cases are as follows.

1. A and B meet their individual interests to an acceptable extent, but not their mutual ones. (For example, the partners in a marriage may be fed, housed, and so on, but have no satisfactory relations beyond that: indeed, may be in a state of 'limited war'.) Relations between units in work organizations are frequently not very different to this, which we might call the *sub-optimization* condition. Its extreme form is intense, mutual exploitation. Its milder form is negotiation and compromise. Realistically, some variant of this condition is likely in most situations.

| | | Mutual (collective) interests | |
		Realized	Not realized
Individual interests	Realized equally	Synthesis	Sub-optimization
	Realized unequally	Domination	Exploitation + fragmentation
	Not realized	Over-socialization	Deadlocked

Figure 3. Outcomes of interface issues

2. A and B meet their individual *and* mutual interests to acceptable (or greater) extents. How different is a marriage or organization where such conditions prevail! At the least, it sustains a valued *status quo*. At best, it enables the enhancement of each individual through energetic, progressive, collective activity and realization of fully mutual interests. We might call this the *Synthesis* or *Synergy* condition. Note that the *character of social relations* (energetic; valuing differences; using conflicts constructively, etc.) is crucial here.

3. Neither A nor B meet their interests to any significant extent (at least when judged by outside criteria) yet they persist. Such a condition seems remarkably common in organizations. A typical example comes from an earlier project in a theatre company (Dale and Spencer, 1977; Spencer and Dale, 1979) where both individual and mutual interests were damaged by a failure to resolve a task issue: nobody liked what was happening, everybody thought the outcomes would be bad, but nobody acted to change the situation. Such conditions are well documented in relation to individuals, but not for larger social units. We might call this the condition of *Deadlocks*.

4. A or B meet their interests at the expense of the other. In the case of marriage, domination by coercion, economic boundage, or other means has by now been so fully documented that it seems pointless to repeat it. Feminists have also made us acutely aware of how such domination can be brought about by various processes of repressing awareness of true interests (such as through a pervasive and one-sided ideology).

Organizations have hardly begun to face the full impact of the recent advances in the understanding of this *dominance* condition, but activist groups and movements of many kinds are forcing them to wake up, however reluctantly!

Two rather strange other possibilities are revealed in Figure 3. First, the *Over-socialized* condition, where both parties gain in terms of mutual interests but not individual ones. (Being happy with each other but starving to death is a classically 'romantic' example from marriage.) An example in a work organization, perhaps, is great satisfaction with the product or service and with the quality of relationships, but an inability to pay people, such as in certain 'job-saving' cooperatives.

Secondly, the condition where individual interests are satisfied unequally but collective ones not at all, seems likely to lead only to *Fragmentation* of social life and *Exploitation* of what is left by the stronger party. It is a case of 'grab-what-you-can-and-devil-take-the-hindmost'.

5. A final possibility is *Separation* or *Decoupling*: an obvious solution both in marriage and organizations, and yet still strenuously avoided in both cases. Note, however, that separation need not be final or complete: various other possibilities exist, such as reducing economic or task interdependence. (In a marriage, by separate personal accounts; in a business, by allowing sub-units a quasi-market autonomy.)

'Decoupling' (in whatever sense!) is actually often good strategy: it strikes at the roots of issues by reducing one cause, interdependence. In many cases the benefits of such a move may greatly outweigh the apparent losses: genuine autonomy may ultimately realize more mutual interests or more important ones.

In all such cases I have argued from the simplest condition, where only two units, A and B, are involved, although using some examples involving more units. Obviously, the possibilities are more complicated with more than two units (A and B may pursue their common individual interests against C, for example). Nevertheless, the same principles apply in describing and assessing outcomes.

Appreciating Interface Issues

I have noted that interface issues involve conflicts, constraints, and interdependent action; that they may or may not be manifested (latent issues); and that other pseudo-issues may also be 'on the agenda'. The first practical problem, then, is *appreciating* the situation.

The Judgements of Appreciation

According to Vickers (1968, ch. 7) this process is a simultaneous judgement of fact (reality) and value, in which an issue is recognized (or not), evaluated, and added to the agenda (or not). Within this general judgement, says Vickers, are four more specific ones.

1. *Importance/Unimportance*, determined by the interests of those involved. In Environmenta, an example of such a judgement was the importance given to the Production/Sales/Customer Services interface issues in relation to the question of the delivery of a contract to a customer on time and as specified. This collective interest was in conflict with the common individual interests of the sales people in securing their commission payments at the time of a sale. Production's interest, however, was in retaining the sales person's involvement with a project after that point, so as to get an accurate, complete, and feasible specification for the contract. (They argued that the commission system encouraged the sales people to neglect these interests.)

2. *Centainty/Uncertainty*, determined by expectations of achieving a result or maintaining a valued situation. An example in Environmenta was the question of the best location for the Customer Services function and the associated difficulty in reconciling the territorial interests of the two Directors, Hildreth and Pickering.

3. *Coherence/Incoherence*, determined by whether the perceived reality is consistent with the existing constructs of those involved. An example in Environmenta was a series of negotiations between sales people, designers, and their managers to produce a commission payment system which would reinforce their declared intention to collaborate flexibly in Regional Groups, each group being responsible for the whole task, from beginning to end of a project. In this

case the highly individualist ways of thought dominant in the company were in sharp opposition to the collective interest of the Regional Groups, and the issues were only partly resolved. The 'solution' adopted, was 'having things both ways at once': retaining an individual reward system whilst strenuously advocating group responsibility and flexible collaboration.

4. *Appropriateness*, determined by whether possibilities are perceived for a resolution of the issue consistent with the value structure of those involved. An example in Environmenta was the avoidance of any serious discussion about the interfaces between the roles of owner, manager, and employee. This was backed up with frequent assertions from the Directors of their belief in the value of capitalism, free enterprise, and strong leadership. In turn, this made it difficult to discuss leadership as a process or function (rather than as a role) and proscribed any involvement of juniors in deciding business policy (thus, of course, limiting the scope of the 'participation' espoused by the Directors). On the other hand, the decentralization into Regional Groups, responsible for whole tasks, was consistent with existing ways of thinking and regarded as fitting well with the prevailing value system.

Regulators

This formulation of appreciative judgements is of considerable practical use, for it can be used to guide the process of noticing, defining, and choosing issues. However, as Vickers points out, such processes do not take place in vacuums, but involve two fundamental interactions. The first of these is a *comparison of what is with what might be* (actual versus preferred and possible states). That is, the situation as it exists, or is tending to become, is compared with rules or goals (if clear) but more commonly with the norms, standards, or values prevailing in the organization. A judgement is made about whether the potential issue is likely to serve or threaten such valued states. In turn, such judgements may lead to responses ranging from doing nothing, through maintaining the *status quo*, to taking steps to restore it.

Such comparisons may also lead to a *change* in the rules, goals, norms, standards, or values themselves. These social things can usefully be thought of as the 'regulators' of the organization. For those involved, the first regulative option is whether to change or retain the 'setting' of the regulators, followed by an appropriate action. A typical example in Environmenta would be a Sales/Design interface issue of whether to accept a sale contract which could not be designed within the price, or some other limitation, to achieve the functional performance standards of the products: should the sale be refused, the standards relaxed, or some other solution found?

In such cases of conflicting criteria, another possible way of resolving the question is to move up to the next level of regulation. Vickers (1973) suggests that there is a natural hierarchy of regulators, with rules and goals at the bottom, standards and norms above, and válues at the top. Galbraith (1973) supports this view, adding that the greater the uncertainty, the more necessary it is to move to the next higher level. A move upwards is also often a good way to resolve conflicts at the lower level. (For example, a dispute over which rules to apply, or whether to apply them, may be resolvable by reference to goals or standards.) In a variety of other projects it has also been found useful to include still 'higher' levels of regulation: the 'orders' or 'images' (ideologies, philosophies, myths, etc.) which express the most basic beliefs and values (Dale and Spencer, 1977).

Repertoires

The interaction of appreciations and 'regulators' is further extended to include the cultural and psychological 'settings' of those involved (regulators being essentially organizational phenomena). Psychological and cultural settings, or *repertoires*, include language, constructs, perceptions, knowledge, and understandings; biases, stereotypes, and attitudes; intuitions, feelings, and sensations.

In appreciating an interface issue, these repertoires work in a similar way to regulators, although often less consciously. Thus, a potential issue is noticed (or not) defined and 'accepted' or suppressed. At the same time the repertoire itself may be changed by the confrontation.

An example of this process at work in Environmenta was the perception of issues between the two levels of management and sales people in the Agency sales division. These were perceived and conceptualized originally as problems of personalities, because the organization lacked any repertoire for noticing and thinking about such phenomena in a more structural way. (A repertoire which *developed* to some extent, however, as the O.P.G. worked on the issues.) Thus, an important option for people confronted by interface issues is to examine and clarify their 'repertoires' for appreciating them. In this way, issues may be redefined, disappear, be sharpened, or otherwise brought to the point where more appropriate actions can be taken.

Other Influences on Appreciation

Such a formulation of the process of appreciation is similar to, although more detailed and practicably useable than, those of Weick (1969) in his discussion of organizing processes; of Pondy (1967) in his discussion of felt, perceived, and manifest conflicts; and of Cohen, March, and Olsen (1972) in their 'garbage can' model of decision making. These authors also point out, however, the influence on the process of such external factors as ecological changes, *other* issues or pressures, the history and interpretation of relationships in that setting, and so on. An example of the latter in Environmenta was the business pressure to achieve sales targets and to develop new products to meet the needs of important customers, which developed just after the O.P.G.'s decision to re-organize the

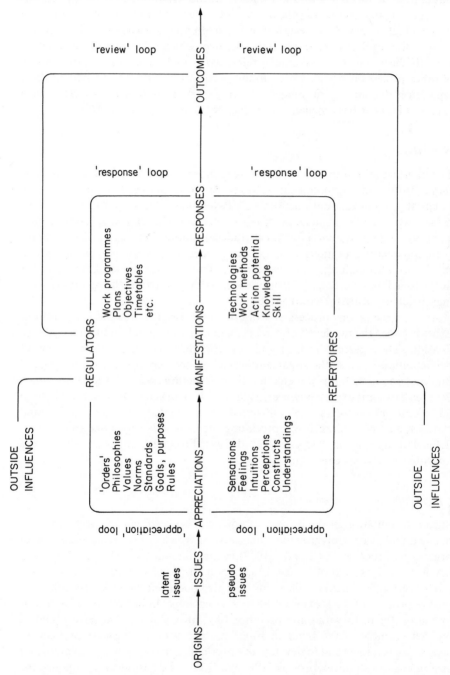

Figure 4. A general model of the process of handling interface issues

Company. These led to a delay of several months before the full implications were appreciated and worked through to conclusive actions.

A General Model of the Process of Handling Interface Issues

We are now in a position to add these formulations of appreciation, regulators, and repertoires to our earlier discussions of the origins, types, manifestations, and outcomes of interface issues. This gives us a general model (Figure 4) with one stage—*responses*—remaining to be considered, together with certain other components of the regulators and repertoires.

The key point about this model is that is represents an active process, and the most important considerations, therefore, are the interactions between the stages in the process and the structures (regulators and repertoires) within which it takes place. The first of these, the loop between Appreciations, Repertoires, Regulators, and Outside Influences, has already been considered. Let us call this simply *Appreciation*. (Weick, 1969, prefers the term 'enactment', and indeed I have been much influenced by his formulations in constructing the model. However, 'enactment' suggests a wholly deliberate and conscious process, which is clearly not the case, so 'appreciation' seems the more descriptive term to use.)

The second loop, including Regulators, Responses, Repertoires, and Outside Influences, will be called simply *Response*. Others call it 'selection', but that term ignores the possibility of inventing a new response not in the repertoire or outside the usual 'regulations'. Responses will be further considered below.

The third loop, including Outcomes, Responses, Regulators, and Outside Influences, will be called *Review*, a process which leads to decisions to retain repertories and regulative structures, or to change them. Again, this process will be further considered below.

Thus, the model can be boiled down to three injunctions: 'Appreciate, Respond, and Review'. Crucially, however, the process is not (or should not be allowed to degenerate into) a single-loop learning system, in which outcomes are compared with appreciations and responses either retained or dumped. It only transcends the purely autonomic if the second-level loops are added, so that there can be fundamental changes in repertories and regulative structures (Bateson, 1973, pp. 133–149). These learning processes also remain to be discussed.

Strategic Responses to Interface Issues

The general model presented in Figure 4 may be used as a guide to the strategic possibilities and constraints in responding to interface issues.

Eliminate the Origins

As we saw earlier, the ultimate origins of interface issues lie in the processes of differentiating and grouping. Thus, although differentiation is the *sine qua non* of organization, it simultaneously creates interface issues and integration problems. Therefore, the first rule of organization design is to *minimize differentiation* of the task structure. (The necessary variety can be achieved in other ways, such as by supporting the greatest possible range of outlooks within individuals.) Obvious though it may be, it is probably the case that this basic option is rarely considered in organizations, where the trends are towards ever-greater specialization and fragmentation.

Of course, most of the differentiation process is actually beyond the control of organization designers or governing bodies, because it arises crescively and on a sentient basis, as well as through enacted task structures. Nevertheless, it seems only sensible to exercise the options which are available.

In Environmenta, this option was exercised in the re-organization by establishing Regional Groups, each responsible for a *whole* task and with deliberately overlapping roles within the groups.

Eliminate the Conditions

Earlier, we noted that issues only exist when there are *conflicts, constraints*, and *interdependent actions*. Thus, issues would be prevented by removing any one of these three components. Conflict can never wholly be removed, however, since it arises from natural variety, so we are left with only two possibilities.

1. *Constraints* can sometimes be removed by the simple expedient of providing more resources. This can be done by such means as larger budgets, better stocks, more or better facilities, looser controls, relaxing deadlines, and so on. Now such suggestions are heresy, of course, because they violate, or appear to violate, values of efficiency and rationality. Yet there are two excellent reasons why they may make good sense. First, constraints which are too tight may endanger other values, such as quality; avoidance of stress or breakdowns, whether in persons or machines; or innovation. Secondly, the relentless pursuit of efficiency by restricting resources *is itself inefficient and irrational*. The reason for this is that the costs of coordination and issue-resolution *between* units become much greater as they compete for inadequate resources. Managers or other resource-allocators have to spend a great deal of expensive time resolving disputes, scheduling the use of equipment, and so on. (See Downs, 1966, ch. 11, for a detailed economic analysis of this phenomenon. Galbraith, 1973, also demonstrates that 'slack' is sometimes a good way of integrating an organization.)

An example from Environmenta arose when an installation team found it had to park its van some distance from the site of the installation. This meant that the heavy components of the product had to be manhandled between van and site, but no aids were available in the van to assist the process. In desperation the salesman concerned bought a two-wheeled barrow with his own money in the local hardware store. When he came to claim the money back from the company he was then involved in an interface issue with the Accounts Department over his right to commit company resources in this way. (He got his money, but barrows are still not standard equipment on the vans.)

2. *Interdependence* of social units in a workflow may be eliminated in several ways. First, if the physical technology allows it, units may specialize by customer or territory, rather than by stage in the workflow, thus eliminating the 'error manufacturing' process of passing each stage in the process on to another person. This solution was used in Environmenta in the Customer Services department: after the re-organization, individuals there undertook responsibility for progressing all stages of a contract for a particular set of customers (within a region or other territory).

Secondly, a quasi-market situation may be created within the firm, whereby a particular unit has the option of gettings its inputs either internally or externally (transfer pricing systems are a necessary aspect of such an approach) so that units can better assess the costs and benefits of 'buying-in'. Quasi-market solutions are common in relation to internal advisory services. In Environmenta they hardly existed, although sales people would sometimes unofficially buy-in components which their own organization had failed to provide in order to complete an installation. See Williamson (1975) for a discussion of these methods.

Thirdly, the maximum possible sub-unit autonomy may be allowed, holding each accountable only in the most general way. Businesses based on profit (or contribution) centres are a common way of achieving this, the extreme case being a franchising arrangement. An example in Environmenta exists in the parent organization in America, where the basic research activity has been hived off into an autonomous corporation. Such arrangements are very common in highly professionalized organizations, such as consultancies, universities, or architectural practices.

Change the Conditions to Create Collective Interests

This option is easier to state than to carry out because, for reasons already elaborated, conflicting sub-unit interests always remain. However, there are a number of possibilities.

1. *Create two-way workflow interdependence.* All too often interdependence is asymmetrical and sequential. For example, in Environmenta Sales provided the factory with orders and the factory provided Sales with products. One could simply 'hand over' to the other. Contrast this with other cases where a joint Sales–production team would visit a potential customer to agree a specification for a challenging new project: in such cases neither could complete the selling stage in the workflow without the involvement of the other. (An example of what Sherif, 1967, calls 'superordinate goals'.) This kind of situation is often very difficult to create, but the 'whole task' concept is one way, where the technology and other factors allow it. Project teams and task forces are often also useful.

2. *Direct the competition for resources externally.* The classical way of doing

this is an extension of the 'profit-centre' concept, so that all members of a system keep any savings or earnings over and above an agreed contribution level. The crucial aspects of this method, however, are that the sub-units within the system share equally in the surplus and that they have real control over the factors which produce it. (In Environmenta neither condition applied. The former could have been changed but the latter could not because the level of surplus or profit was manipulated by use of the transfer pricing mechanism operated between the various parts of the Company internationally. For example, if a sale was urgently wanted, the transfer price used for components could be low, the sale price low, and the 'profit' still look respectable. So much for profitability as an objective measure of performance!)

An excellent example of this approach is described by Searle (1979). So-called Integrative Bargaining, to jointly act to increase the 'size of the cake', is a parallel example developed by specialists in industrial relations. See Walton and McKersie (1965) for a discussion of principles and methods.

Improve Appreciations of the Issues

If it is not possible or appropriate to prevent issues arising, then we may move to a consideration of how to handle them. Note that the concern in either case is *not* to prevent conflicts, but to identify and handle their action implications. As a first step, there are many things which can be done to improve the appreciation process.

1. *Accurately register the existing situation.* That is, identify

—the outside influences;
—the interests and likely outcomes for the various parties;
—the nature of interdependencies and constraints, plus the important corollary of *areas of autonomy and opportunity*;
—the true issues, latent issues, and pseudo-issues;

and then clarify each party's judgements of

—importance/unimportance;
—certainty/uncertainty;
—coherence/incoherence (actual 'fit');
—appropriateness (value 'fit').

The opening Workshop of the Organization Study Project in Environmenta was an example of a method of registering existing appreciations.

2. *Define differences and agreements.* That is, clarify areas of

—collaboration and integration (even where conflict remains);
—competition, bargaining, etc;
—sub-optimizing, or even 'decoupling'.

Part of this process often involves:

—moving up the hierarchy of regulators to clarify issues at lower levels (e.g. from rules to values);
—moving deeper into inter-unit communication, by such means as exchanging perceptions; examining ways of thinking; and by using intuitions, feelings and sensations as ways of expressing and understanding the real concerns of self and others.

Much of the work of the O.P.G. in Environmenta was devoted to defining differences and agreements, in association with the following subsequent step.

3. *Modifying appreciations.* That is,

—redefining issues and interests; and
—changing judgements of importance, certainty, etc.

At the same time,

—changing the 'setting of the regulator': that is, modifying rules, standards, values or whatever; and
—changing the 'repertoire': that is, developing different understandings, feelings, etc.

Respond to Issues (That is, 'Solve' Them)

In many situations this is the beginning of the process, but our approach in Environmenta was to delay this stage until the preceding ones had been worked upon.

There is a huge literature of organization design which offers ways of devising solutions and, of course, we drew upon this (as well as the participants' own experiences) in the O.P.G.'s seminar, their two-day conference, and the subsequent activity to re-organize the Company. Whilst this is hardly the place to attempt a summary of this vast literature, there are a few theoretical points of great importance to this essay and a number of general solutions which can be listed. (For more detailed discussions see Child, 1977; Galbraith, 1973; Handy, 1976; and Jaques, 1976.)

1. *The general problem is integration,* or how to 'make whole' that which has been differentiated.

2. *The first class of solutions are structural.* They include:

—The Regulators already referred to, to which we must now add Work Programmes (Plans, Targets, Timetables, etc.).
—Direct supervision and use of authority by bosses in an appropriate number of hierarchical levels (see Billis and Rowbottom, 1977).
—A matching of authority and accountability, and of types of authority (see Jaques, 1976).

—Lateral relationships (committees, task forces, project teams, coordinators, etc.).

—'Combination' structures, such as the matrix form (see Knight, 1977).

   2. *The second class of solutions are procedural.* They include:

—The 'repertoires' already referred to, which must now be extended to include knowledge, skills, work methods, standard operating rules, and technologies.

—Information systems of all kinds, both vertical and lateral.

—Budgets and other resource-allocation methods.

   3. *The third class of solutions are general policies and practices.* They include:

—Rewards and payments system.

—Physical proximity of those whose work must be integrated.

—Selection of people who 'fit in' to the culture.

—Induction and socialization to that culture.

—Training of the groups who must work together, or at their interfaces.

—Use of organizational symbols, logos, badges, uniforms and propaganda; explicit 'philosophies' and 'styles'.

—Rotation and exchange of people between units where interface issues exist.

Most of these options were considered by Environmenta. The structural solutions and some of the procedural and general ones were described in the opening case history. For example, the new commission system for sales people still rewards individuals for getting a sale, does encourage more collaboration between them, but does not reinforce the message to collaborate more actively with the factory in achieving a workable and accurate specification for the contracts. Other solutions, such as team-building and inter-team training, have yet to be tried.

Review

This process has a number of components.

   1. *The actual outcomes in relation to interests* (who actually gets what?). This results in a re-definition of interests and/or conclusions about the validity of the responses to issues. In turn, this leads to a consideration of the following point.

   2. *The outcomes in relation to regulators.* This may result in decisions to strengthen, retain, or change the regulators, at any level from rules to philosophies.

   3. *The outcome in relation to repertoires.* Was the response appropriate? Should it be strengthened, retained, or eliminated from the repertoire? Are new responses needed?

   In Environmenta the process so far has been in relation to Repertoires. Work is now proceeding to strengthen them through training and the improvement of work methods. In relation to Interests and Regulators, the feedback time is necessarily longer and results are not yet clear.

Developing Capacities to Handle Interface Issues

In the preceding section we saw how the model can be used to guide improvements in the processes of handling issues. Such interventions should normally result in increased *capabilities*: that is, actual changes in appreciations, responses, regulators, and repertoires. Yet, we all know that such improvements are frequently not the outcome of interventions, but that issues may remain unnoticed, deadlocked, or otherwise unresolved. Why is this? To consider the question, we must return to the origins of interface issues.

We have already noted that interface issues between social units result partly from natural variety and the process of differentiating. Reducing differentiation is one way to reduce the number of interface issues. However, we have also seen that a certain level of variety and differentiation is necessary to cope with a given level of complexity: as complexity increases, so does the 'requisite variety'. Furthermore, as conditions change, new categories may be required but, at the same time, some of the old ones become inappropriate: it is not simply a matter of adding categories, but of replacing or moving existing ones. In short, what is needed is the capacity to constantly adjust categories to suit conditions (whether actual or desired).

The problem is that once a category is established, there are several strong forces which tend to maintain it. We have already noted that members of a social unit have or develop common and collective interests which are separate from the enacted task differentiations which bring them together in the first place. That is, they have interests in maintaining the *status quo*—interests which may be instrumental, psychological, social, moral, political, or whatever.

However, there is a deeper reason why, once established, social categories tend to persist, which is that the social units often come to be thought of as 'things' with fixed boundaries, rather than as processes. Thus, we talk of organizations, not organizing processes; groups, not the processes of grouping; and so on. This imposes a kind of orderliness on the world which appears to reduce uncertainty (and hence, anxiety). However, it also increases uncertainty when external conditions change, because fixed categories cannot handle new conditions, and thus unsolved problems may become more frequent (Hedberg *et al.*, 1976). Nevertheless, much energy is invested in maintaining the established categories since those involved *initially* learnt that they were a means of reducing anxiety and the primitive fear that chaos and destruction will follow disorder.

Leach (1972) and other anthropologists have further demonstrated that social categorization of this kind is intimately linked with the categories of language itself. For example, the verbal category 'leader' very easily becomes equivalent to the social category, thus ensuring that leadership is treated as a role to be performed by one person rather than a process which may be performed by many. The area of overlap between two categories is, *a priori*, 'messy' and hence often also 'dirty' (dirt = 'matter out of place'). It is also ambiguous and, therefore, likely to raise anxieties. Thirdly, it is an area of inter-penetration and, hence, both potent and threatening. The combination of dirtiness, threat, and anxiety leads to *taboos* on activity within the area of overlap, or at least to very severe constraints upon it. The process may be illustrated more clearly as a diagram (see Figure 5).

This is perhaps most obvious in the case of the categories 'man' and 'woman' and the sexual relations between them. In organizational life the categories 'leader' and 'follower' are often associated with similar taboos: for example, a taboo about examining 'management's prerogatives'. In all such cases, much energy may be invested in maintaining the verbal categories, as well as the social ones, to keep anxiety at bay.

Thus, people become trapped in nets of their own making (Watts, 1973) which prevent them handling new issues as they arise. Even when strenuous efforts are made to confront the issues, the unconscious attachment to fixed categories may make it impossible to resolve them. This attachment may not necessarily be even to particular categories, but to the *way of thought* which divides the world into fixed exclusive categories so that, for example, an individual is regarded as either a 'leader' or 'follower'. The fundamental 'interface issues' are those between verbal categories and between different ways of thought.

The project, then, is not only to be able to change the verbal or social categories when necessary, but to *transcend the process of categorization itself*. How might this be possible?

Remaking Social Reality

In spite of the difficulties, social realities and ways of thought do change. In the extreme case, crisis may force the change upon us. However, I assume that this would not be the preferred means of learning for most of us, so let us examine some alternatives.

The construction of verbal and social categories is itself a social process in which people interact to bring order to the world. Any new group confronted with some kind of challenge quickly establishes such an order: the problem is how to *re*-new it. In principle, this may be done by recreating the fluid conditions which exist at the beginning of the life of a group, but without initially destroying it. The way to achieve this in practice is to take the social units (individuals, a group, or groups) *out of place and out of time*, so that experiments may be made with dissolving or moving the boundaries between categories, often with the aid of *appropriate ritual*. For example, taking members of two departments to a conference centre, working unusual hours, and having a consultant create and legitimate unfamiliar ways of working, is a common method. (The consultant

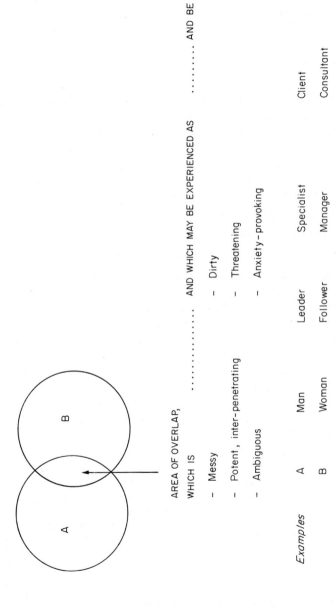

Figure 5. Overlapping categories

here performs, among others, the role of priest or shaman, facilitating the crossing from one state to another.) I think that ritual is helpful, and possibly essential, to such a process, for it is a public, collective expression of the project. It may take many forms, from 'trust-building exercises' conducted by a consultant, to rounds of drinks and jokes in the bar, but the underlying meaning is always similar: 'we are in this together to try to find a new way of thinking about and organizing our world'.

Transcending Categorization

New ways of thought may well be constrained by individual capacities, but I do not propose to pursue that issue directly here. Instead, it is sufficient to note that alternative ways of thought already exist both within and between societies: the project is to practise using them. Some examples will illustrate the point.

First, we can practise using two or more categories simultaneously, such as recognizing that each individual may be simultaneously leader and follower; strong and weak; adult and child; or whatever. (The Eastern idea of Yin and Yang, each contained in the order, is similar.) We could extend this further by deliberately experimenting with categories such as

—work, play (why not 'plork'?);
—(un) employment, play (why not (un)emplayment?)

to see what new social structures or policies are suggested.

A very striking example can be found in Deakin's (1973) account of a family in which the four children had all reached astonishing levels of achievement for their years. There was no rigid separation in the family between work and play: the two were often going on simultaneously. Thus, the twelve-year-old son, who was largely educated at home and had already passed examinations of university entrance level in mathematics and science, would ask 'to play at mathematics work'. The nine-year-old son, winner of a national piano competition open to people up to eighteen years old, seemed actually unaware of the work/play distinction in his life, and to shift, ignore, or transcend several others. When still only nine, he announced that he wanted to go away to boarding school and this was arranged with support from the local authority. When he arrived

He had, he felt, come to play the piano for them, to learn about music fully and seriously. It was *they* who must accommodate themselves to him. Such—to him—quite rational idiosyncracies as refusal to wear heavy school shoes, eat school food, or keep to a timetable restricting the four hours practice he was accustomed to each day would just have to be tolerated by the adult authorities. There was no room for debate, he was not intending to change his attitude. The school gulped—and to their great credit complied; not that they really had much choice. This boy, they came to see, meant 'no' when he said 'no' and 'yes' as literally. . . .

His practice house, his permission to attend Quaker meetings and his need to wear slippers most of the time, were vital to him, and that was that. What became clear at school was that everything was really an adjunct of his piano playing—it was not just an activity, it was a central part of life itself (Deakin, 1973, p. 103).

A second approach is to pursue the line that one person is multi-faceted. For example, instead of having specialists for everything, a counter-trend which already exists widely in our society is the do-it-yourself movement and the de-professionalization (or 'barefoot doctor') one. Here, the categorization of activity and thought continues, but is separated from role. Instead, each individual learns a wider variety of skills and frameworks, thus reducing the incidence of interface issues between him/her and specialists on whom s/he is dependent. Such an approach may easily be extended into organizations.

A third approach is to make much more use of synthetic (rather than analytic) modes of thought and symbolic (rather than categorical) ones. Examples can be found all around us in the form of graffiti, stories, jokes, myths, cartoons and so on, which frequently cut through all the wordy categories and reveal the central concerns which people share. It is relatively easy to practise such modes of thought and expression in organizations: for example, by groups of people constructing stories or making physical pictures illustrating how things are or might be.

Single- and Double-loop Learning

There is an apocryphal story, attributed to James March of Stanford University. Three chickens lived in a cage. Their owner fed them by throwing handfuls of seed in through the wire of the cage. The first chicken walked clockwise in a circle and learnt that it found enough food to eat that way. The second chicken walked anti-clockwise and learnt the same lesson. The third chicken stood still and learnt the same lesson again.

Of course, none of the chickens could reflect upon their experience, so that they learnt only to reproduce a behaviour pattern. One wonders what they would have done had the owner changed the feeding process.

The chickens exhibited single-loop learning: simply checking results (food) against their behaviour. There was no double-loop learning to ask why and whether such behaviour would always be appropriate. The project in organizations is similar: how to learn from experience, rather than merely repeating it; how to *review* not only outcomes but the original appreciations, responses, regulators, and repertoires; and to change any of them if appropriate. In short, to learn how to learn, or how to increase the *capacity* of a social unit. A number of sustained attempts to induce or support double-loop learning have been made in recent years, notably by Argyris and Schon (1975) and by Watzlawick *et al.* (1974). These and other methods are beginning to be used in organizations and show much promise of developing capacities.

Security and Boundaries

All of these approaches require a measure of emotional security in those involved. Paradoxically, it seems to be the case that a strong 'home base' group membership is necessary to develop an identity which is sufficiently clear, strong, and flexible to allow individuals to move freely in and out of *other* groupings. To cross or dissolve boundaries requires that certain other boundaries are firm (Hjelholt, 1976).

The implication of this for organizations is clear. Most individuals need some kind of 'home base' group to which they can return and which provides a 'platform' from which to take off and experiment elsewhere. Without such a platform, rapid re-groupings seem to be anxiety-provoking, alienating, fragmenting, or even disabling for most people. It is not realistic to expect that interface issues can be confronted if people are very anxious, alienated, or isolated! Indeed, some strengthening of the 'home base' may be necessary before change can be contemplated. For example, groups of factory workers may need to discover and strengthen their collective identity before being able to engage in negotiations about, say, new ways or organizing. We may indeed learn much from those suffering extreme insecurity, such as single parents. Such people have had much success by first supporting each other in self-help groups, gradually developing stronger identities, and *then* taking action to improve their relations with other groups with whom they must interact.

Conclusions

Interface issues arise from natural variety on the one hand and, on the other, from processes of social and conceptual categorization. Most approaches to handling interface issues in organizations suffer from a simplistic and bureaucentric view focused on the enacted task of the organization, and ignoring much of the variety and competing interests which exist. An alternative model has been presented. This may serve as a guide to understanding the origins and nature of interface issues and to finding realistic ways of handling them. Ultimately, it may be necessary not so much to handle interface issues as to transcend the processes which create them in the first place.

References

Argyris, C. and Schon, D. A. (1975) *Theory in Practice*, Jossey-Bass.
Ashby, R. (1962) 'Principles of the self-organising systems', in H. Von Foerster and G. W. Zopf, eds., *Principles of Self-Organisation*, New York: Pergamon.
Bateson, G. (1973) *Steps to an Ecology of Mind*, Paladin.
Berne, E. (1964) *Games People Play*, André Deutsch.
Billig, M. (1976) *Social Psychology and Intergroup Relations*, London: Academic Press.
Billis, D. and Rowbottom, R. (1977) 'The stratification of work and organization design', *Human Relations* **30**, 1, 53–76.

Burns, T. (1955) 'The reference of conduct in small groups', *Human Relations* **8**, 4.

Child, J. (1977) *Organisation: A Guide to Problems and Practice*, London: Harper and Row.

Clegg, S. (1979) *The Theory of Power and Organisation*, Routledge and Kegan Paul.

Cohen, M. D., March, J. G., and Olsen, J. P. (1972) 'A garbage can model of organisational choice', *Administrative Science Quarterly* **17**, 1.

Dale, A. J. (1980) 'Organisational research is bureaucentric', Working Paper, Institute of Organisation and Social Studies, Brunel University, England.

Dale, A. J. and Spencer, E. (1977) 'Sentiments, norms, idelologies and myths: their relations to the resolution of issues in a state theatre company', Working Paper, Brunel University, England.

Deakin, M. (1973) *The Children on the Hill*, London: Quartet.

Downs, A. (1966) *Inside Bureaucracy*, Boston: Little Brown.

Galbraith, J. R. (1973) *Designing Complex Organisations*, Addison-Wesley.

Giner, S. and Silverstone, R. (1978) *Innovation, Communion and Domination: Some Notes Towards a Theory of Culture*, Brunel University, England, Mimeo.

Handy, C. B. (1976) *Understanding Organisations*, London: Penguin.

Hedberg, L. T. Nystrom, P. C., and Starbuck, W. H. (1976) 'Camping on seesaws: prescriptions for a self-designing organisation', *Administrative Science Quarterly* **21**, March.

Hein, P. (1969) 'Grooks', London: Hodder Paperbacks.

Hjelholt, G. (1976) 'Europe is different: boundary and identity as key problems', in G. Hofstede, and S. Kassem, *European Contributions to Organisation Theory*, Van Gorcum.

Jaques, E. (1976) *A General Theory of Bureaucracy*, Halsted Heinemann.

Katz, D. and Kahn, R. L. (1966) *The Social Psychology of Organisations*, London: Wiley.

Knight, K. (ed.) (1977) *Matrix Management: A Cross-Functional Approach to Organisation*, Gower Press.

Leach, E. (1972) 'Anthropological aspects of language: animal categories and verbal abuse', in P. Maranda, ed., *Mythology*, London: Penguin.

Lewin, K. (1973) *Resolving Social Conflicts*, London: Souvenir Press.

March, J. and Olsen, J. (1976) *Ambiguity and Choice in Organisations*, Universitetsforlaget, Norway.

Merton, R. (1968) *Social Theory and Social Structure*, New York: Free Press.

Miller, E. and Gwynne, G. V. (1972) *A Life Apart*, London: Tavistock.

Miller, E. and Rice, A. K. (1967) *Systems of Organisation*, London: Tavistock Publications.

Molin, J. (1979) 'Demokrati Som Organisations Forandrings Strategi: Et Case', working Paper, Institute of Organisation and Industrial Sociology, Copenhagen School of Economics, Denmark.

Moscovici, S. (1976) *Social Influence and Social Change*, London: Academic Press.

Pfiffner, J. M. and Sherwood, F. (1960) *Administrative Organisations*, Prentice-Hall.

Pondy, L. R. (1967) 'Organisational conflict: concepts and models', *Administrative Science Quarterly* **12**, 2.

Sartre, J-P. (1977) *A Critique of Dialectical Reason*, London: Merlin Press.

Searle, D. (1979) 'Team organisation in a construction firm', in K. Knight, ed., *Putting Participation into Practice*, Gower Press.

Shaw, G. B. (1971 edition) *Man and Superman*, London: Penguin.

Sherif, M. (1967) *Group Conflict and Co-operation*, London: Routledge and Kegan Paul.

Simmel, G. (1950) *The Sociology of Georg Simmel* (trans. Wolff), New York: Free Press.

Spencer, E. and Dale, A. J. (1979) 'Integration in organisations: a contextualist approach', *Sociological Review* **21**, 4.

Spink, P. (1975) 'Groups, Boundaries, Networks', Discussion Paper HRC 990. Tavistock Institute of Human Relations, London.

Sumner, W. G. (1906) *Folkways*, Boston: Ginn & Co.

Trist, E. L., Higgin, G. W., Murray, H. A., and Pollock, A. B. (1963) *Organisational Choice*, London: Tavistock.

Tuckman, B. W. (1965) 'Developmental sequence in small groups', *Psychological Bulletin* **63**.

Vickers, G. (1968) *Value Systems and Social Process*, London: Pelican.

Vickers, G. (1973) *Making Institutions Work*, London: Associated Business Press.

Walton, R. E. and McKersie, R. B. (1965) *A Behavioural Theory of Labor Negotiations*, McGraw-Hill.

Watts, A. (1973) *The Book on The Taboo Against Knowing Who You Are*. Abacus.

Watzlawick, P., Weakland, J., and Fisch, R. (1974) *Change: Problem Formulation and Problem Resolution*, New York: Norton.

Weick, K. E. (1979) *The Social Psychology of Organising*, Addison-Wesley.

Williamson, O. E. (1975) *Markets and Hierarchies*, New York: Free Press.

Author Index

261

Subject Index